120

Nanking

Yangtze River

Shanghai

30

Kiukiang

Ningpo

25

Foochow

FORMOSA

Amoy

20

SOUTH
CHINA

120

125

CHINA RACES

Austin Coates was born in London in 1922. He went to India as an officer in Royal Air Force Intelligence in 1944, and has lived almost continuously in Asia ever since. In 1949 he joined the Government of Hongkong as Assistant Colonial Secretary, subsequently becoming District Officer and Magistrate in the New Territories. Between 1957–9 he was Chinese Affairs Officer and Magistrate in Sarawak, and in 1959–62 First Secretary in the British High Commission, Malaya. By this time author of several books, he left government service to devote his time to writing. In 1966 he returned to Hongkong, and has resided there since, producing a succession of books on Asian and Pacific themes.

China Races

Austin Coates

Commissioned by the Royal Hong Kong
Jockey Club to mark its Centenary in 1984.

HONG KONG
OXFORD UNIVERSITY PRESS
OXFORD NEW YORK MELBOURNE

Oxford University Press

Oxford London Glasgow
New York Toronto Melbourne Auckland
Kuala Lumpur Singapore Hong Kong Tokyo
Delhi Bombay Calcutta Madras Karachi
Nairobi Dar es Salaam Cape Town

and associated companies in
Beirut Berlin Ibadan Mexico City Nicosia

First published in 1983

ISBN 0 19 581540 8 (cloth)
ISBN 0 19 581541 6 (limp)

Cover illustration: Racing at Pao Ma Chang,
Peking, in the 1920s.(By courtesy of Andreas, Baron
von Delwig.)

Designed by Colin Tillyer.
Printed by Hip Shing Offset Printing Fty.
95 How Ming Street, Kwun Tong, Kowloon.
Published by Oxford University Press,
Warwick House, Quarry Bay, Hong Kong.

Contents

Foreword

The idea for this book was suggested by the late Peter Gordon Williams, Chairman of the Board of Stewards of the Royal Hong Kong Jockey Club from 1974 to 1981. His point was that whereas the current Hongkong racing scene is famous throughout the sporting world, very few people today realize that Hongkong's racing traditions stem from nearly 200 years of racing, in Macao, in Hongkong, and in China itself.

This earlier period traversed one of the most turbulent centuries in China's history. The racing community, of many nationalities, were not infrequently enmeshed in situations which in retrospect are alarming.

They were survivors, however, prepared to put up with minor inconveniences such as heavy artillery and mass-murderers. On at least one occasion races were held within earshot of warfare. Nobody seemed to mind, not least the thousands of Chinese who turned up to attend the races.

It was amateur racing. Millionaires rode their own horses, or watched their sons race for them. The financial scale of it is without parallel in the annals of amateur racing. In this respect it was far from amateur, as too in matters of horsemanship, in which standards were of the highest.

Just before the Revolution of 1911 Chinese joined the racing fray, with the same high standards of sportsmanship and expertise. In the Chinese race clubs European jockeys rode for Chinese owners, Chinese jockeys for European owners. Seemingly insuperable barriers melted away.

Here, then, is an unusual chapter of racing history, worth rescuing before it passes into oblivion.

China Races has been commissioned by the Royal Hong Kong Jockey Club to mark its centenary in 1984.

The historian who would attempt
to write the story of racing in
Shanghai and guarantee it to be
correct is not to be envied.

North-China Herald,
Shanghai,
7 March 1934.

Nor is he who would write the
story of racing in China, for that
matter.

A.C.

1. The Barrier Gate

Previous page: The Barrier Gate, Macao. Sketch done from the earliest known photograph, 1902. This was the Portuguese Barrier Gate, erected after the Sino-Portuguese Treaty of 1888, when Portuguese controlled the barrier. Beyond it, however, remained the original Chinese barracks, restored after their destruction by the British in 1840. (By courtesy: Department of Tourism, Macao.)

China and the Horse

On the first English trading voyage to China the diarist Peter Mundy, who was the expedition's commercial officer, went to the races in Macao. It was a Sunday in November 1637. The races were held in a large open square, artificially levelled, in front of the church of São Domingos in the heart of the attractive little Portuguese city, which was then already eighty years old.

'Every Cavallero was bravely apparelled . . . each having their Negroes or Caphir, Cladd in Dammaske, an ordinary wear here For slaves and Servauntts. These carried launces with pendantts, whereon were painted their Masters Armes.'

'Their Horses,' Peter Mundy noted, 'are very smalle, butt quicke and Couragious (like our Cornish nagges), beeing of this country breede. There were among the rest 2 or 3 off a farre larger size, butt those are brought From Mannilla.'

In fact, the 'Couragious' horses were not bred in China proper, but were almost certainly from Mongolia; and both they and the Philippine horses had been imported into China.

This brings out a key factor relating to horses in that country. The horse cannot be bred successfully in China due to the calcium deficiency in all organic matter, including water. The T'ang horses immortalized in bronze and pottery were not Chinese. They were brought to China across thousands of miles of wasteland from the kingdom of Ferghana, in what today is Soviet Uzbekistan. In China they gradually dwindled and died out. The same is true of the horses painted by the Jesuit artist Castiglione, most of which were Kazakh and Afghan horses, some of them brought to China as presents for the Emperor. Traditionally, China has depended on horses imported from less daunting distances, principally the lofty grasslands of Mongolia, from which thousands of horses were brought down annually to be sold at fairs in many parts of North China.

It is worth bearing in mind that throughout the centuries, when the horse was the most important military animal and the fastest means of communication, China, the world's largest, oldest and most prestigious nation, was in an almost incredible position. Unable to breed horses of her own, she was dependent on subduing her barbarian enemies, from whom solely could be obtained the essential organs of military despatch and of cavalry warfare against the mounted hordes imperilling her.

Difficulties with a Dragon

FORTY years after Peter Mundy's visit, Macao is referred to in an East India Company report as 'dreadfully impoverished'. Not until a hundred years later, towards the end of the eighteenth century, do Chinese sources speak of foreigners, clearly meaning Englishmen, exercising horses on the Campo.

In 1773 the East India Company moved into a considerable amount of rented property in Macao, and became permanently resident. The Company, the largest and most powerful commercial organization on earth, included the Bengal Army with its cavalry, and had the pick of the finest horses in all Asia. Its ships furthermore were the largest and most stable in the world. Obtaining a good mount from Calcutta for riding in Macao presented no problems. There was the drawback that Company personnel were in Macao for only three months of the year, the hottest months of summer, when racing is out of the question. For the rest of the year they were in Canton, where they were confined to a small section of the waterfront, so congested it was almost impossible even to go for a walk, but which was the only place in China where foreigners were allowed, and then only during the trading season, which was usually from September to April. Still, even with these limitations, some felt it was worthwhile owning a horse.

The Campo, where they are reported exercising them in Macao, consisted of just under two miles of open countryside beyond the city wall, as far as the narrow neck of the Macao peninsula. The neck was so narrow that it looked like a man-made causeway, though in fact it was natural. Beyond this was the Barrier Gate, past which no foreigner was allowed.[1]

The first race-meeting probably took place around 1798–9. By this time there were more Britons on the coast: not only East India Company personnel either, but men engaged in the 'country' trade between China and India, defying the Company's monopoly. Above all, English ladies had taken to arriving with their husbands, or to joining their husbands, in defiance of the adamant Chinese rule that no foreign woman must come to China. The Chinese authorities turned a blind

1. In Portuguese the Campo referred to a recreation ground which once existed just outside the city wall, beyond the present-day Rua do Campo. In Chinese the equivalent word refers to the whole area between the city wall and the Barrier Gate.

eye, provided that the ladies remained in Macao and did not venture up to Canton.

The site chosen for the racecourse was the most remote possible, and the most secluded. Just short of the neck of the peninsula was a natural oval of flat grassland concealed by low rocky hills. There they laid down a three-quarter-mile track, and raced where no one could see them, except from the sea. This was the first English racecourse in China. One side of the course ran along the edge of the shore. The sand here was black, giving the locality its name, Hak Sha Wan or Areia Preta (Black Sand).

Macao: The 'Casa Garden', residence of the head of the East India Company in China. On race days in the early 1800s the cavalcade to the course started here.

Immediately to the right of the Casa Garden, the cavalcade passed down Rua dos Cavaleiros, which in those days led to open countryside.

When the East India Company personnel departed for Canton at the start of a new trading season, a skeleton staff was left in Macao to attend to essentials. This staff consisted of clerks, a notary or two, occasionally a surgeon, all of them juniors and most of them young. It is reasonable to suppose that horse-owning senior officers asked these young men to see that their steeds were looked after, and to exercise them while they were away. It is more than likely that these juniors were the ones who got things going, particularly, one would suspect, after ladies appeared on the scene. And it is unquestionable that from the start the races enjoyed the full support of the President of the Select Committee, head of the East India Company in China. Races came to be held around Chinese New Year, when business in Canton came to a standstill for at least three weeks and Company men could take a few days off and come down to join their wives.

In 1802 it was decided to construct a proper road from the city to the racecourse — mainly for the convenience of the ladies. This provoked an outburst from the 'gentry' of Mong Ha, a village one had to pass in order to reach the racecourse. 'Gentry' meant those few who were literate. Their outburst took the form of a petition to the Tsotong, the mandarin directly responsible for Macao. 'Villainous barbarians,' the Tsotong was informed, 'are employing labour to make a road from the Kennel Gate to the Red Tea-Garden Hill, a road for rambling play and running horses abreast.'

The Kennel Gate was the smaller of the two gates in the city wall, giving access to the Campo. The Red Tea-Garden Hill was the hill embracing the racecourse and concealing it. According to Chinese records, the building of the road was stopped. The Tsotong must have taken some action, since otherwise the 'gentry' would have petitioned a higher authority and he himself would have been in trouble. Nevertheless, whatever the Tsotong did, the road was completed.

The gentry of Mong Ha are next heard of 10 years later, in 1812. This time they resorted to *fêng shui* (geomancy), meaning this was serious business. They complained that labour was again being employed. The labourers had 'assumed the liberty of pushing down the great rock of the Coming Dragon at the Red Tea-Garden Hill,' the plan being to make 'a Horse Road'.

Accustomed as one may be to all hills in China being the abode of dragons or tigers, one is bound to admit that the

Coming Dragon is particularly ominous. It should be noted also that no distinction is made between the racecourse and the road to it; both are 'Horse Road'. What they were really objecting to was the races.

From the sound of it the Select Committee ordered a large rock and part of the hill to be cut down at the upper end of the course, which was thereby extended in the direction of the peninsula's narrow neck. This became known as the Barrier Turn. The Tsotong on this occasion ordered the erection of a stone forbidding the building of a Horse Road. It did not prevent continued racing on an improved and enlarged course.

The next outburst from the gentry occurred in 1828, in the first moon, drawing attention to

the audacity of several scores of barbarian slaves, each carrying a military weapon. At the narrow path for cowherds and woodcutters, near the Red Tea-Garden Hill, where there is an Imperial vein of the Coming Dragon, they dug up and lowered away a piece of rock to widen the path of the Horse Road. Old grave booths and tomb cumuli that impeded their Horse Road were at their pleasure scooped away that they might have the sport and play of coming and going on a broad Horse Road.

Reference to the first moon suggests that at the Chinese New Year race-meeting it was decided to widen the track and, by the sound of it, take away some more of the hill to make the Barrier Turn less sharp. It was also decided to widen the racecourse road and straighten it. Between the city and the racecourse there were numerous Chinese tombs, and it is evident that the original road snaked its way among these. To straighten the road would mean removing tombs. Since there would be difficulties about this, East India Company troops were brought in, armed though not in uniform. This is the earliest indication that racing had become important. The East India Company was having no nonsense.

The troops had not been at work for more than a few days before, on 8 March 1828, the Heungshan Magistrate, the Tsotong's immediate superior, sent word to the Procurador of Macao forbidding 'the opening of a track for horses, since it passes the Mong Ha tombs and will interfere with Chinese burials and with fishermen's huts' — there were a few of these along the beach at Areia Preta.

No notice was taken, and work proceeded. Then, on 23 May the Tsotong came out with a thundering pronouncement:

The foreign barbarians shall remain within the Kennel Gate. The Horse Road is FOREVER prohibited. We will maintain the Laws immovably as a mountain; positively not the least indulgence will be shown. You must all tremblingly obey! Do not oppose! A Special Proclamation.

When this had no effect either, he resorted to a typically mandarin ruse. Stable straw and horse fodder were stored in Chinese shops along the Rua da Palha (Straw). An order was now given to all Chinese concerned, forbidding the storage and sale of straw in this locality because of the danger of fire: no straw, no horses, no races.

By this time it was June. The troops had evidently done their work on the tombs and rocks, and in July it would seem that they were withdrawn, with the road still incomplete. Around the time they withdrew, the Governor of Canton learned of their presence, and was reportedly extremely angry. The Tsotong was summoned to Canton to give an account of himself, and, it is said, left in fear of his life. During his absence, according to the gentry of Mong Ha, 'native vagabonds lost to all goodness' obtained for the British all the labour they required to complete the road.

The Governor of Canton now ordered the Procurador, described as the Foreign Eye, to inspect, interrogate and report. In due course it was announced that the barbarians had shown deep repentance, had acknowledged their crime, and would not again repair the road. On the Governor's orders stones were engraved declaring an everlasting prohibition on the dreaded innovation of the Horse Road — the races. These were set up in various places on the Campo. Next night a party of Portuguese went out secretly and removed one of them. The Portuguese, it must not be forgotten, enjoyed the races just as much as everyone else.

By this time, of course, the road was built. It was the best road in Macao.

Company and Country

IN 1827, the year preceding the Horse Road excitements, the *Canton Register* came into being, the first English newspaper in China. It was printed on a small hand-press loaned for the purpose by one of the principal country traders, James Matheson, and his disagreeable nephew Alexander.

The earliest meeting covered by the *Canton Register* was held on 20 and 21 April 1829, with an off-day following, and the newspaper commented that the races 'have afforded so much rational amusement' and were 'a source of great gratification to the surrounding society', meaning the Portuguese and the Chinese.

Though the races were still very much an East India Company affair, a number of prominent country traders took part. This would have been out of the question in the earliest days of racing. The Company regarded the country traders as riff-raff, and would have nothing to do with them socially. Things began to change in 1819 with the coming of James Matheson to the opium trade. Educated at Edinburgh University and the younger son of a baronet, Matheson could not be dismissed as riff-raff. Nor could the Company assume its usual lofty attitude when shortly after this Dr William Jardine came to the coast. As a former East India Company surgeon, Jardine was 'one of them'. From this time forth the country traders came to hold their proper position, often a leading position, in society.

The largest country firm in 1829 was Magniac & Co., and at the race-meeting their personnel were conspicuous by their absence. The Magniacs had left China by this time, the senior partner in the firm being Dr William Jardine, with James Matheson as junior partner, the two of them well on the way to creating what was to become the colossus of the China trade. Lancelot Dent was present at the race-meeting, prominently so. Dent & Co. was a firm rivalling Magniac's in the opium trade. Between Lancelot Dent and Dr William Jardine lay a deep and implacable antipathy, the reasons for which will probably never be known.

The races were run in heats. These were of endurable length, allowing for six races each day. It is probable that most of the horses were Arabs. At any rate, when the famous artist George Chinnery sketched horses in Macao, a few years after this, they were Arabs and very fine ones. Conforming with the social situation existing — the East India Company presiding and racing — all the events were stake races; there were no prizes, cups or plates.

The Tsotong honoured the concourse with his presence on the second day. Whether it was the same Tsotong, recovered from his ordeal with the Governor of Canton, or a new incumbent is not clear. Whoever it was, his presence at the races was extraordinary. After all that commotion over the racecourse road and the widening of the course, here was the representative of Chinese authority patronizing the barbarian horse games.

Here one comes to the kernel of this odd nut. Whatever his public pronouncements, the Tsotong knew as well as anyone that horse-racing was extremely popular with ordinary Chinese, gave a great deal of entertainment, and did no harm. And this, the popularity of the races, was the most extraordinary feature of the matter. Chinese had traditionally regarded Europeans and everything to do with them with complete indifference . . . until this. With the advent of English racing, Chinese and Europeans alike found a common ground of interest and pleasure.

The Tsotong took his seat in the Ladies' Stand, and 'entered into the spirit and amusement' of the occasion, making innumerable inquiries in respect of the different breeds of horses and the countries they came from. Explanations were given to him by Europeans speaking Chinese.

This of course did not prevent him, exactly a week later, from informing the Procurador that it had been brought to his attention that foreigners were conducting horse-races along a path long used by people coming and going on foot. The danger existed of a disaster befalling such wayfarers, leading to disorders between Chinese and Europeans. Let the Procurador allow it to be known that horse-races near the Barrier Gate were to take place no more. This Edict was to be obeyed from the moment of its publication; any who opposed it would be rigorously punished. No excuses of not having been warned in advance would be accepted. Let no one oppose!

Harriet Low at the Races

THE November meeting that year was attended by the pretty and vivacious Harriet Low, the first American girl to come to China, whose portrait by George Chinnery is one

*Harriet Low, who gave one of the earliest descriptions of a China
race-meeting. Portrait by George Chinnery, done in Macao, 1829.
(By courtesy: Mrs Francesca Wiig, Honolulu.)*

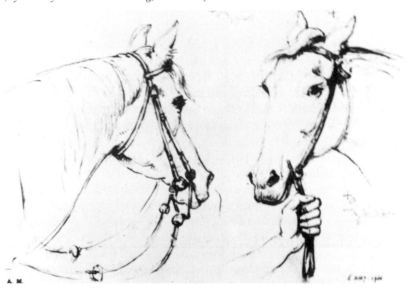

*Arab horses sketched by George Chinnery in Macao, 1840. (By courtesy: Victoria and Albert
Museum, Crown copyright.)*

of that artist's masterpieces. Harriet was 20, and had come from her native Salem, Massachusetts, accompanying her aunt Abigail, who was joining her husband, a partner in the great American firm of Russell & Co.

Harriet kept a journal, written in the form of letters to her sister back home. In her entry for 5 November 1829 she described a race-meeting at Areia Preta. She and her aunt had been in Macao for four days.

The race-ground is at what is called the Barrier, which prevents all foreigners from passing over that spot . . . It is a delightful place, and I was much amused by the novel scene. There was a temporary house of bamboo built for the ladies, and I assure you, my dear sis, it was very interesting to look upon the motley group below us. Chinese of all descriptions, dressed in their most singular costume, some with those large basket hats, many of them with nothing on their heads, but carrying a fan which they hold up to screen them from the sun. Some of them had bags on their backs about half a yard square, in which they put their babies. The poor little things were knocked about in the crowd as if they had been so many bits of wood.

Portuguese and Lascars were mixed with the Chinese, and to hear the mixture of languages — none of which I understood — made me think of the confusion of Babel . . .

Some of the races were very good, and some large bets were made. We returned about seven.

The bets Harriet refers to were evidently made by Europeans, but as her description shows, this was a large and bustling crowd of Chinese, Portuguese and Indians, and no one in their right mind would imagine that several hundred Chinese would have walked two miles out into the country to watch races without betting on them, privately and in their own way.

And the view from the Ladies' Stand must have been delightful. The Stand was erected in the curve of the hill, with tumbling slopes covered with bushes and fringed with flamboyants and bamboo on either side, and ahead the broad Pearl River, with Castle Peak and Lantao Island far away in the blue distance. The moments when the horses galloped along the edge of the shore, and one had a perfectly unimpeded view of them against the background of the sea, must have been fine indeed.

The Opium War

IN 1833 the East India Company's monopoly of trade with China was abolished by Act of Parliament. The Company closed down its China station.

With the Company's departure the races needed new patrons. A Race Fund came into being, and prizes and plates were offered by sponsors, foremost among whom was Lancelot Dent, who took over the mansion of the President of the Select Committee — today the Camões Museum — and in a sense replaced the President as the head of Macao society.

Under the new circumstances not all racing enthusiasts had the contacts or the means with which to obtain Arab horses from India. Somewhere along the line Manila ponies re-entered the scene. Three Philippine ports had recently been partially opened to non-Spaniards, and, after going through many formalities and giving numerous bribes, ponies could be procured. They were cheaper than Arabs, and of course needed no acclimatization. There were now special races for them.

There is no record of the races during these years. One of the reasons for this is that both the newspapers — there were now two — were printed and published in Canton, and often did not get wind of a race-meeting until too late. One thing can safely be assumed. Racing continued with unabated vigour. Macao in the years leading up to the Opium War was almost bursting with Britons. Social life had become positively English.

In January 1841 the British took possession of Hongkong, where in conditions of chaos and anarchy a colony struggled into some sort of existence. Racing does not seem to have been affected. Numerous Britons remained in Macao, whither in February 1842 there was a 'general pilgrimage'[2] from Hongkong to attend the races, and another such in the following year.

Between these two race-meetings the entire scene changed. In August 1842, with a British Expeditionary Force on the river beneath the walls of Nanking, the Southern Capital, the Emperor sued for peace and acceded to foreign demands. A few days later the Treaty of Nanking was signed. Hongkong became a British possession, and five South China ports — Canton, Amoy, Foochow, Ningpo and Shanghai — were opened for foreign trade, Britons having the right to reside

2. E.J. Eitel, *Europe in China*.

ashore at these places, living under their own laws administered by such authorities as the Queen chose to appoint.

If the evidence of the British in Macao was anything to go by, there were soon going to be some more racecourses.

Racing before Ratification

AMOY was first off the mark. When the fleet sailed up the coast in prosecution of the Opium War, the first measure taken, in August 1841, was to subdue the garrison at Amoy, where Sir Henry Pottinger, the Queen's Plenipotentiary in China, left a body of troops stationed on the small hilly island of Kulangsu, on the west side of Amoy harbour. The fleet then sailed on up the coast.

Kulangsu had about 4,000 inhabitants, and here and in the old town of Amoy the British encountered none of the hostility evinced for foreigners in Canton. The people of Amoy had long experience of foreigners, not only in Amoy itself, but in Singapore and Penang, where they were the leading traders, and where the Amoy dialect was the principal language of native commerce. Good relations existed from the start.

Kulangsu, small and hilly — it is just over a mile long — had an area of flat land where there was no cultivation. Indeed there was very little cultivation anywhere around Amoy, whose choppy hills, seen from the sea, looked a livid yellow.

When, a year later, news was received that the Treaty of Nanking had been signed, and that Amoy was to be a Treaty Port, one of the first things that happened was that the Army laid down a racecourse on Kulangsu, where some time in the autumn of 1842 the first race-meeting was held. There is no record of this meeting. The next, held in April 1843, was reported in detail in Hongkong's first newspaper, *The Friend of China*. From this account it is plain that there had been a previous meeting. Both meetings took place before the Treaty of Nanking had even been ratified.

The Amoy Spring Meeting which opened on Monday, 9 April 1843, was dominated by the vagaries of *Planet*, a very fast but temperamental horse owned by an officer named Money, whose colours were black and white. The meeting was clearly an enjoyable one, though the amount of bolting which took place is almost unbelievable, specially for officers of the Bengal Army, most of whom were excellent horsemen.

Whenever there was a good start and no bolting — which was rare — *Planet* won. In one heat, however, he 'made a desperate and irrecoverable bolt, and was entirely thrown out.'

Another very fast horse at this meeting was *Small Bones*, owned by Sir Charles Burdett, who was a kinsman of the legendary Angela Burdett-Coutts, of Coutts & Co., the bankers. *Small Bones* did not bolt quite so frequently as *Planet*, but nearly.

Meanwhile in Macao the usual annual meeting was held throughout the week of 20 to 25 February 1843; and it would seem that virtually every European who could get away from Hongkong went over for the races — many of them with relief, one would imagine, because Hongkong was not only a place of much insecurity, but also disease was taking a terrible death-toll. Macao was universally held to be a healthier place.

The races were held on alternate days, Monday, Wednesday and Friday, with an off-day on Saturday. The Opium War was over, and a number of Bengal Army officers were around with their own horses — the British Expeditionary Force was raised entirely in India — and the sport was expected to be excellent. The horses entered included 15 Arabs, and of course there were the Manila ponies.

The Bedouin Cup, value $100, run in heats on the second day, was won by *Little Wonder*, raced and owned by a Bengal Army officer named Rivers. Significantly he raced three horses, all Arabs. In those days, even in war, it was not unusual for officers to bring two horses, one for duty and one for sport. Rivers evidently collected a third as he went along.

Twelve horses, a large number for the Areia Preta course, ran in the Barrier Plate, weight for inches, 12 hands, 126 pounds. Towards the end of the third day the Winners' Cup was run: $50 from the Fund, Arabs only. Rivers won it on his own *Skylark*. Twenty-five years were to pass before the idea of a winners' race with forced entry recurred — the Champions' Stakes in Shanghai, which was to be the greatest event in the China races.

Interspersed in the programme were the races for Manila ponies, 'this small fry', as the *Canton Press* correspondent loftily described them. Admittedly starting them was difficult. The Manila pony — black, dun and chestnut mainly, used as a farm animal from one end of the Philippine Islands to the other — is ideal for a sedate ride, wonderfully patient as a draught animal, but once given his rein becomes excited, and is not an easy animal to race.

The disdain of the uninitiated for this type of horse was singularly misplaced on this occasion, for it was at this Macao race-meeting that the first hero of the China races made his appearance, a Manila pony small even by the standards of his breed, named *Tetoy*, whose remarkable record will be given in a later chapter. Suffice it for the moment to say that if ever there were to be a Golden Record of the great horses of the China races, the name of *Tetoy* would head the list. He is described later on in his career as 'having afforded the community a good deal of amusement from first to last', from which it is to be suspected that he was one of those ponies given to antics when they win; and win he usually did.

On the off-day at this meeting there was one field, the rest being match races. The weekend followed, allowing time for the return to that difficult, out-of-sorts island, Hongkong, from which the Macao races had provided a temporary, merciful deliverance.

Whereby it was Ordained

THUS it seemed set to continue. There was no thought of having races in Hongkong. Why should there be any? Macao had all the racing facilities; there were hotels, or one could stay with one's friends, many of whom still maintained spacious old houses there. Besides, it was a pleasant visit, and good for one's health. By January 1844 all the usual arrangements were being made for the February meeting, and everyone in Hongkong was looking forward to their annual escape to more salubrious surroundings.

Then, on 26 January, about a fortnight before the races, the Government of Hongkong published for general information the text of the Consular Ordinance, No. 1 of 1844. Issued by Sir Henry Pottinger as Plenipotentiary in China, it authorized British Consuls to deal with all misdemeanours committed by Britons in any part of the Chinese Empire, and blandly went on to state that for the purposes of the ordinance the territory of Macao was 'deemed and taken to be within the dominions of the Emperor of China.'

This, calling into question Portugal's sovereignty over the Macao peninsula, produced fury in the Portuguese community there. It ended with exchanges at the highest level between London and Lisbon, but that mattered not a jot when the Hongkong Government's insulting pronouncement came out. The Portuguese reaction to the British was so hostile that it would have been impossible for the British to have landed either themselves or their horses there, let alone hold a race-meeting.

There was no meeting in 1844, and it brings out a point often overlooked. The Portuguese, not the Tsotong or the Governor of Canton or anyone else, were the key permissive factor in the inauguration and development of English racing in China — because they enjoyed it. It has been seen how the Procurador, when assailed on the subject, issued pleasing Chinese noises, ensuring that any development concerned with racing would peacefully continue.

Question Portugal's sovereignty over Macao, however, as Sir Henry Pottinger unwisely did, and that was the end of that. Not another race-meeting was ever held on the remote and pleasant Areia Preta racecourse.

Meanwhile the thwarted horse-racing enthusiasts in Hongkong turned their attention to the only significant piece of flat land on that mountainous island. This was a much larger but noxious area, looked down upon from surrounding slopes by derelict houses where the occupants had either died of disease or fled from it. Swampy and smelly, it was not unreasonably known by Chinese as Yellow Mud Stream — Wongneichong — after the village whose offerings principally contributed to the stink.

Some comic on the English side had named it the Happy Valley.

2. Boom Town

Powerful Small Horses

THE Treaty of Nanking was ratified in August 1843, and in November HMS *Medusa* sailed into the Whangpoo river to Shanghai, bearing 34-year-old Captain George Balfour of the Madras Field Force, who had been appointed British Consul. He began his mission by calling on the Taotai in the walled city.

Here again, as at Amoy, there was none of the hostility and stone-throwing witnessed in Canton, with children screaming in terror at the sight of a foreigner. The people of Shanghai showed much interest in the foreigners, parents holding their children up to see them better.

The Taotai was a mandarin of considerably more importance than the Tsotong of Macao. Of approximately the same rank as the Governor of Canton — he was an Excellency — his jurisdiction covered Shanghai and several prefectures of Kiangsu province. In due course he returned the Consul's call, and aboard the warship a businesslike discussion was conducted through interpreters regarding the site for a foreign settlement.

The port of Shanghai, such as it was, lay for 13 miles along the muddy Whangpoo river, from the walled city, in a generally northern and winding direction, to the river's confluence with the Yangtze at Woosung. The site chosen for the foreign settlement was an area of sparsely settled countryside of groves and ponds lying a short distance north of the walled city, with 1,000 yards of muddy river frontage between Soochow Creek and a smaller and somewhat smellier creek called Yang-king-pang, destined one day to become the famous Avenue Edouard VII. The river frontage was to become the Bund, the most famous thoroughfare in Asia.

Because the frontage was muddy, it gave rise to the absurd statement, repeated *ad nauseam* in nearly everything ever written about Shanghai, that the foreigners were given a mud-flat to build on. It was nothing of the kind. This entire area at the mouth of the Yangtze is alluvial, the land kept dry and solid by an amazing criss-cross of deep ditches, itself a scientific marvel and a never-ending source of excitement when cross-country racing started. The foreign settlement was an entirely presentable area, indeed a pleasant place. In the flat hinterland beyond it lay over a hundred square miles of cotton fields, rich in pheasant and other game.

It is a strange reflexion, though, that while the walled city remained much as it had always been, having no bearing on the future, from the peaceful area of groves and ponds there developed the fifth largest city in the world.

The first settlers arrived early in 1844, and on the initiative of the young Consul a simple plan was made for a town. This being a British settlement, it goes without saying that the plan made provision for a recreation ground surrounded by a riding track. This was next to the site for a church, later to become a Cathedral. Beside it there was to be a fives court.

The Consulate was sited beside the Soochow Creek, with Jardine, Matheson & Co. next door on Lot No. 1; and with Dent's, Sassoon's and other opium firms moving in, soon it was quite an array. Some of the early houses were prefabricated in Hongkong and sent up by ship. Labour was available from the walled city, and numbers of Cantonese who spoke pidgin English came up to become intermediaries in the new trade and make their fortunes in the process.

Foreign ships in the early months arrived at a rate of one a week, which was promising. At the end of the year the foreign resident population numbered only a few hundred, but their numbers were rising steadily. Quite soon there was racing: heats run for two hours on Saturday afternoons during the cooler months of the year — not in the winter snow, one would imagine, though with the British one never knows. An old hand looking back on those early days wrote of 'those very first meetings on the racecourse situated near the Soochow Creek, with clumsy, sour-tempered, fiddle-headed ponies that ran in heats.'

And here we re-encounter Peter Mundy's 'Couragious' horses, and peer dimly at the introduction of the China pony into English racing, the pony who was to be the composite hero of the China races, though from the foregoing description one would hardly imagine so.

Shanghai held something entirely new and unexpected for the British, being situated just within the orbit of those large northern parts of China where the horse was widely used for travelling, as a farm animal, for drawing passenger carts and bearing loads, and as the invariable ceremonial escort to senior mandarins on important occasions. The towns along the Yangtze were in fact the southernmost points at which annual horse fairs were held.

The horses were driven down from the wilds of Mongolia in mobs of a hundred or so — thousands of horses each year

— shaggy, furry little creatures looking as much like large dogs or bears as horses. They were quite wild. For the first four or five years of their lives they had roved free in their thousands in the vast grassy uplands, where there are more horses per human being than anywhere else in the world. They were the Mongols' staff of life, used as a mount in peace and war, to carry loads, for mare's milk, and for sale to the Chinese for silver, or more commonly as barter for Chinese goods, mainly food and clothes.

The nearest large horse fair was held at Chinkiang, where the Grand Canal meets the Yangtze. A lesser fair was held near Shanghai in the country outside the walled city. To cater for the foreign settlement there arose a regular horse bazaar, not only for sales, but where horses could be stabled, fed and groomed at a very modest charge. The horses themselves were cheap, 25 taels[3] of silver or thereabouts, and it cost only 10 taels a month to maintain a horse and employ a mafoo (groom). A prospective buyer at a fair simply went in and made his choice. If it proved a good racing pony this was sheer luck. The animals were so furry that it was impossible to see anything of their features.

The horses in the mob were between 12 and 13 hands, at once prompting the question, 'Are we dealing with horses or ponies?' A great deal of learned opinion was expressed on this over the years. Put simply, we are dealing with Mongolian horses, which Europeans have always called China ponies. Some of the best and most authoritative writing on the subject of the China pony is that of Andreas, Baron von Delwig, who raced and trained such ponies for 25 years in Tientsin and Peking. His definition is this:

The name China pony, though widely used, is and was misleading, because first of all no horses were ever bred in China proper but were imported from Mongolia and Manchuria, and second they are not what is understood as 'ponies' on the European continent, but are powerful small horses of almost unbelievable endurance, a great weight-carrying capacity, and for their size a great speed.

The official history of the Shanghai Paper Hunt Club, written when Europeans were rich in experience of the China pony, gives these as his characteristics:

Large head, short ewe neck, deep chest, short legs, long body, thick

3. 1 tael = 1.33 ounces.

hocks, often sloping hindquarters, shaggy long winter coat, hairy fetlocks, heavy mane and thick low-set tail. He shows an extraordinary variety of temperament, from the gentleness of a lamb to the ferocity of a tiger. He has speed, sturdiness, soundness and stamina, is a wonderful weight-carrier, and can bear equally well torrid heat and Arctic cold. He has all the qualities sportsmen admire, undoubtable pluck, staying power, amazing cleverness over a country, and the determination from start to finish to get home first, which is the mark of the true racehorse.

He is also one of the most antique of horses. If one wishes to know what the horse was like thousands of years ago, before there was any line-breeding or cross-breeding, the Mongolian 'powerful small horse' is one of the answers. He is the horse in its natural state, coming from lands where there was only one kind of breeding. The horses 'ran around half wild in herds of a thousand or more. Each stallion would take forty or fifty mares into his own pack. He was the king of the pack because he was the biggest and the strongest and the best fighter,' to quote George Sofronoff, who trained many a winner, adding, 'The foals grew up on the best grass you could get anywhere — just like Kentucky blue grass.'

Driving the mobs down to places as far south as Shanghai and Nanking was a feat in itself. A hundred wild horses is no one's idea of bliss or a sound night's sleep. The fairs were held in the autumn, and by the time the mobs reached the southernmost fairs it was nearing winter. A sensible owner, with the coming of snow in mind, kept his new acquisition unclipped until the spring. (Later, when the Horse Bazaar became wiser to foreign proclivities, the dealers themselves kept the horses through the winter, selling them just before training started for the Spring Meeting, when the price went up.)

Then, with the coming of spring, to quote Baron von Delwig,

In about the month of March all their fur would be clipped off, and only then one would see their shapely legs, which almost always are absolutely perfect, and their powerful well-ribbed bodies with strong backs. What spoils their appearance to a certain extent are their short necks, though many have them quite pretty and fine.

To make a China pony arch its neck was out of the question. As someone once remarked, there was not enough neck. They walked as they raced, with their necks straight out, all in a straight line as it were; and since they invariably locked the bit behind their teeth, controlling their speed was far from easy. Another point not mentioned in the description given above: China ponies have Roman noses. Someone spotted this in the very early days, as will be seen in a moment. China ponies, incidentally, come in all the horse colours from snow white to jet black.

Though some of the ponies in the mob had been ridden before in a rough and ready way in Mongolia, no one could pretend that a new pony had been properly broken in. The first month with one's China pony was one long tussle, marked by many bruises and some bites. The new ponies were frightened of human beings, specially of Europeans, and the mafoos were frightened of both. One tamed one's pony oneself. It took at least a month to achieve even a semblance of obedience. Even after that, mounting the animal was a major operation. Somehow a hind leg had to be seized and raised, while two men struggled to hold the pony's head. Once mounted, much depended on how the pony was feeling that day. The first thing might be a bite on the shin. They had mouths like iron. They did not feel the bit, and paid no attention to the reins. However hard one tried to make a pony move in a given direction, it would usually start by going exactly where it wanted, no matter if its head was facing a different way, crashing your leg into a wall *en route* maybe. If you fell off, the pony was liable to savage you, the terrified mafoo completely useless.

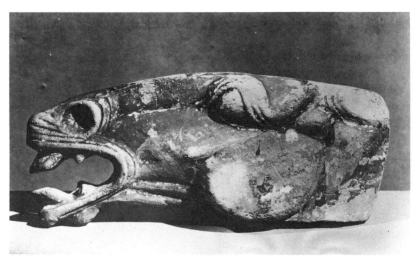

'China ponies have Roman noses.' An earthenware horse-head (Six Dynasties, AD 220–589). (By courtesy: B.B.C. Hulton Picture Library.)

Even when nominally tamed, they bolted whenever they liked. Europeans galloping wildly in no special direction, resolutely concentrated only on staying aloft, were a common feature of life in China. As the foreign settlement in Shanghai gradually became urban, galloping horses in narrow lanes became an installed hazard, not least to shoppers and shopkeepers. When carriages were introduced it was even worse. A galloping carriage in a narrow Shanghai lane was no joke, not least to those inside the carriage. Frequent pleas appeared in the press begging that ponies, whether ridden or driven, be debarred from various parts of the town.

Yet these wicked little animals were to prove themselves true racehorses, providing nearly a century of sport as exciting as, and on a scale larger than, anything Asia had ever known.[4]

Soochow Creek

RIVALRY between Shanghai and Hongkong was a feature of these times, with Hongkong in the grander position. Hongkong had a Governor who was in addition the Queen's Plenipotentiary in China. The Court, as it were, resided in Hongkong. Shanghai had only a Consul and themselves. Prior to the formation of the Shanghai Municipal Council in 1854 there was no government, not even a committee of residents. The 'Treaty' Consuls, British, French and American, exercised a vague sway over their nationals — the American over himself, because he was the only one — but in the words of one old-timer, 'We just thought out what we wanted to do, and went ahead and did it.'

Seen from Shanghai, power and security — meaning the China Station of the Royal Navy — dwelt in Hongkong; but while doubtless this made Hongkong kingpin, Shanghailanders themselves rather preferred to be where they were. Seen from Hongkong, the foreign settlement in Shanghai was brash and parvenu. The head office of every foreign institution of any importance in China was in Hongkong. It was a situation which led to differences of opinion and a certain edginess on matters of 'firsts' and 'largests'.

4. Nor did they change much. An eye-witness account of 1924 records a new pony in Shanghai bucking his rider so viciously that he performed two complete somersaults before reaching earth.

So before going any further let it be clearly stated that Hongkong's first race-meeting was held in the year 1845, notching down a probable though not entirely certain 'first'.

The first Shanghai race-meeting of which there is any record was held on 17 and 18 April 1848, and it is plain from the report of it, published at length in the *Japan Gazette*, that it was not the first meeting. Nor would it seem to have been the second, otherwise surely the correspondent would have mentioned the fact. Judging by the report, racing in Shanghai .was already an established institution by 1848. So it may have started in 1846, or even — perish the thought — in the same year as in Hongkong.

The Shanghai races were for China ponies only, and that pony's amazing weight-carrying capacity had been discovered. The first official standard weights in Shanghai were 140 pounds for 12 hands, and 3 pounds for every inch above. 'Very heavy,' an old hand commented, 'but so too were the jockeys.'

1848 was a somewhat early date for embonpoint to have assumed much of a figure. There were no welter races; the Hack Stakes were as far as it went. Here it is of note that the seven entrants included some of the best ponies, reminding one that these racing ponies were their owner's daily ride. Virtually every Briton in Shanghai owned a horse and rode every day. The knowing ones in fact watched the riders and their ponies carefully, not just when they were training, but on ordinary daily rides, and made mental notes.

The Hack Stakes was an exciting race, with two outstanding ponies, *Roman Nose* and *Kiss-me-quick*, equally favoured. '*Kiss-me-quick* made a bad start,' the *Japan Gazette* correspondent reported, 'but nevertheless on reaching the Willows was just in the wake of *Roman Nose*; at Hicks' Corner he reached his girths, and at the distance post was not more than a neck behind him. Then followed a beautiful race, *Roman Nose* winning by not more than a head. *Kiss-me-quick* was bought immediately, but the winner was not claimed, though he might have been within a quarter of an hour.'

Buying ponies after they had raced successfully was to be a prominent feature of the China races, accentuated by the condition that from the mob you had no idea what you were buying. Betting was keen; a lot of money was changing hands, even in these early days. For a young man, let us say a clerk in one of the big firms, to sell your 25-tael (cost) winner for 250 taels — double that a few years later — made good sense, provided that you did not mind another set of bruises and bites, the outcome of your next 25-tael investment.

Another exciting race that day was the Scurry Stakes, which gave a fine demonstration of the quality of the China pony. The course was narrow, and 12 ponies ran — about the maximum possible. Inevitably there was trouble getting them started, but 'at last the flag dropped and away they went in the most beautiful style, all together too, until they came nearly up to the Grand Stand; even opposite to it there was not the difference of a length among the whole twelve.'

The last event of the second day was a Native Purse for Chinese riders. Ten started, presumably all of them mafoos, in the full paraphernalia of Chinese horsemen — bells, high saddles, bamboo whips, no spurs. The race, run with 'great pluck', was won by a rider with the splendid name of Tattersall.

There is something delightfully rustic about these races. Music was supplied by the birds singing in the woods around the course. One horse bolted and galloped away into the countryside. Most enchanting of all are the Willows. Once round and a distance was known officially as 'Once round from the Willows.'

Henghua Hue and Cry

SHORTLY after this race-meeting a movement was set afoot to acquire a new and larger recreation ground and race-track further inland from the Whangpoo river, just east of a place called Muddy Flat.

The Old Park, as the original recreation ground came to be called, had been purchased from its Chinese owners by a group who, as the Shanghai Recreation Club, held interest-bearing shares in the venture. It was now proposed to pay for the New Park by the sale of the Old Park, and by issuing 5,000 new shares.

The Shanghai Race Club — originally the Race Committee of the Recreation Club — inevitably went along with this, though in fact, owing to its special finances and needs, it was separate from the start, linked only by the racing organizers being Recreation Club shareholders. It was all very informal. For the 1848 meeting the Clerk of the Course — almost certainly Chay Beale, of whom more later — got a group together, fixed the date, made all the arrangements himself, and looked after the cash afterwards. It became a Club in 1855, still run on the same informal lines to begin with, though with the important difference that only members and their bona fide-owned horses could race.

Early in March 1851, when an attempt was made to lay out the line of a road to the New Park, two Europeans were assaulted, following which inflammatory placards appeared in Chinese, referring to

stinking barbarians, brute beasts, tigers and wolves, who having been taught good manners, reason and law, still remain incorrigible. The only thing left for Chinese is to by death utterly exterminate these barbarians rushing into our midst and erecting devilish towers [houses of more than one storey], bringing opium and smuggling and desecrating tombs. Now they wish to open a Horse Road and establish a cavalry parade ground. Let each Chinese select a leader, collect guns and ammunition, and on a future day, by understood signal, make a combined descent on the foreigners, put them to death, and distribute their goods as rewards.

The perpetrators of this were not Shanghai Chinese, but Henghua from Fukien province, noted even by their Chinese neighbours for their unendurable quarrelsomeness. Taotai Woo, the second Taotai the British dealt with in Shanghai, publicly condemned the placards, advising foreigners to 'give no ear to them.' Nevertheless the purchase of the land required for the road and the course was an interminably slow business. Not until 1853 was everything more or less ready. In that year the horrors of the Taiping Rebellion afflicted Shanghai, and racing was suspended.

Meanwhile there had been various developments in the races themselves. At the Autumn Meeting of 1850 Manila ponies raced for the first time in Shanghai, the Manila Stakes being solely for them, and the Union Cup, run in heats, being for the two breeds of pony racing together, Manila ponies carrying 7 pounds extra. The same year quite a number of horses were imported, though not as yet for racing.

Around this time someone in Shanghai, evidently someone with experience of India, jokingly called his new pony a griffin, a word used to denote a newcomer to India, or a novice; and the name stuck. The first Griffins' Plate was raced in Shanghai in April 1851. From then on, China ponies fresh from the mob and racing for the first time were called griffins. They came to have a special appearance. 'Though beautifully clipped and groomed to a high gloss, their manes and tails were often left long, the tail looped up with bright braid, to show their status.'[5]

This was the last time the Spring Meeting was held in April. March in Shanghai is wintry; April is wet; June brings intense heat and the heavy summer rains. May in between is uncertain, sometimes wintry, sometimes very hot and windy, but generally fairly dry. May was chosen for the Spring Meeting of 1852, and this became the order of the day.

And despite the annoyances over the New Park, at 'Once round from the Willows' there was still a very good spirit. In April 1853 someone congratulated the committee on this. 'We are not a racing community,' he went on, 'and until we are, and a regular Tattersall's is established, sport and nothing but sport should be our object, even though some of our arrangements might astonish the ideas of the knowing men of Newmarket, as much as a whirl round Fives Court Turn might astonish their nerves.'

The Battle of Muddy Flat

THE Taiping Rebellion, one of the most ghastly episodes in recorded history, in the course of which not less than 20,000,000 people met their deaths, most of them in massacres, broke out in 1852 in the remote south-west, in Kweichow province. The rebels came rapidly north, gathering adherents as they went, and seized Nanking, where their leader declared himself Emperor. Nanking, the Southern Capital, was in addition the provincial capital of Kiangsu, in which Shanghai was situated. The state of affairs was ominous, the foreign settlement totally defenceless.

The leading citizen at this juncture was Alexander Grant Dallas, a partner in Jardine, Matheson & Co. and head of the firm in Shanghai. At his instigation Defence Creek was dug some distance beyond the New Park, defining the settlement's western perimeter, and the Shanghai Volunteer Corps of all nationalities came into being.

Meanwhile the Small Swords, a criminal society, took advantage of the prevailing disorder in Kwangtung province

5. Ann Bridge, *The Ginger Griffin*.

to launch a campaign of plunder, murder and rapine. They came rapidly north through Fukien province, and in September 1853 infiltrated the walled city of Shanghai by stratagem, and murdered the Magistrate. Two Englishmen bravely rescued Taotai Woo, bundling him over the city wall. From the relative safety of the settlement he then called Imperial troops to his aid.

There was no race-meeting that autumn. November, when it should have taken place, witnessed 'the most awful butchery of human life', in broad daylight, within a hundred yards of the settlement. A Spring Meeting for 1854 was optimistically announced, but was not held. Instead, the new recreation ground witnessed the Battle of Muddy Flat, one of the epics of Shanghai's history, in which a British and American force of 400 sailors, marines and volunteers, with three guns, forced an Imperial army 10,000 strong, which was threatening the settlement, into retreat. The advance was made across the exposed and dangerous ground of the racecourse and recreation ground, using tombs as cover. The engagement lasted just over half an hour. On the Allied side there were only 2 fatal casualties, 24 wounded.

The settlement was revolutionized by these events. From being a small, rather English country town it had become a city. Thousands of Chinese had fled from the walled city and taken refuge in the settlement, where in a single year the Chinese population rose from less than 500 to well over 20,000. In the usual sensible way in which things happened there, the rules were changed; henceforth Chinese could purchase and own land and property in the settlement. There was no other way. That year the Shanghai Municipal Council, composed of all nationalities, came into being, destined to be known with affection and pride as 'the model government', which indeed it was.

There was no autumn race-meeting that year. Though a victory, the Battle of Muddy Flat had been an unnerving experience. Confidence had not yet been regained. The first race-meeting at the New Park was held in May 1855, when there was 'no fear of warlike interruption', and for the first time horses — Arab, English, Australian (from Sydney) and studbred — raced in Shanghai. The band of USS *Powhattan* played between races.

Among the great horses of these years was *Cheerful*, owned by one of the Jardine men, either Grant Dallas or Coll McLean, or possibly by each in succession, and who had a fine record of wins. A horse of great pluck, he was very popular with the public, though if the weather was wet the knowing ones placed their money elsewhere, since he had an irremovable dislike of a wet course. An idea of his quality can be had from a remark made about him in 1859: 'We can be proud of a horse running two miles within four seconds of *Voltigeur* and *Flying Dutchman* in their great match at Doncaster — as *Cheerful* did on Saturday, carrying three stone more.'

Other great horses were the Sydney-trained *Canrobert* and *Sydney*, owned by Mackenzie of the big import-export firm of that name. The most exciting races were those in which *Cheerful* and *Canrobert* were entered together. *Canrobert* was much smaller than *Cheerful* and not nearly so powerful, but he showed more breeding. The two best horses on the course, they were beautifully matched and it was anybody's guess which would win. *Canrobert* at his very first appearance in November 1856 actually beat *Cheerful*, and did so again at the next meeting, and by two lengths. It was not allowed to happen again, until four years later when *Canrobert* won in what was the nearest thing to a dead heat. But then, as one need hardly explain, that day the course was wet.

Cheerful is last heard of at Tientsin in 1863, racing for his Jardine owner, Coll McLean, who was the first of the hermaphrodite owners, his racing name being 'Mr Florence'.

The Court put to Shame

HONGKONG had raced horses from the start, as was only fitting in Court circles. Inevitably, when Shanghai took to racing horses, a polite challenge travelled south across the seas. Why not send up some of your horses to our races?

The racing men of Hongkong seem to have been doubtful about this. Perhaps they knew those brash young men up there. Instead of sending a horse, they presented a Cup — rather decent of them, but slightly patronizing? The Cup was courteously received, though with a just perceptible yawn.

The polite challenge was repeated. In the spring of the following year, 1856, the racing men of Hongkong allowed themselves to be drawn. Taking no chances in the matter of Hongkong's unquestionable superiority to backwoods areas like Shanghai, the champion Arab, *Omar Pasha*, was sent up.

Omar Pasha's achievements in the Hongkong races were known in Shanghai. Approval was shown at Hongkong sending its best. *Omar Pasha* was a hot favourite, entered for the major race of the first day, the Paoshan Cup.

He was a complete let-down. 'He proved himself the most contemptible cur that ever ran round a course,' said someone

Happy Valley racecourse, Hongkong, 1858. (By courtesy: Illustrated London News Picture Library.)

Arriving at Happy Valley, 1858. (By courtesy: Illustrated London News Picture Library.)

The Mafoos' Race, Happy Valley, 1858. (By courtesy: Illustrated London News Picture Library.)

The One-Shilling Stand, Happy Valley, 1858. (By courtesy: Illustrated London News Picture Library.)

who had evidently lost money on him. On the second day, *Omar Pasha*, apparently deterred by defeat, went to the post and refused to move. The race was run without him.

Shanghai had a field day. 'If they want to try the speed of our races, let them send up a horse, not a moke,' they crowed.

To give everyone their due, *Omar Pasha* was entered for the Autumn Meeting. This in Shanghai produced the desired effect. He was evidently still game for a win, and wagers were made accordingly, with due regard to the fact that he was racing against *Cheerful*. This was the meeting at which *Cheerful* was beaten by *Canrobert* for the second time. A disappointing day for him, one would say. Not for Shanghai. *Cheerful* beat *Omar Pasha* by three lengths.

'Send him back to Hongkong,' said the racing men of Shanghai in their most exuberant tone — they had never expected such a walkover as this — 'where he may perhaps again shine in the short distances. He is quite unfit for the Shanghai turf.'

Satisfactory when dealing with the Court; it is, after all, the sport of kings.

Hongkong tried again. In the spring of 1857 they sent up two of their best, *Tartar*, an Arab, and *Druid*, an Australian who was a star of the Hongkong races. *Tartar* had no chance against Shanghai's best Arab, *Sultan*, while *Druid* showed up miserably. 'Our Hongkong friends do not shine in the specimens they send here. We would appeal to some Hongkong sportsmen to send up something more worthy of our competition. We are quite prepared to meet them.'

Worse followed at the Autumn Meeting, the principal feature of which was

the début and hollow defeat of another Hongkong animal, *Yellow Jack*, from the same stable as *Tartar* and *Omar Pasha*, trained personally by 'Mr Chance'. He did nothing in Hongkong, but in Singapore he was a real 'flyer'. It is said he is disposed of to the Shanghai Municipal Council, and will be harnessed to one of those nice little traps in the Lord Mayor's yard.

Delivering the *coup de grâce*, Mackenzie the following February took *Canrobert* and *Sydney* down to Hongkong, rode them himself, and won four out of the six Cups. Hongkong shied off Shanghai's challenge to the May meeting after this.

Respectable Betting

R ACING at the New Park was from the start a big affair, drawing crowds of thousands. The British went in their best, of course, grey top hats, extravagant waistcoats, gloves, field-glasses, the ladies in their crinolines and peg tops and long-sleeved gloves. An intriguing feature was that the Chinese had exactly the same idea about the races. They were to be seen in their best silk robes.

The cavalcade to the racecourse became a real show, with traps, gigs, four-in-hands, even a phaeton or two, much to the admiration of the Chinese, who thoroughly enjoyed it. Race days became holidays. As early as 1861 the Spring and Autumn

Meetings were described as 'the grand festival of Shanghai.' The place literally closed down for a week twice a year. The only thing which could interfere with the races was the unexpected arrival of the mail, when there would be a sudden exodus and return to offices.

Wagers and bets were clearly on a large scale, though of course a veil of shyness surrounds this subject. Lotteries were held at various places in town. Lotteries were respectable. Stray comments indicate that in the grandstand and enclosure young men were keeping books, all rather discreet and in low murmurs. Chinese always claimed they went to the races for the sheer enjoyment of it, which means they were betting.

It was not good form for ladies in the grandstand to wager money. They started by wagering gloves instead, and by 1860 were wagering all kinds of things, bonnets, hats, cigar boxes, fans, even umbrellas. To get the picture clear it must be added that they were not wagering just *one* fan or umbrella. At the Spring Meeting of 1861 a husband was overheard restricting his wife to wagers of ten dozen gloves, times being so bad — Shanghai was having one of the biggest booms in history — while another husband was heard strictly prohibiting his wife from staking jewellery. Remembering that out of courtesy the ten dozen gloves would have to be the right size for the lady concerned, some idea can be had of the peculiar orders received by fashionable dress-shops in faraway Europe.

The Tartan and the Scarlet

THIS was the heyday of the racehorse in China, and it was shortlived. Numerous puzzled answers have been given on the question of the racehorse's demise in that country — poor economic conditions, lack of interest, owners going away, and so on. In fact, the racehorse's demise was inevitable. Racehorses, in a country where horses cannot be bred, require wealthy owners, and this was amateur racing by gentlemen owner-riders, most of whom were far from wealthy. There were very few stables in Shanghai with racehorses. Fields of three were not uncommon, and as early as 1857 there were rumours that in some races all the horses were from the same stable.

The years of the racehorse in Shanghai were artificially prolonged by the strange and peculiarly intense rivalry between the Jardine and the Dent families. It will be remembered that between Lancelot Dent and Dr William Jardine there lay an implacable antipathy. These being family firms, a grain of this was perpetuated in the next generation, and surfaced unexpectedly in racing. John and Wilkinson Dent succeeded Lancelot and became major figures in Hongkong racing. On the Jardine side there was a regular clutch. Dr William Jardine's elder brother had six sons, all of them connected with the firm, and all of them 'horsey'. The youngest, Sir Robert Jardine, became a famous name in the English sporting world.

In Shanghai, Dent's was Dent, Beale & Co., and Thomas Chay Beale was much respected as one of the founders and first organizers of Shanghai racing. When he died, aged 46, a few days before the November meeting of 1857, the meeting was postponed for a week out of respect.

Beale was a descendant of Thomas Beale, who in Napoleonic times was head of Beale and Magniac, the firm which after several changes of name became Jardine, Matheson & Co. When Beale was a ruined man in Macao, Dr William Jardine could have helped him, but would have nothing to do with him. Old Beale eventually committed suicide. Chay Beale at one time worked with Jardine and Matheson, but left them to join the Dents. In other words . . .

The racing rivalry between the Jardine and the Dent stables for the most valuable stakes and best Cups began in Hongkong. The stables were not organized by the actual firms, but by individuals within the firms, racing under various names, the Jardine taipan being 'John Peel', his colours blue and white. In Shanghai, to which the rivalry spread, the stables were known respectively as the Tartan and the Scarlet, the latter sometimes referred to as 'the other stable', which the Dents would not have relished much, though with the public they were the more popular.

In 1859 the Hongkong Challenge Cup, value 500 guineas, the largest prize yet offered, was presented for the first time, for all horses, two miles, to be won two years in succession by the same horse and owner. Strange to relate, only one horse — Snowdon, owned by Muirhouse of Jardine's — came to the post, and had a walk-over win.

What the Dent fraternity were doing is not recorded, but from that day forth the rivalry intensified. The Tartan had a sure winner in Spider, while the Scarlet had a smaller horse of equal merit, Pons Asinorum. The Dents were taking no chances, however. One of them organized the purchase in England of a valuable English horse fit to be an indisputable champion on the China coast. There being no doubt of his quality, he was raced as *Godolphin*, and at the Shanghai Spring Meeting of 1861 he lived up to his celebrated name, carrying all away.

The Jardine side resorted to the same tactics, each side veiling their moves in the deepest secrecy, each determined that the other would not win the Hongkong Challenge Cup, which incidentally a Shanghailander, possibly jaundiced, described as 'probably the ugliest piece of plate which was ever run for on a racecourse.' The outcome was that each year one or other side purchased at high price a valuable English or Australian horse. These raced first at the February meeting in Hongkong, and were then brought up for the May meeting in Shanghai.

When the Tartan's *Eskdale* beat *Pons Asinorum*, the Scarlet stable bought *Niger*. Shanghai had its own Challenge Cup by this time, with the same value and conditions, and the Scarlet stable carried it away, *Niger* winning twice in succession.

The Jardine side next purchased *Sir William*. When he showed unmistakable signs of winning the Hongkong Challenge Cup race twice, the Dents bought *Exeter*, a splendid Australian horse who was to have a fine career in the China races. *Exeter* outran *Sir William*, whereupon someone in the Jardine fraternity bought *Haddington*, who beat *Exeter*. The Tartan and Scarlet horses simply dominated the Shanghai races, amid tremendous popular excitement — 'frenzy' was the word used 15 years later. Each side had its enthusiastic supporters. Shanghai was experiencing a stupendous boom. Wagers and bets were reportedly enormous. When racing started in Tientsin, in 1863, the inveterate struggle spread there too.

'This friendly rivalry', it was called. It may have been. The word 'friendly', though, occurs too frequently to inspire confidence. Certainly in origin the rivalry was far from friendly. At any rate, the public enjoyed it vastly, and Shanghai in particular had some terrifically exciting racing with superb horses.

But it could not possibly last. No one in Shanghai had racehorses which could compare with these, and no one in their right mind was going to enter into so expensive a competition as this, particularly when the boom was over. When *Sir William* and *Exeter* were entered for the Home Cup in 1866 — 100 guineas, 1½ miles — it became a match race. Other owners wisely held back. The same happened next year when *Exeter* and *Haddington* were entered together. That year there were six races for horses, and the largest field in any race was three.

Worse than this, the Shanghai Race Club was controlled by a clique of the principal owners, who were using the Club's money to allot high prizes for events in which their own horses were to be entered, prizes paid for out of the entry fees paid by pony owners. Throughout, in fact, the principal owners were simply making their own private arrangements. As an example, *Sir William* was allowed a walk-over for the Bachelors' Cup because a sufficiently lightweight rider 'could not be found' for *Exeter*. In the Champagne Cup, when *Lawyer* won over *Rochester*, the latter being visibly held back, *Lawyer*'s jockey was booed and hissed at the winning post, and on entering the enclosure lashed out with his whip at those nearest him. An unpleasant scene followed.

It bore all signs of being a nadir. In fact, it came to an end that very year, 1867, when in circumstances which were never made clear, and with mysterious suddenness, Dent & Co. collapsed and went out of business. The *raison d'être* for the great struggle no longer existed. The Shanghai races returned to their core element, the China ponies.

In July 1868 a pitiable auction was held at which the horses and ponies of the Scarlet stable came under the hammer. Business was not good, and bidding was languid. Significantly, a China pony fetched the highest price, 900 taels. The splendid *Exeter* went for only 500 taels, while Shanghai's champion Arab, *Sultan*, with a decade of victories behind him, was knocked down for a mere 50 taels.

Prior to this there was a thorough shake-up in the Race Club. A full-time Secretary was at last appointed. The clique was not thrown out. It vanished at the first mention of open voting by members.

The Third Course

BETWEEN 1856 and 1860 the Second Chinese War took place, conducted on the Allied side by Anglo-French forces acting with the moral support of the United States and

Russia. By the Treaties of Tientsin, 1858, more Treaty Ports were to be opened, and the Powers were accorded the right to have diplomatic missions resident in Peking.

In June 1859 an Anglo-French fleet escorting the new plenipotentiaries to Peking was attacked from the Taku forts guarding the entrance to the Peiho (North River) and suffered a crippling defeat at the hands of the Chinese. The Royal Navy lost three warships, one sunk, two left abandoned on sandbanks. For the size of the force, casualties were higher than in any previous engagement in Royal Naval history. What remained of the fleet limped back to Shanghai to wait while a larger force was assembled for a second attempt.

In August 1860 this force, after another deadly encounter at the Taku forts, in which the Chinese fought to the last man, reached Peking, sacked the Summer Palace as an object-lesson to the terrified Emperor, who had fled to Jehol, and made further demands, which included the dismantling of the Taku forts and all other military positions impeding access to Peking from the sea.

Before this happened, however, the Taiping hordes streamed eastward from Nanking, bringing mass slaughter and destruction on an almost unimaginable scale. In May 1860 they seized Soochow and Hangchow, massacring some 3,000,000 people. Entire populations rose and fled from this terror. In June 1860 half a million people — men, women and children — poured into the foreign settlement in Shanghai. It was impossible to stop them. They would rather be shot than turn back. Once more the settlement underwent a dramatic change.

In August it became clear that the Taipings were heading for Shanghai. An Anglo-French force on its way to Tientsin was diverted to the defence of Shanghai, and within a week the horde was upon them. The terrible mass, advancing on the walled city, hesitated when they found it guarded by British troops, and withdrew when they were shelled from warships on the river. Next day they seethed into the settlement and reached the racecourse and recreation ground, but again withdrew when they were shelled. They withdrew entirely a few days afterwards, but remained in the vicinity of Shanghai and Woosung.

When the military operations in the North were over, the Anglo-French force defending Shanghai was more than doubled. The threat of attack and massacre remained for nearly two years, until early in 1863, when Charles George

Gordon took command of the Ever-Victorious Army, and opened the campaign which finally crushed the Taipings, their 'Heavenly King' committing suicide in 1867. After 1863 no sounds of war could be heard in the country around Shanghai.

It would be thought that a menace of this appalling character would have entailed suspension of the races. Not a bit of it. All the usual meetings were held. They were in fact splendid and brilliant occasions. Shanghai in the years from 1860 to 1862 was quite indescribable. The value of land, of course, rocketed with such a swollen population. Unwanted pieces of land were being sold three or four times in a week, sometimes several times in one day, increasing in price each time. Fortunes were being made on all sides.

To cap it, these were the years of the American Civil War, when American cotton exports dried up. Chinese cotton, which had never been of much interest, suddenly held prime place on the international market. Anyone who could get cotton out of China stood to make a fortune. The Taiping menace meant that the price was abnormally high, but this made no difference, such being the world demand for cotton.

During this boom the sportsmen of Shanghai pulled off an exceptional coup. The New Park had never really been satisfactory. The committee had not succeeded in buying the whole of the recreation ground land. There were still tombs in the midst of it, and parcels of private land. When good Chinese refugee money was offered, tombs quickly lost their sanctity, and soon after the New Park opened, buildings started going up in the middle of the racecourse, some of them blocking the view from the judges' box and grandstand. The New Park was steadily being absorbed into the city.

Seeing the inevitable occur, the Recreation Club, in conjunction with the Race Club, purchased land for a new park on the outer, western side of Defence Creek. This was early in 1860, before the Taiping eruption from Nanking; and this time they bought the land in its entirety. In June the population of the settlement rose by half a million and the land boom started. It rapidly became plain that nothing could prevent the new site from being engulfed by building, and racing had always been a country affair. Why not take advantage of the land boom, and move further out still?

This they did. The third racecourse was purchased in 1860 for 2,245 taels. It was sold in 1861 for 49,425 taels, a figure which aptly demonstrates what was happening all over Shanghai at the time.

When the fourth racecourse and recreation ground was purchased, the Race Club wisely separated itself from the Recreation Club, owning solely the course and adjacent land required for the grandstand, enclosure and stables.

But in the prevailing atmosphere the members lost their heads and settled for a large and splendidly ornate grandstand combining complete club facilities, a large and elegantly furnished dining-room and ballroom, card rooms, billiard rooms, an indoor bowling alley, even a reading room. When the racecourse opened, for the Spring Meeting of 1862, this extravaganza was still incomplete, and shortly afterwards the Club ran out of money. William Keswick of Jardine's came to the rescue, and the building was finished on the basis of a mortgage which the Club was still struggling to pay off twenty years later. The munificent William Keswick never referred to the matter. (This, incidentally, was the second generation of nephews. William Keswick's maternal grandmother was Jean Jardine, sister of Dr William Jardine.)

This time the leaders of the community, evidently realizing that around the third racecourse they had let valuable land go by default, perceived that the land around the fourth course was fit for 'desirable residences'. Jardine's installed themselves in terrace houses overlooking the course, with their stables nearby, and others followed suit. Across the other side rose the mansion of Henry Morriss, who among other things had the controlling interest in the *North-China Herald* and *North-China Daily News*. Known as the Mohawk Chief, his house was named Mohawk Lodge, and the street became Mohawk Road.

The Jardine fraternity were on Bubbling Well Road, which indeed led to a bubbling well if one went far enough. Like everything rural in the fast-growing city, it disappeared, leaving only its name. But this move by leading citizens to occupy prime sites around the course ensured the neighbourhood and the course itself of a settled future, giving the Shanghai Racecourse a characteristic unique in the annals of racing in any part of the world, that of being surrounded by the equivalent of Mayfair, with racing stables.

The third racecourse, between what became Tibet Road and Sinze Road, was used for only four meetings, those of 1860 and 1861. The Spring Meeting of 1861 was one of the most colourful and exciting of any hitherto. Shanghai was bursting with army and navy. The mail had arrived two days before, so everyone could relax and enjoy themselves. General Montauban and Admiral Protet, with numerous French officers, were present. The band of the French flagship played at the course. When the Dents' *Godolphin*, making his first appearance, won the Oriental Cup, his rider received an ovation — the truth is people preferred the Dents to the Jardines — and none of the Hongkong 'favourites' showed up for the rest of the day.

The view from the grandstand was described as 'exquisite, the vivid green of the new crops forming such a magnificent ground for the scarlet trousers of the French and the red uniforms of the Punjabees, while the contrast was toned down by the intermixture of such a horde of Chinese [wearing blue] as was nearly incredible.' At least 10,000 Chinese attended each day. The Taotai came and stayed an hour, all European ladies being presented to him. He left preceded by a ceremonial guard consisting of four flags, two spears, one umbrella, some long swords borne by soldiers, and two servitors on ponies. All began to howl and shout as they neared and departed from the grandstand.

The Screws

IT has to be admitted that the China pony dealers were not petty crooks. They were real crooks, meaning they were easier to deal with, because when a real crook makes a mistake it is a real mistake, sometimes leading to beneficial results, in that it wakes people up.

This was how it was in Shanghai.

At an inopportune moment, when it almost looked as if the racehorse might oust the China pony, someone in Mongolia learned that somewhere far, far away in the south, in China, was a town called Shanghai where foreigners bought ponies for more than they were really worth. This was of course true. A price of 25 taels seemed wonderful to a young Shanghailander, where a Chinese might have bought the same pony for 20 taels or even less. The same visionary also learned that these foreigners purchased ponies per picul. This too was true. Since you had no real idea what you were buying, height — meaning also weight — was as good a criterion as any, and heavier ponies fetched a higher price.

So in 1856 the visionary selected a batch of a hundred old screws, and sent them down to Shanghai, where they were sold for much more than the previous year's batch. But of course like all real crooks he went too far. The whole lot were duds, and he was revealed. The dealer at the Shanghai Horse Bazaar, who was of course responsible for it all, had to face some pretty aggressive Britons that year, though as so often with Britons, specially in anything concerned with horses, no one can help rather liking a good crook, and this one, known as Llama Miaou, was a real specimen.

For after all, if the Mongolians could select a hundred dud ponies, they could equally select a hundred good ones, could they not?

This quaint incident in fact marks the beginnings of selection, which within 15 years became the general rule. All ponies for the racing cities of China were selected by the dealers in Mongolia, and were sent down in smaller numbers, with more care and attention. Those for Shanghai were either shipped from Tientsin, or else came by inland water-craft down the Grand Canal to Chinkiang, whence they reached Shanghai by river steamer.

Around 1862, after the Second Chinese War had ended, many officers disposed of their chargers in Tientsin and elsewhere, and numbers of these were taken to Mongolia and Manchuria, where they interbred with China ponies. At that time selective breeding was beyond the competence or imagination of even the most intelligent Mongol duke. The chargers mated as they liked, as did their offspring. But it brought about a distinct change in the ponies delivered to the racing cities. In the ensuing years the number of 13-hand ponies rose till this became the normal height of a racing pony.

The remarkable feature here is that these interbred ponies retained all the characteristics and qualities of the 'original' China pony. 'Powerful', that word so carefully used by Baron von Delwig when describing them, has more than one meaning.

The Shanghai Racecourse — the fourth and famous one — opened for the Spring Meeting of May 1862, with 'warlike demonstrations against the rebels fairly close.' It was a broad turf track with a circuit just over $1\frac{1}{3}$ miles, a steeplechase track beside and within it, and a cinder track within that, the whole encircling 72 acres of recreation ground.

3. Peking and the Racing Ports

Previous page: The Tienanmen, or Gate of Heavenly Peace, in the Inner City, Peking. Two more courts and two more gates further in is the entrance to the Forbidden City. Photograph taken around 1912.

Dust in the Mouth of Man and Mount

THE inclusion of Tientsin among the Treaty Ports brought the racing world a step nearer the source of griffins. Not that anyone would ever get the better of the dealers. But at least in the North there was a more extensive commerce in ponies, there were more dealers and more information — of a kind. It was only some nine days' ride to Kalgan, the entry point in the Great Wall through which the greatest number of ponies came in each year. Tientsin became the point of final selection for the batches of griffins annually sent down to Shanghai and other cities of the South.

It was a terrible place. Edward Bowra,[6] of the Imperial Maritime Customs, described it in 1863 as 'a dirty little hole of a town with about six Europeans and a hostile population of half a million.' But a good pony cost only £8, or $40, with $5 a month for a mafoo and another $5 for fodder. 'Thus for £2 a month I have a luxury which at home would cost me £100 a year.'

This may have been the pony he wrote of two years later when he won a steeplechase in Peking: 'When I first had him, he was the wildest, maddest animal I ever saw, vicious and uncontrollable; but by feeding him myself, and by kindness, he had become as docile as a dog, would eat out of my hand, follow me about the place, and do everything but talk with me.'

This was to be the experience of many Europeans.

The British Settlement was sited well away from the city, and with good reason. The city, a place of unredeemed ugliness, literally stank from quite a distance around due to rubbish being dumped over the city walls, whence it drifted out into the swamps by which the city was judiciously surrounded. Outside the city were the soap-boilers, the smell being so awful that no European could go near them without covering his nose and choking. The land about was dead flat for miles, and treeless. It was one of the most important places in the Empire for the storage of salt, owned by the Imperial Salt Monopoly. So featureless was the landscape that the mounds of salt, beneath mat coverings, looked like a low range of hills in the distance.

A peculiar feature of early racing in Tientsin was sudden emergency changes of racecourse, sometimes within two or

6. Grandfather of Sir Maurice Bowra, Vice-Chancellor of Oxford University, 1951–4.

three days of a meeting. A furious dust storm would obliterate every feature of the course, creating an urgent need to find somewhere else, or a dyke would break somewhere and the whole place would be under water. By the fifth year of racing they were already on their third racecourse, and there were to be several more.

The first meeting was held in May 1863, and despite the drawbacks it was done in style, the Tartan and Scarlet stables in full force. 'Mr Florence', first head of Jardine's in Tientsin and a great racing man, seems to have brought his entire Shanghai stable of horses and ponies there. Hector Coll McLean was the son of a former partner in Jardine Matheson. He himself worked for the firm on the China coast from 1855 to 1894 with only one stint of leave. His daughter married Sir Robert Ho Tung, the Hongkong millionaire philanthropist who was compradore of Jardine Matheson from 1880 to 1900. Coll McLean is buried in the cemetery overlooking Happy Valley racecourse in Hongkong, doubtless as he would wish.

At the Autumn Meeting that year there were more races for ponies than for horses. This trend continued, until after five years there were pony races only.

Inevitably, with Peking only 80 miles away, when racing started there as well it was not long before people were competing in each others' races, racing ponies sometimes being ridden between the two cities, though more often making the

Peking Races, 1867. An artist's impression from a verbal description. The crowds round the course and on the hillocks were far larger than this. The hillocks were entirely covered with blue-clad Chinese, the hillocks themselves being described on such occasions as looking like blue pin-cushions with the pins stuck in. (By courtesy: B.B.C. Hulton Picture Library.)

journey by river. With two other Treaty Ports, Newchwang in Liaoning province, and Chefoo on the Shantung peninsula, both in the Gulf of Chihli with easy steamer access to Tientsin and each other, a network of 'Races of the North' developed, with owners and riders bringing their ponies to compete in 'away' events, or attending simply as visitors on holiday. These were the years of the German ascendancy, particularly in the North where they were concerned with heavy industry and mines. The Germans in Newchwang and Tientsin took an active part in racing, contributing much to the success of the sport, as did their diplomats in Peking.

Largest on Earth

THE Peking races were started by the student-interpreters of the British Legation and the Imperial Maritime Customs. The atmosphere surrounding the student-interpreters was that of an English public school near end of term — anything to escape from the rigours of diplomatic behaviour and Chinese studies. The auspices were favourable. Sir Robert Hart had just taken over as Inspector-General of Customs and was thoroughly in favour of racing. Bismarck, the Prussian Minister, promptly entered *Ironsides*, an Arab. It has to be remembered that the Ministers came from European countries where riding, hunting and good horsemanship were part of life for a certain class. The response from the Diplomatic Corps could not have been more satisfactory.

The races were held on Thursday, 17 December 1863, on the Anting plain north of the city. All the Ministers, indeed everybody, turned up. Even a missionary was seen. He was in for a shock. The student-interpreters had become very bored with missionaries. One of them had had a horse named after him, *Revd Mr Mitchell*, and it raced. Another was called *Excommunicated* and another *Devil*. To make it worse, *Excommunicated* won a race; his rival, well ahead, bolted within yards of the winning post.

But the most interesting feature of the meeting was the dense crowd of Chinese, Mongolians and Tibetans assembled near the winning post, deriving unlimited satisfaction from the riding and the speed of the horses and ponies. Once again in China, this time in the august and magnificent capital, the magic of the races, their most extraordinary quality, had completely taken possession.

At the following April meeting more than 50,000 people came, the largest gathering yet seen at a China race-meeting. Thus it continued, with ever more and more attending. As was said at the time, the crowds at the Peking races would be beyond the imagination of people in Europe and America. These were the largest race-meetings in the world.

For the meeting in April 1864 the Imperial Government gave as a racecourse the dry bed of a large lake in the neighbourhood of one of the palaces. The vast throng surrounded it, yelling their heads off as the ponies passed, booing lustily at any pony dropping behind, the entire enormous human mass maintaining complete order. There was not a policeman in sight.

The student-interpreters surpassed themselves. They introduced a Trotting Race. Before a crowd of 50,000 Chinese, Mongolians and Tibetans this was courting disaster. Trotting was one of the equine arts of the North, always a beautiful spectacle, nowhere to be seen better than in Peking. In Chinese trotting races you ride your pony, sitting him firm, never rising from the saddle, having trained him to give you a completely smooth ride, as constant and unwavering as the flight of an arrow.

Here the Russian Legation came into their own. Glinka, Pestchouroff, Pogojeff — such names sprang to the fore. The Russians had the same system as in Peking, knowing how to train a trotting pony so that its rider's head moved past in a perfect horizontal. The half-mile race was run with thunderous approval. Afterwards the drilled Manchu battalion formed by Captain Coney at Taku in 1862 marched under Manchu officers, and went through several evolutions before the grandstand. The entire foreign community was present, including all the Excellencies.

It was a three-quarter-mile course. The major race, in which all the best ponies were entered, was once round. Just for fun, the students called it the Derby.

They had no idea what they had started. It took time for anything about Peking to penetrate far-distant Shanghai, where in any case Peking was regarded as the world's end by Chinese and European alike. When at last it dawned on the members of the Shanghai Race Club that Peking had a Derby *twice* a year, it was no longer exactly a joke; it was a matter of principle. Shanghai must have a Derby.

Which it did in 1868, and to make sure that there was no nonsense with those aristocrat cavaliers in Peking, for good measure they had a St. Leger as well. And Shanghai went one better. They decided that the Derby would be for griffins, making it the most exciting of all races.

The first winner of the Shanghai Derby was the Scarlet stable's *Zündnadel*, the pony who two months later, at the Scarlet stable auction, fetched the top price of 900 taels. Soon there were several Derbys. By 1873 even Hongkong had one. Not that they were following Shanghai's example, of course, not on your life.

The Peking races moved to a new venue in April 1866, six miles out from the west wall of the city, a site surrounded by low hillocks or mounds on which crowds larger than ever seen before gathered. It was impossible to make even a vague estimate of how many tens of thousands of people were there. The weather was glorious, the enormous Peking sky a deep blue. The course was larger. The Derby — still the only Derby in China, and as usual once round — was now a one-mile race. Among those racing that day was Algernon Freeman-Mitford, the future Lord Redesdale, at the time an attaché in the British Legation.

The Derby, value $30, one mile, had become a fixture. The real race, however, was the Hai Kwan Challenge Cup, value 100 taels, 1½ miles, presented by the servants of the Imperial Maritime Customs (Hai Kwan). No missionary had ever again been seen at the course, but no one was taking any chances. When Bismarck entered *Faust* for the Hai Kwan, Murray of the Customs entered *Mephistopheles*. The devil won.

The Comte de Rochechouart, the French Minister, was a Steward at the Spring Meeting of 1871, and Bismarck was Starter, an intriguing combination in the year of the Franco-Prussian War and the fall of Paris. Several senior Chinese officials attended the two-day meeting, despite high winds and dust storms. Their Excellencies the Ministers of the Tsung-li Yamen presented the Maiden Plate.

The Tsung-li Yamen was the Chinese Foreign Office, though in fact it was a combination of several ministries, including defence. It was also the exalted screen set up to prevent heads of diplomatic missions ever being received by the Emperor.

More important in one way than the Ministers was Sir Robert Hart, who as Inspector-General of Customs controlled the coffers of the Empire, and would not allow spendthrift

Ministers or anyone else to get their hands on them. Hart was the most influential European in China, in fact more influential than all the Europeans in China put together. That year, evidently at the insistence of his staff, his name appeared on the Hai Kwan Challenge Cup, and continued to do so. The Cup and its name were his idea, of course.

In April 1872 the Peking races were held on a new course east of the city. The old course had a swamp in the middle, excellent for shooting snipe in the autumn. The spring rains were unexpectedly heavy, the swamp flooded, and the course was described as 'now unfit for anything but boat racing.'

The new course was at a place called Miao-chia-ti, and was just under a mile round. The weather was perfect, bright and calm, with no dust, and once again it was a brilliant affair, 'more like a Derby Day than anything seen in the East.' This refers to the mass of Chinese side-shows, booths and cooked-food stalls brought out to the racecourse. To cater for the wants of anything up to 80,000 people the number of food stalls there must have been is almost unimaginable. The Diplomatic Corps and the entire foreign community attended with their wives. The Foreign Ministers of the Tsung-li Yamen paid visits on both days.

The Grandstand was on a high mound with sides sloping to the course; from this position the entire race could be viewed. The paddock was three hundred yards away below, and the view from there was most interesting. The sea of faces which rose tier above tier from the course to the Stand on three sides of the mound, and the concourse of Chinese that surrounded the entire course, and who, although there was nothing to keep them back in the shape of ropes or railings, behaved themselves in a most exemplary manner, was a grand sight. Loud and long cheers rose as the ponies passed, and fortunate was a bad last not to be recognized.

Shorn of Victorian verbiage such as 'exemplary manner', this is an astonishing description. Due to the swamp having flooded, the new course had been set up in a hurry. There may have been time to paint a white line to mark the outer rim of the course, but there was certainly nothing else; and here was a vast crowd entirely surrounding the course, and they were excited. Surely the first thing excited people do is run forward? None did, apparently. This scene is simply without equal.

Miao-chia-ti was used for the Peking races until 1882, in May of which year the first race-meeting was held at the famous Pao Ma Chang. Meaning simply Racecourse, it gave its name to the whole locality, and is generally acknowledged to have been the most attractive of all venues of the China races. In fact, this was a return to the former site, with the difference that the course was laid down so that the swamp was outside it, where if it flooded again it would do no damage.

Getting to Pao Ma Chang was rather a business. Starting from the Legation Quarter the choice lay between a Peking cart, a chair, a pony, or a donkey. The Peking cart, made of wood, was one of the most uncomfortable conveyances ever devised by man. One sat on its wooden floor; it had no springs, and when its wooden wheels encountered the least unevenness one shot up and hit one's head on the wicker roof, which was as hard as wood, with another bang on one's behind when landing. A chair entailed endless haggling with bearers. A pony or a donkey was to be preferred.

Moving anywhere inside Peking entailed an everlasting series of encounters with unpredictable obstacles: camels, goats, mules, men carrying burdens on long poles suddenly altering course, geese and turkeys. After passing down Legation Street one worked one's way through to the Chien Mên, the central and southern gate of the Tartar City, then made one's way along the wall of the Chinese City to the West Gate and out into the country. Three miles along a sandy road among trees and graves and temples, then three miles more over fields, and one came upon the one-mile course, surrounded by willows and some low mounds, with at all times a perfect view of a spur of hills running down from the Great Northern Range.

It was already very hot, 84°F, but 'the view of the Western Hills some eight miles distant was grand — all nature was bursting forth, while from the plain in all directions were rising little cyclones of dust which were whirled in a straight line right up almost to the clouds.'

Dense crowds of blue-clad Chinese covered every height and vantage point. A quarter of a mile of Peking carts several rows deep were drawn up beside the track. There was a large turn-out of the better class, and everyone, even the humblest, seemed to be wearing their best. Three Ministers of the Tsung-li Yamen attended 'with no end of secretaries, servants and attendants.' The whole thing was on such a scale that it was difficult for anyone to find words to describe it.[7]

7. The arrival of senior mandarins was most impressive. They usually came in closed chairs borne by either 12 or 14 bearers running completely smoothly at great speed, a proceeding adopted for the last quarter-mile of the journey.

No one will ever know how many tens of thousands of people were there. It is safe to say that these were among the largest gatherings in world sporting history. The Colosseum in Augustus' Rome and the Hippodrome in Justinian's Constantinople had never seen anything like this. For those Colosseum and Hippodrome crowds were unruly and dangerous. Here at the rustic Pao Ma Chang near Peking were crowds larger than those, completely orderly, jolly, clad in their best, enjoying themselves, with not an armed man to be seen, the whole vast crowd getting there and back without the aid or obstruction of a single policeman, and with no guards at the course.

It is worth dwelling for a moment on those who, inspite of themselves, had the privilege of being the organizers of this incomparable and truly immense scene. The Stewards were the Belgian Minister, Comte de Noidans; Count Tattenbach, the German Secretary of Legation; Cyril Maude, Second Secretary in the British Legation, who had a win on *Macaroon*, his own pony; Professor C.H. Oliver; and Boyd Bredon of the Customs, who was Sir Robert Hart's brother-in-law. The Starter was the fiery and forthright German Minister, Baron von Ketteler.

The Ministers of the Tsung-li Yamen gave the Yamen Prize, 75 taels for the winner, 25 taels for the runner-up. The Hai Kwan Challenge Cup's lettering now ran: 'Presented by Sir Robert Hart, K.C.M.G., and the Gentlemen of the Chinese Imperial Maritime Customs.' Cyril Maude of the British Legation rode Sir Robert's *Sunshine* to a win.

The three Chinese Excellencies of the Tsung-li Yamen lunched on turkey, ham and champagne with evident enjoyment.

Patronage and Crowd Participation

FROM these extraordinary scenes, without parallel in racing history, held in an idyllic landscape, in an almost unreal atmosphere — if one moved an elbow one was liable to bump an Excellency — let us turn to the South, to something equally edifying, but different.

In 1864 the foreign community of Ningpo resolved to hold an inaugural race-meeting on the Queen's Birthday. Very silly of them, considering this was 24 May. As they afterwards admitted, most of the jockeys nearly died of sunstroke.

However, it was a start, and the organizers had the good sense to invite the racing men of Shanghai, 120 miles distant by steamer, to participate, which they did, sending two of their best.

Ningpo was formerly more important than Shanghai. The principal port of Chekiang province, it was a large and well-ordered walled city, noted for its clean and well-paved streets, and for its internal firebreak walls. The foreign community was installed across the river on a promontory where two branches of the Yung river join. The city was seized in 1862 by the Small Swords, causing thousands of people to cross over to the foreign settlement, which consequently became congested and rather a mess.

Land was always a problem in this area, much of which is below sea-level and has to be meticulously guarded. The settlement was bisected by a straight road forty feet wide and a mile long, where the foreign gentry galloped their ponies. There was no argument about this. Chinese just had to get out of the way. But there was nowhere for racing.

The Consul therefore called on the Taotai of Ningpo, and requested permission to use a piece of deserted land — there had once been a town there — west of the city, across the river from the settlement. The Taotai expressed immediate approval, gave permission, and a Cup.

Now, this meeting was to be held on the birthday of the Queen whose forces had twice humbled China in war, and it was going to have a strong patriotic flavour. This did not prevent one of the principal races being the Taotai's Cup.

At this point it is as well to dwell for a moment on this other extraordinary feature of the China races: the patronage conferred by high officials.

From Manchu officials one could understand it, Manchus being almost born on horses. Most of the officials hitherto encountered, however, were Chinese, who had probably never seen a horse-race in their lives. Yet one and all, from the petty Tsotong of Macao to the exalted Ministers of the Tsung-li Yamen, gave their patronage to these strange foreign horse games, which held a fascination for Chinese people which is unaccountable. Racing, indeed, was the one thing about foreigners which Chinese did *not* think mad.

To understand it, one needs to look back to Macao. The reason that Areia Preta was chosen as the racecourse was almost certainly because senior Portuguese citizens asked the English not to race too near the city, fearing that racing would be a cause of civil commotion among the Chinese, and would bring down the wrath of the mandarins on Macao. Instead, the races, despite being concealed behind hills, spontaneously became a festival; and Chinese civil authority must always associate itself with festivals, provided these are respectable. Thus, far from commotion and wrath, there was enjoyment and patronage — the very last thing anyone would have expected in China.

Yes, but how was the Taotai of Ningpo to know that this might prove to be a festival? Here was a small clutch of foreigners holding races solely for their own amusement, totally uninterested in any Chinese unless he was a mafoo. It was most agreeable of the Taotai to give a Cup, but why did he do so? Also, the ever-related problem, how did so many people in Ningpo discover that the mad foreigners were holding races, and pour out in thousands to watch? Something in the region of 70,000 people in Peking knew without public announcement when the race venue shifted from the east to the west side of the city. But then Peking is that kind of city; everyone knows everything. How did the people of clean and well-ordered Ningpo know there were going to be foreign races? From the mafoos, presumably. Yet why, when they never went anywhere near foreigners if they could help it, did they stream forth to watch the foreigners race?

Here we face the inexplicable. To take a parallel, they never went near a foreign football match, and there were plenty of them. One is tempted to wonder how they would have reacted if the Europeans had introduced elephant fights. They might have attracted a kind of exotic attention for a year or two, but they would not have drawn the well-to-do. And this is a key point. From the very start the races attracted the leading and the best, wearing nice clothes too. Nothing shoddy about racing. Mystifying, but there it was.

The Taotai, of course, knew what was going to happen, and thus gave a Cup which signified his sanction for a festival. He knew because the mandarinate was the biggest old-boy network on earth. Young men who had taken the classical examinations in the same year, though they might never meet again, had a tendency to keep in touch throughout their careers, and all were in some kind of contact with Peking. An extravagant feature of life is noted more quickly in China than in any other land. The fact that foreign-devil horse-racing provoked a spontaneous response of approval among well-to-do Chinese citizens and a well-behaved crowd would have been known throughout the mandarinate; thus, without ado, the Taotai's Cup, Ningpo 1864, and never mind that it was Queen Victoria's birthday.

In the third year of the Ningpo races, held more sensibly in April, the Taotai had the races take place closer to the city, just outside the walls between the East and South gates, on the former Tartar parade ground.

The energy of the Stewards converted this, with the aid of bamboo fencing and matting, into a very fair enclosed course, with capital stables at a corner — the only place possible — and with three Stands in descending order of grandeur nearby. There was a very sharp turn near the stables, so sharp that the ponies thought it must be the end, and there were great difficulties keeping them on course, and several spills and swerves. *Confucius*, the favourite, fell for this, to his owner's disappointment. In the Quang Yuan Cup — it was a handsome silver tankard — *Ironsides* crashed into *Confucius*, whose rider fell off. *Ironsides* carried on, but with no struggle left in him. The race was won by an outsider.

HMS *Weasel*, a gunboat, was in port. There were sailors' games, including blindfold racing, with sailors running in all directions, the Chinese crowd giving desperate instructions to put them on course. There was chasing a greasy porker. A sailor won by throwing himself on top of it, while another seized the tail. A desperate struggle ensued, arousing such excitement that several Europeans were pushed from behind into the mêlée in hilarious confusion. The pig survived. The same two sailors bore him off. No one knows how it was settled.

A dense and enormous crowd attended. More than 10,000 Chinese were present on each of the two days. On the second day the Stewards improved the corner, but not enough. The ponies would not get it into their minds that a bamboo fence was an obstacle. So a line of Europeans holding bamboo staves lined this part, and asked the Chinese, several thousand strong, to yell vigorously whenever a horse approached. This they did splendidly. After that 'hardly any pony succeeded in throwing his rider there and stopping more than five minutes in each race. The Chinese obeyed their instructions with an intelligence beyond praise.'

In the Balance Cup *Confucius* made straight for his stable, followed by two others. The Chinese yelled, Europeans cursed and waved their bamboos, and *Confucius* passed astoundingly on. On the second time round *Great Hopes* threw his rider and fell over him, and *Confucius* was forced to go on round or ride over them. On the third round yells and bamboos reduced a bolt to a swerve, and *Confucius* went on in the lead. But by the fourth round he had recovered from his surprise, charged straight through the fence, threw his rider, and scattered the Chinese like chaff before the wind. He was caught, led back, bambooed, and started; but again he turned short inward toward the breach in the fence, and sent his jockey flying. A last effort to get him past was successful, but by then he was in the rear. The gentlemen with bamboos, faint from their exertions, went to refresh themselves on champagne.

One rider was thrown in every race he entered. Every pony flung his rider on average once in each race, and some two or three times. In the Challenge Cup *Great Hopes* omitted to do this and won in consequence, simply because he had no competitors left.

There were more sailors' games. The greasy porker scuttled under one of the Stands, and six came out holding him. In the Sailors' Race the ponies cantered through the breach in the fence in Indian file, depositing their riders each and severally on the turf. They remounted and tried again, but only one survived. One pony was lost sight of completely; even his rider did not know what happened to him. Another pony judiciously threw his rider near the road, and was last seen cantering quietly home. The sailor who reached the winning post did so only after six falls, with all the other ponies cantering around riderless.

'Seldom has a race-meeting surpassed this in point of amusement,' was the summing-up.

Far up the Great River

RACING started in the foreign Yangtze settlements of Kiukiang and Hankow in April 1864, and the meetings were arranged so that residents could attend each other's races, the main feature of which was competition between the Kiukiang and Hankow stables.

Kiukiang (Chiu-chang), near the outflow of the great Po Yang lake, is some 450 miles inland from Shanghai, and 140 miles from Hankow, even further inland. But as was said at the time, transit by river steamer was becoming so regular and convenient that it could be expected that many Shanghai residents would repair for a week's relaxation thither, which indeed occurred. It was not uncommon to find some of Shanghai's best ponies racing at Kiukiang and Hankow.

Here we encounter River ponies for the first time. There were separate races for them, a distinction being made between them and China ponies. The Mongolian horse is to be found over such a vast area — Manchuria, Mongolia, Tibet, and Chinese Turkestan — that inevitably there are regional types. These, presumably so-named because they were brought down by river through the gorges, were probably of the type usually called Tibetan in standard works on horses, though actually most of them come from Chinese Turkestan. In Hankow they were easier to obtain than China ponies, and almost certainly cheaper; but they were slower. There is no record of a River pony ever winning a race in Shanghai.

Kiukiang, with a very small foreign community, mainly British, never achieved what was expected of it in foreign trade, though it had its charms, as a visitor to the first race-meeting testified:

When an Englishman steps out of a palanquin or alights from a sampan and sees a level piece of turf, his first question is, 'When are your races?' This is a small, flat, but prosperous port (so the inhabitants say). The course, in the bright sunlight, backed by the lofty hills of Si-shan, not yet entirely divested of snow, and surrounded by the swift-flowing Dragon's river, the music of whose falls rendered the presence of a band unnecessary, enlivened by crowds of Chinese in holiday attire, and flags that floated from the Stand and the various temporary stables, and rendered homely by the presence of the venerable Aunt Sally, the jockeys in their bright colours — this is a scene seldom met in the sombre valleys of the Yangtze. These little outports have few opportunities of amusement, but when they do arise they are seized with enthusiasm and zeal.

Fields were good, 10 or 11 ponies running in every race. Meetings lasted for two days. The Kiukiang meeting that year was held in May, when it was already very hot. By August the temperature at Kiukiang rises above 100°F. The Si-shan range, incidentally, to which the visitor quoted above referred, is over eight miles from Kiukiang, but has the peculiar effect of seeming much nearer, dominating the scene.

Though 600 miles from the sea, Hankow is situated in an area where, with rivers and lakes, there is distinctly more water than land. The oldest of the three cities which go to form Wuhan, where the Han river joins the Yangtze, it developed under foreign impetus into China's first great centre of modern industry.

The international settlement was sited just down-river from the Chinese city. The river here rises and falls by never less than 18 feet in the course of the year, often considerably more than this. A massive stone riverfront wall was the first requirement, which because of a shortage of money took several years to complete. In addition, nothing can be built in this area unless it rests on an artificially raised platform of earth, which in the case of villages is protected by walls of brick or timber, somewhat after the manner of Venice. Thousands of tons of mud had to be scooped out of the river and dumped on the settlement to bring the earth level up to a safe height for building. The foreign settlement, in fact, was something of a masterpiece.

In the course of time the Russians asked for a concession of their own, the French and Germans followed suit, and so too did the Japanese. When the Japanese completed their section, around 1910, Hankow had the longest Bund in China, a spacious tree-shaded carriageway running for nearly five miles beside the great river.

Hankow was particularly international from the outset. The French and Germans were interested in the region's coal and high-quality iron ore. For the Russians it was the headquarters of the large and important brick tea trade, the tea bricks starting from there on their fabulous journey by river steamer, coastal steamer, and armed caravan to the samovars of Moscow and Petersburg.

Unlike other places, where each nationality had its own club, the Hankow Club was international, and remained so throughout its existence. The Hankow Race Club held a loosely defined position as part of the Hankow Club, a situation which does not appear to have bothered anyone, all the members belonging to both clubs, and which occurred only because there were no 'national' clubs. The informality of the arrangements is demonstrated by the fact that though racing started in 1864, the Hankow Race Club was not incorporated until 40 years later, in 1904.

They were exceptionally fortunate, in this region of more water than land, in acquiring an extensive and valuable piece of land two and a half miles out from the settlement. Within the racecourse there came to be a golf course, a polo ground, and facilities for cricket and football. Around 1910 a swimming pool was added — welcome in a place where in summer the temperature can shoot up to 105°F.

In April 1870 there was terrible rain the night before the races. They had to be deferred. This, as always, caused a major alarm, the reason being that lotteries, wagers, and advance bets bore a date. It was worse when a meeting occurred near a weekend and had to be deferred. Lotteries and wagers did not stand over a Sunday.

Everyone in Hankow with a barometer was nearly driven mad that night with people dashing in to consult it. There was great excitement at the Club when in the early hours a two-tenths rise in pressure was announced. Verdict was given that the races would be held that day. Wagers would stand.

When one reflects that all the Shanghai ponies and riders participating were going to miss the Shanghai Spring Meeting, it gives an idea of the way in which the Hankow races were viewed, and the friendly, let-live spirit between the racing ports. Here was a group of visitors prepared to forsake the high stakes of Shanghai to ensure the outport races were a success. They had a pleasant holiday, of course, but the spirit was there, one of the most pleasing aspects of the China races.

Happy Valley racecourse, 1869. A very early photograph. The second structure on the right is the Grand Stand. (By courtesy: Mansell Collection.)

And the distances themselves give pause for thought. For a Shanghai pony to race in Hankow meant a return journey of 1,200 miles by river. For a Hongkong pony to race in Shanghai meant a return journey of 2,112 miles by sea. Even forty years after the time being discussed here, people were saying that taking horses such distances to race would in England be thought incredible.

While on the subject of high stakes, a strange incident must be recounted from Shanghai. At the Spring Meeting of 1863 the Fuhtai (the Deputy Taotai) attended with the Governor of Chekiang, who was on a visit. The Governor was a Manchu, and appeared with a large entourage of mandarins inside the course, and a mass of armed bannermen at the gates. Mandarins seemed to be everywhere, clearly in a holiday mood. When it was reported that some of them were in the weighing room, a ghastly thought occurred to someone: what *were* they going to make of 'leading'? Here amid the high stakes, with people laying bets on horses winning, was a secret chamber in which a group were weighting the horses down with lead to *prevent* them from winning, clearly in dastardly pursuit of privy gain. A Chinese-speaking European was hastily despatched to the weighing room, from which with decorum the mandarins were herded out as fast as possible.

Further South

FOOCHOW, 34 miles inland on the Min river in Fukien province, was the principal port for the export of tea to Britain, including the most prized of all the China teas, 'the fragrant Bohea'. The foreign settlement there was the most picturesque of any in China, the residences scattered over low wooded hills across-river from the city, with exquisite views of other wooded hills and distant mountains. But because the residences were so scattered there was less community spirit than elsewhere. The place became noted for narrow cliques. For many years there was no Club. Races were sometimes held, but in a half-hearted way compared with other places.

Not until 1868 — the settlement dated from 1843 — did racing get into its stride, with from the beginning a close tie-in with the Amoy races. In Amoy, only ponies were raced, though these were of many kinds, Arab and Cabul ponies, Straits, Japanese and Manila ponies, and Amoy ponies, which being 12 hands 2 inches and over were evidently China ponies. By 1868, when Foochow joined in, the races were for Japanese, China and Manila ponies, and there were special races for ponies of Foochow and Amoy ownership. The Japanese ponies were simply China ponies which had raced as griffins on the course at Yokohama, where English racing started in 1862.

The first Foochow meeting, held in January 1868 at the Tartar Camp, was a tremendous success. Every European lady in the place turned up, together with all the mandarins and all the consuls. Foochow being the provincial capital, mandarins were numerous. Excellent tiffins were served. Shanghai jockeys came in force.

By 1870 there was still no grandstand, and no outer ring — British sailors kept the crowds in place — but it was all very enjoyable. A large assemblage of Chinese attended, including several mandarins in plain clothes. The Viceroy of Fukien and Chekiang came disguised as a coolie, and was observed eating a 10-cent toffee cake at one of the stalls. The British Consul had recently married, and was making his first appearance with his wife. As they passed by, the cynosure of all eyes, the Viceroy's mouth was full of toffee, and he had to turn his back on the British Consul, pretending not to recognize him.

By December 1872 there was a grandstand, and instead of the Stewards serving tiffin for ninety people, as in the previous year, there was now a public tiffin which proved very popular.

The next meeting was held four months later, in April, which is about the last time possible in Foochow before it becomes too hot. The Shanghai contingent was on its way home from the Hongkong races, where they had made a clean sweep of wins, and stopped off in Foochow. Naturally they were the favourites for everything. Foochow ponies, however, had three wins — something of a marvel against competition such as this.

In December a real galaxy came. Unfortunately they held the meeting just before the Winter Solstice, and were disappointed when only 2,000 Chinese of the lower sort came, most of them for the purpose of watching the Europeans eating.

From Foochow the ponies and riders went on to the Amoy races. These were no longer held on Kulangsu, but on the island of Amoy itself. The racecourse was on a small plain beside the outer harbour beach, with a background of the sharp craggy hills typical of Amoy. The consulates, foreign banks and offices all being on Amoy Island, the venue was convenient.

Kulangsu was entirely residential. One crossed over to work each day by boat, and the boats were first-rate, made by Amoy Chinese to foreign specifications. The Amoy Regatta was a major sporting event in China. Kulangsu had become a most attractive place, famed for its gardens which, in so arid a region, were outstandingly beautiful, the houses dotted about in no special order, some of them perched on improbable eminences. On a race day, however, Kulangsu conveyed the peculiar sensation of having been abandoned; it was described on such occasions as being 'given up to buffaloes and missionaries.'

The Amoy races were popular with Hongkong people, as was Kulangsu itself as a holiday resort. A feature of the Amoy races was that betting among Europeans was noticeable, gentlemen bookmakers being quite open in the matter. In Foochow there was more shyness. Betting in Foochow was 'very minor' (they said).

After the Amoy races, the Shanghai contingent were nicely in time for their next onslaught on the Hongkong races. Whether anybody ever did any work is a question best left unasked. They must have done, though how is a mystery.

4. Happy Valley

The Detested Governor

HONGKONG was a different kind of place from those encountered so far, a slow-moving place, frustrated, afflicted by unseemly quarrels and scandals. There was no question in Hongkong of thinking out what to do and going ahead and doing it. Hardly anything could be done without reference to the Governor; and he could authorize hardly anything without reference to the Secretary of State for the Colonies in London. Before the invention of the telegraph, this was a slow and enervating business.

The Happy Valley, the only conceivable place for racing on Hongkong Island, had proved itself a deathtrap, the high incidence of disease and death there being attributed to the Wongneichong villagers' ricefields, and the stagnant water about them, which occupied the flat centre of the valley. It was held that in the interests of health the villagers must be expropriated from their fields and the valley drained. Sir John Francis Davis, who took over as Governor in May 1844, concurred, though he was not entirely convinced that the fields were the real cause of disease.

Expropriating villagers from fields meant reference to the Secretary of State. (Imagine anything like this happening in Shanghai. They would simply have bought the fields, with goodwill on both sides.) A Commission was appointed to investigate and determine the compensation to be paid. The Commission's report, with an explanatory despatch, was sent to London. A year of queries, justifications, and more queries passed before permission was at last guardedly given. In 1846 the valley was drained. In all, 18 months passed — from the date of the last Macao race-meeting, three and a half years — before there was a racecourse.

Prior to this, some time in 1845, the racing enthusiasts held a meeting on a very small course in the Pokfulam area, on the west side of Hongkong Island. This area is so mountainous, with so little flat land, that it almost passes belief that even a very small course could be formed. Yet from this event the Hongkong races were to be numbered and dated. Nothing is known about the meeting except that it took place in the year 1845.

The first meeting at Happy Valley was announced for 17 and 18 December 1846. In November of that year David Jardine in Canton wrote to his brother Andrew in Scotland:

There are great preparations making at Hongkong for a race meeting to come off in the beginning of next month. Sir J. Davis has given a cup of $200!!! for which Joseph & I have decided to start Saint Andrew, as we think it would be a pity that he should leave China without one trial for the object for which he was more immediately sent on. Joseph says he has got him into splendid order. Joseph is jockey; we shall send him home to you in January or February by the first good ship & Captain that offers.

The note of ridicule in referring to the Governor of Hongkong was inherited. In his earlier days Sir John Davis was a member of the Select Committee of the East India Company in Macao and Canton, and Dr William Jardine, who at one time had to see a good deal of him, regarded him as a ridiculous little man. Uncle William's opinions of people tended to hold.

The Plenipotentiary's Cup, first presented by Sir John Davis in 1846, became the principal race at all the early Hongkong meetings. Whether Joseph Jardine on *St. Andrew* won it is doubtful. *St. Andrew* was not, in the event, sent to England, but stayed in Hongkong, where he raced for several years, always good for a place, only occasionally a winner.

As with so much else in Hongkong, the draining of the valley was not properly done. One of the nullahs ran beside the course and in front of the grandstand. Whenever there were heavy rains the nullah flooded, spewing sand and mud over much of the course. The middle of the course, where the ricefields had once been, was now a swamp.

The course itself was not an easy one, the turns at the upper end being fairly sharp. Even the Shanghai jockeys, when they later started coming down, admitted that Happy Valley was a challenge. The Black Rock, beside the upper end of the course, became the Hongkong equivalent of the Willows in Shanghai. As a vantage point it was very popular with Chinese, who swarmed all over it on race days.

These years were marred by a disgraceful public squabble between the Governor and the Chief Justice, J.W. Hulme, whom Davis accused of drunkenness and had shipped back to London. The donnish Sir John, with his Latin and Greek epigrams, was cordially disliked by the Hongkong Britons. When Hulme returned exonerated, there was jubilation, and on the second occasion when Davis offered a $200 Cup, no one entered their horses for it, and the race was not run. When Davis left in 1848, none but his staff saw him off.

In fact, the racing public had much to thank Sir John Davis for. With his memories of Macao he knew the social importance of racing, and not just for Europeans. The Hongkong Chinese were Her Majesty's subjects. Anything which could bring them even remotely within the social framework of a British colony was of value. Racing, at that time, was the only thing which could.

Davis knew that if anyone in Whitehall discovered that villagers were being expropriated to make way for a racecourse — which in London was what it would look like — there would be an imperious disallowance. Thus throughout his patient correspondence with the Secretary of State he never mentioned a racecourse — dwelling solely on health, and in the vaguest terms. Had it not been for his shrewd silence, the introduction of racing in Hongkong could well have been deferred for twenty or more years, because the Colonial Office would always take the part of the villagers.

The grandstand was a matshed structure, and remained so for 25 years. Forty years passed before there was a race club. These are examples of how slowly things moved in Hongkong, due in part to the complicated and restrictive colonial form of government, which had a dampening effect on everything.

Annoyances mainly, and Cups

A JOURNEY to Happy Valley was a country excursion. One took a picnic lunch. The varied conveyances — traps and gigs, an occasional carriage, and chairs swiftly borne by trotting coolies — made their way out of town along the peaceful waterfront road, past Spring Gardens and the sleepy village of Wanchai, following the exact line of the present Queen's Road East and Wanchai Road, turning into the Valley exactly as today, and making for the matshed grandstand, which was exactly where the grandstand of the Royal Hong Kong Jockey Club is now situated.

The Navy and the Army were much in evidence at meetings, and there was usually a military band, either regimental or that of the flagship. The heads of the Services were Honorary Stewards. Numerous officers raced, some of them on their own horses, most of them as jockeys for others, who included the new Plenipotentiary and Governor, Sir George Bonham, who had a stable.

Always a large crowd of well-dressed Chinese attended. There were not many Chinese of the better sort in the Hongkong of those days, and it is clear from the descriptions that a high percentage of them went to the races, setting a precedent which has been followed from that day to this.

Rising on the slope of the hill behind the grandstand was the cemetery.

We could wish that some other spot might be selected for our races than that prettiest but most melancholy of all, the Happy Valley. It tells too sad a tale, and is teeming with too mournful memories to make it a fit place for amusement. Balls are not held in charnel houses, and we do think that scenes of amusement should be removed as far as possible from those of burial.

This was not to be. The racecourse could not be moved. The cemetery was there before the racecourse, and it remained there. As the memory of the first terrible years faded, it slowly became less spectral.

From an early date there was the peculiar feeling of the town emptying on race days. Even a hundred years later, when the population was much larger, there was something of this feeling still. A correspondent of 1863 noted that the silence became so pronounced that the click of billiard balls in the Club, and the sound of beer being poured for the two players, could be heard from the Court House steps.

In fact, things went less easily in Hongkong than elsewhere. One year the committee, evidently a clique, only 'partially' announced the meeting and held a Race Ball in the original Club without giving the members prior notification, causing

'Dogs were a regular nuisance at the course', and in this sketch, done in 1881, it can be seen why. The weighty gentleman's dog has neither collar nor lead. The Parsi gentleman following in a more modest though in fact more comfortable conveyance, is overtaking, and will reach the Valley first. (By courtesy: Mansell Collection.)

justifiable annoyance, one member threatening to bring an armchair into the ballroom and smoke a cigar.

Dogs were a regular nuisance at the course. Year after year people were asked not to let their dogs loose, and year after year someone or other did, their dog being different. The Hongkong Britons were not an easy lot to deal with. In 1859 a dog dashed out at a winning horse, and there was nearly a serious accident.

The Jewish community presented a Cup in 1869, and were roundly snubbed for their pains. These were the declining years of the racehorse, and one of the conditions of the Hebrew Cup was four horses or no race. Only three horses came to the post, and it looked like no race. Then, after a pause, *Exeter* joined them, making it from all angles a certain thing. When the flag fell, *Exeter* went away on his own. One of the others cantered after him for a furlong or two, then turned back when his rider saw the other two horses had gone back to the stables. The Jews were widely blamed for making such difficult conditions, when in fact they had been aiming to enliven matters by getting a proper race, instead of the match races and walk-overs to which horse-racing had been reduced.

When Sir Hercules Robinson, Hongkong's youngest Governor hitherto (he was 35), indicated that there should be a separate enclosure within the Stand for the Governor and his guests, this was refused as being an insufferable effrontery. The Governor did not attend the next meeting, and gave no Cup.

So it went on. Nearly every year there was petty nastiness of one kind or another. Hongkong was that kind of place.

A pleasing feature of the races was the degree of participation. All the principal communities, the Germans, the Parsees, the Portuguese, the Americans, gave a Cup. Even the Muhammadans gave a Cup — for Arabs, naturally. The Germans always made sure that their Cup was among the most valuable, the Hongkong Challenge Cup excepted. The Germans were in a curious position in Hongkong. The volume of their trade exceeded that of the British, as did the tonnage of their ships using the port. As a consequence, the German community was always careful to participate to the hilt in anything of social consequence, such as the races, even though they themselves seldom raced.

The Fakei Cup, given by the Americans, was the most magnificent in point of design and execution. *Fa Kei*, meaning Flowery Banner, is the Cantonese name for the Stars and

Stripes. The first Fakei Cup was made in Canton; later ones were from Tiffany's of New York.

The Jardine brothers gave unfailing support in the matter of Cups, as did the Dents. In 1858 (Sir) Robert Jardine gave a gold Cup. The Dent reaction is not of record.

The finest Cups of all were those made in Belgium and presented at the Peking Races, often by the Belgian Minister. In general, the Cups made in Europe were superior in design to those made in China, though in execution they could not compare with those made by Chinese. Chinese-designed Cups tended to be too florid to suit European taste, despite staggeringly good workmanship. This, however, throughout the world, was an era of extravagant racing Cups.

Tetoy

AUSTRALIAN horses dominated the early races. When one thinks that the first horses, of mainly Spanish blood, reached Australia with the First Fleet in 1788 — the first English thoroughbred, *Rockingham*, in 1799 — the fact that by the 1840s the Australian horse had made its mark at the races as far afield as Calcutta, Madras, Colombo, Singapore and Batavia, and dominated the Hongkong races, is little short of phenomenal.

The real hero of the early Hongkong races, however, was the Manila pony *Tetoy*. He was brought from Manila for the Macao races of 1843 by Adam Scott, a merchant whose elder brother and partner owned one of the original lots on Queen's Road Central, the alley connecting with the waterfront beside their office being known as Scott's Lane.

Tetoy — the actual word in Tagálog is *totoy*, meaning 'little chap' — stood only 12 hands 1½ inches. In 1846 he won 4 races against 27 ponies. Next year he won the Valley Stakes and the Victoria Plate, both of which he had won the year before, against 13 ponies. He ran for the Ladies' Purse with a handicap weight of 14 stone 3 pounds, and was beaten, but only at the post, by *Beauty*, a pony who was not handicapped and carried only 9½ stone.

Beauty later committed suicide by jumping overboard on the way to Shanghai. Someone wondered whether it was remorse.

In 1848 *Tetoy* won the Valley Stakes for the third time in succession, each time carrying 7 pounds more, against 8 ponies. He lost the Victoria Plate and the Ladies' Purse to *Charlie*, a pony of 13 hands 2 inches, who was allowed an advantage of 14 pounds in both races.

Next year *Tetoy* won the Valley Stakes for the fourth time in succession, and the Victoria Plate for the third time. He did not enter for the Ladies' Purse, a 9-stone race, since he was handicapped at $12\frac{1}{2}$ stone, and it had become ridiculous. He won it next year instead.

Whether horse or pony, it is a rare animal who can come up to this. *Tetoy* was a marvel. By 1851 his racing days were over, but as was said that year, and truly, 'If he should die in his owner's hands, and a monument be voted to him, its appropriate site would be somewhere near the winning-post.'

He did not have a monument. When one considers that the Governor of Hongkong in those days had to ask permission of the Secretary of State before erecting a flagstaff, had he asked permission to erect a monument to a horse, it needs no stretch of the imagination to realize what would have happened next.

Instead, *Tetoy* was more modestly commemorated, in 1864, by the Tetoy Plate, the mark of a veritable champion, the first to be so named in the Hongkong races.

China Ponies at the Valley

S HANGHAI'S disastrous challenges to Hongkong, recounted in an earlier chapter, made Hongkong racing men aware, though only dimly at first, of the China pony and his possibilities. The trouble was that to those who had never seen China pony races the riders looked so peculiar, with their legs dangling well below the girth, the riders in some cases looking almost bigger than the ponies.

In this context a story used to be told in Tientsin and Peking of a paper hunt gentleman who for years rode a pony called *Goliath*. The gentleman was 6 foot tall and weighed over 200 pounds. *Goliath* was only 12 hands 2 inches. He completed many hunts, and never had a fall.

'How is it,' said someone, 'that this pony never falls?'

'He dare not,' was the answer, 'for fear of being rolled upon by his rider.'

China ponies first raced in Hongkong in 1856. 'Won easy — all bolted,' runs the record. Next year there were three of them, and they were not a success. More arrived in due course, and each year there was at least one race for them. Interest in them was muted, and when entered with Manila ponies they were nowhere.

Happy Valley, 1881. The small central edifice is the Grand Stand. (By courtesy: B.B.C. Hulton Picture Library.)

It is evident from the early days of the China pony at Happy Valley that Hongkong was not getting good ones. This is understandable. In Shanghai, if a purchaser made an unlucky pick from the mob, he could rectify the matter after the next races by buying someone else's winner. Not so the Hongkong purchaser, who made his pick and shipped them. If they turned out to be duds, there was nothing he could do about it. Add to this the wiles of the Horse Bazaar, and the fact that Hongkong men had a tendency to be somewhat at sea in Shanghai, where everything was different, and it comes as no surprise that Hongkong was getting duds.

Later, when Tientsin became a Treaty Port, and when, later still, there were the beginnings of selection where racing ponies were concerned, Hongkong still did not get the best, for different reasons. To take an analogy from cricket, if Tientsin was the bowler and Shanghai the batsman, Hongkong was long stop, catching only what the batsman missed and the wicket did not collect — in short, bowler's errors. At the end of two decades of China pony races in Hongkong, not one name of significance had appeared.

The Last Challenge

THE earlier reference to petty quarrels and annoyances associated with Happy Valley — these were no worse than in any other branch of Hongkong activity — should not overshadow the fact that the Valley witnessed great racing. Certainly in the Treaty Ports the Hongkong races were regarded as second only to those of Shanghai.

It may be well, therefore, to look in some detail at what is, for historical reasons, one of the great races in the annals of the Hongkong turf, the Challenge Cup raced on Wednesday, 20 February 1867, which in retrospect might be seen as the grand finale of the racehorse in China.

The Challenge Cup, it will be remembered, value 500 guineas, for all horses, two miles, had to be won twice in succession by the same horse and owner. *Exeter*, owned by Wilkinson Dent, had won the race the previous year. *Exeter* had in fact for the past two years been winning most of the best prizes. The previous day he had won the valuable German Cup. It was an all-out challenge to the Jardines.

The weather was dull and gloomy, but steady. Five came to the post. All were from either the Dent or the Jardine stables. There was a large crowd.

Jardine hopes were pinned on Captain King's *Haddington*, who had beaten *Exeter* in Shanghai, and on Muirhouse's *Sir William*, though with the proviso that *Sir William*, once in the lead, could not stand being passed; he lost heart.

Dent entered two of his best, *Exeter* and *Pathfinder*. Prior to the race he declared to win with *Pathfinder*. This, causing suitable betting confusion, was to become a familiar practice in Hongkong and Shanghai when a single owner entered two possible winners in the same race. By declaring to win on one, and with a nice arrangement of his wagers, he sometimes stood to gain as much or more if the other horse won.

The start was a good one [the *China Mail* correspondent reported], all getting away on pretty equal terms. Passing the stand the first time, *Haddington* was leading by a clear length, *Sir William* second, *Pathfinder*, *Exeter*, and *Queen Mary* bringing up the rear.

At the turn *Sir William* drew past *Haddington* and went away with a good lead, and at the Black Rock was about twelve lengths in advance of *Haddington*; *Exeter* and *Pathfinder* close together about a couple of lengths behind, *Haddington* and *Queen Mary* falling away. At the village [Wongneichong, tucked away in the upper part of the valley] *Sir William* still held a commanding lead, and appeared to be going strongly, and passing the grand stand the second time was still the same distance ahead.

It looked all set for a Jardine win.

Exeter and *Pathfinder* then raced up to *Haddington* and passed him at the hill, and *Exeter* being let out, gradually drew up until at the village he reached *Sir William* and passed him at the turn into the run in. At the distance *Pathfinder* was called upon, and responded in the gamest possible manner, passing *Sir William* about a hundred yards from the winning post.

For *Sir William* to be passed twice was disaster. He was out. The correspondent, however, continued in all innocence:

But though *Exeter* was hard pulled, *Pathfinder* could not quite reach him, thus making *Exeter* the winner of the Hongkong Challenge Cup, he having won it two years in succession.

Exeter being 'hard pulled' can only be described as sleight-of-hand. *Pathfinder* was beaten by a diplomatic — or financial — half-length. *Sir William*, beaten by three lengths, was led off the course 'dead lame' — psychosomatic, probably.

So Wilkinson Dent carried off the ugly but desirable Cup. They had won, beating the Jardine brigade at last.

That was in February. By October, Dent's had collapsed and was no more.

Defeated, their firm bankrupt, yet they won in their — no, not friendly — contest.[8]

8. The contest was at its worst in Hongkong, where the two families confronted each other. In Shanghai and Tientsin it was conducted by surrogates, and was therefore more relaxed.

5. Races of the North

Chefoo

O F the Races of the North the most unexpected and pleasant, with an atmosphere entirely their own, were those of Chefoo, one of the lesser and smaller of the Treaty Ports, on the north coast of the Shantung peninsula.

Chefoo as a Treaty Port was misnamed. The port is actually Yent'ai. Chefoo was an anchorage nearby which had nothing to do with the port. Europeans somehow got the name wrong, and so it remained.

Yent'ai was only a small place — about 20,000 inhabitants in 1861 — but as the French were the first to realize, it was of strategic importance, being situated just outside the entrance to the Gulf of Chihli and commanding the sea route to Peking. That the Chinese too had long been aware of its strategic importance, could be observed from the numerous disused and ruined forts to be found in the wooded countryside along the coast.

The foreign settlement was on the west side of the town. Like most of the settlements, it had no fixed boundaries, but unlike most of the others, it had no plan. Europeans, mainly German and British, simply built houses where they liked. This allowed room for Chinese of the better sort to come in as well, giving the place an atmosphere of pleasant informality.

The racecourse was situated about an hour's walk along the coast westward. It was on completely solid sand, above tide level and beside a long sloping shore of sand, way out in the country, a place of great natural beauty, with a distant view of the purple hills of the promontory guarding the Gulf. It being axiomatic that horses cannot race on sand, the track in fact consisted of solid earth covered by a thin layer of fine sand, making it look as if it was part of the beach.

Chefoo was singularly well placed for obtaining good ponies. Only 120 miles away to the west was Laichou, facing the bay of that name. Laichou was the scene of some of the most important horse fairs in China. The organizers of these were in touch with one or more of the places beyond the Wall where particularly good horses were bred. These places were not yet known to Europeans; they came to be later on. Because of the special quality of the ponies sold at Laichou, they were distinguished from others as Shantung ponies, even by Chinese.

The Chefoo Race Club was formed in March 1864. When its chairman, Detmering of the Customs, announced a race-meeting for May, when the weather would be perfect, there was an immediate response from Tientsin. The Chefoo riders were somewhat worried, fearing that their Shantung ponies would be no match for the proud ponies from Tientsin, whose achievements at the Peking races were already well known. 'Contrary to all expectation, the Shantung ponies quite eclipsed the animals brought up from Tientsin.' The Chefoo men were in fact riding some of the finest ponies in China.

Shantung ponies were bigger than average. At this date the largest ponies in the China races were 13 hands, and there were not all that many of them. Among the Shantung ponies many stood 13 hands 2 inches, and at Chefoo this was the height taken as the basis for the scale of weights. Chefoo, 4 May 1864, is an important date in the annals of the China races, being the first enunciation of the talismanic 13 hands 2 inches, which in due course became the scale height for racing ponies. At the first Chefoo meeting the weights were 11 stone 7 pounds for 13 hands 2 inches, with an allowance of 4 pounds for every inch under.

The meeting was only a modest affair, attended by a small group of enthusiasts, with fields of six on average; but there was exciting racing, and the Race Club was clearly there to stay.

Two years later, in 1868, this had entirely changed. Chinese had learned of the races, and streamed forth in hundreds, on foot and by boat, to watch. Those coming by boat had their chairs meet them, the chair-bearers wading into the sea to ensure that their masters and mistresses disembarked and came ashore without getting wet. The Taotai of Yent'ai, who graced the occasion by his presence, arrived in this manner. It was a long way for a senior mandarin to come, and speaks volumes for the strange importance and prestige of the races in China.

A trap paraded past the grandstand, three ponies in tandem, the driver dressed Derby-style, white hat with veil and spectacles. The other two ponies had postillions, one vigorously blowing a horn. They were received with tremendous enthusiasm by the Chinese.

The postillions were of course Shantung men wearing Derby attire, the hornblower clearly enjoying himself no end. And this brings out another interesting small point. Here in Chefoo, as in Shanghai on many similar occasions, Chinese loved seeing their own people dressed up in some outlandish foreign costume. Far from being jeered at or scorned as lackeys of foreign imperialism, they were greeted with acclaim.

This meeting was noted for its 'vivacity and success' even as far away as Shanghai. Tientsin, having learned a lesson the first time, sent better ponies, one of which won the China Cup, the main race.

Another feature of the meeting was the Mafoos' Race at the end. Mafoos' races in the South were very funny. The mafoos were terrible riders. Nearly all of them fell off, to everyone's great amusement, including their own — 'Celestials become Terrestrials', as someone in Hongkong put it.

Here in Shantung things were different. The men of Shantung are among the toughest and strongest in China, many of them excellent horsemen. The Mafoos' Race was going to be good, and was treated in style, two miles, with a prize of £70 for the winner, an enormous sum, enough to keep a mafoo and his family in comfort for three years, unless he gambled it away, as he probably would. It was in some ways the best race of the day. All the riders were good, some were very good, and of the winner it was said that he could easily have made a professional jockey.

The mafoos of Tientsin were not quite up to Shantung standards, but they too were good riders, and the mafoos' races there were taken seriously, as at Chefoo. Because the ponies were racing with men of the proper weight for them, mafoos' races offered one of the soundest means of judging the true qualities of a pony. Though the race still came as the last event at the end of a meeting, owners watched carefully, and drew their conclusions.

The grandstand at Chefoo, with a roof of dried kaoliang leaves, was put up each year. It was comfortable, with furnishings brought from town, and always beautifully decorated with bunting and flowers. At the end of a meeting the course was dismantled (there was no outer rail) and set up again the next year. A correspondent of 1866 captured much of the charm of it:

As the afternoon waned, the wind, which had been high, died away, and the whole atmosphere became bathed in that golden haze which Cuyp loved so well to paint in his sunny cattle pieces. The public slowly streamed homewards on foot and in boats, the ponies were walked gently back — glad, no doubt, that it was all over — and the sandy race course was left to another year's rest and silence.

Naval Meetings

CHEFOO was the healthiest of the Treaty Ports. Its climate is one of the nearest to ideal in China. It has three months under fairly deep snow — December to February — and two hot months, July and August, when the temperature goes up to 90°F. But at all times it has the sea air, a wonderfully dry and exhilarating climate, a clear sky, and except during occasional tempests in autumn, a perfect deep blue sea. It was ideal for swimming, and in its simple way a delightful place for a holiday.

Not surprisingly, it ranked high on the list of ports of call — resorts would be a better word — for the Royal Navy, and for the navies of other nations with squadrons in the China seas.

With the coming of the hot weather the China Squadron sailed north from Hongkong. To save coal the ships went under sail at a majestic four knots, timing their movement so as to be at Chefoo for the races. Ships of other navies converged there at the same time. From the racecourse it was a magnificent sight as the great ironclads with their huge white sails slowly took their places and anchored in ceremonial array, some distance out, within view of the course, the respective navies giving salutes of guns for each new arrival.

After the Meiji Restoration of 1868, and the development of modern docking facilities in Yokohama, the Royal Navy found it more convenient to call at Chefoo on the return voyage, and the Race Club accordingly shifted the date of the races from May to September.

The 1872 races took place over two days, with 22 ponies racing. HMS *Iron Duke*, the United States frigates *Colorado* and *Alaska*, and a French corvette were among the ships in the bay. Many of the officers attended. Captain Arthur of HMS *Iron Duke* was Judge, and the ship's band played at the course. Sailors policed the course and kept the front of the grandstand clear, though this was merely ceremonial. The Chefoo crowds were as orderly as those of Peking. The entire foreign community seems to have been there, and there were a number of lady visitors from Shanghai and Tientsin, always a point to be noted.

For ten years the presiding eminence at the Chefoo races was W.A. Cornabé. He was English. Wilson, Cornabé & Co. started business in Amoy, and were first in when Chefoo opened. Starting, as so many did, as straight import-export

The Hongkong Derby, 1882. The Grand Stand was built with foundations for a one-storey building. Two more storeys were added. The top storey became so precarious it had to be closed. A larger and more substantial Grand Stand was built in 1892. Note the private matshed Stands lining the final straight, and the nullah, which was not nearly large enough, and spewed sand and mud all over the course whenever there were heavy rains. (By courtesy: B.B.C. Hulton Picture Library.)

merchants, they became shipping agents and shipowners, dealt in imports of heavy machinery, and had interests in mining. At Chefoo they had a fleet of lighters, and owned all the water-boats. They were exporters of straw braid and silk.

Cornabé was the heart and soul of the Chefoo racecourse. He had a large stable, and raced against himself under different names — including 'Mr England' and 'Hokee', the name of his lighter company — providing great opportunities for the young men who raced his ponies for him. Aside from his, there was no other racing stable, though of course, as ever in the North, virtually every European owned a pony and rode every day. Most of these, however, were hacks.

When Cornabé moved to Shanghai in 1876, there were no races in Chefoo for two years. There were simply not enough racing ponies. Then, in 1879, the Club appealed for help from Shanghai and Tientsin. This was immediately given, and combined with local people's determination to enter, a highly successful meeting was held. William Keswick, taipan of

Jardine's, sent *Lalmahal*. Ten Broeck, star owner at the Shanghai course, sent *Wild Whim*. Shanghai ponies took most of the Cups.

The Taotai, who always gave a Cup, value 100 taels, inquired in advance the time of his race, arrived punctual to the minute, and presented the Cup personally. *Wild Whim* won it, with a local pony, Jaeger's *Bosnia*, putting up 'a good show'.

It sounds for a moment as if the Shantung ponies were not much good. In fact, the problem was training. Because the Royal Navy liked the races to be in September — and without the navies much of the fun, and the glamour, would be lost — training had to be conducted in the fearful heat of August, in the very late afternoon, the only time possible. Add to this the fact that it was a long way to the course each day, and it is understandable that the ponies did not show up well when pitted against animals brought up from the perfect training conditions of Shanghai.

There was jubilation in 1881 when Cornabé returned to Chefoo with a boat-load of ponies, including *Gay Deceiver* and *Scot's Grey*, both of which he had raced successfully in Shanghai. The Taotai came on the second day to witness his race, and lunched in the Winner's Tent, where 'sumptuous viands' were provided by the delighted Cornabé, whose ponies won 8 out of the 12 races, and the Mafoos' Race. Overwhelming superiority of this kind did not matter in Chefoo. The great thing was that there was once more a racing stable.

Remembering again the quality of the Shantung ponies, it seems at first strange that there is not a single famous name in the Chefoo races. The reason for this is that none of the ponies were entered in the greater arenas, where fame was to be had. When at last a Chefoo pony did enter the great arena, the truth was out.

After some years of racing, Tientsin started getting ponies similar to those called 'Shantung', and Chefoo owners gave up buying from Laichou. Generally, it was simpler and safer to have new ponies shipped from Tientsin, despite Tientsin owners having first choice in any new batch.

In 1875 there were two unallocated new ponies in Tientsin, a bay and a black, one of them required by Cornabé of Chefoo. Two of the leading owner-riders decided to ride them in a private trial race, and keep whichever pony won. One of the riders was Harry Hutchings, one of the few Americans in the China races, and an outstanding man. Known as Wild Harry, he rode short stirrup to a degree never seen before in China.

People said that in a race he looked like a monkey on a pole. However, as pointed out in his racing notes by Sir Henry May, Governor of Hongkong 1912–19, Harry Hutchings was simply sitting as Tod Sloan taught English jockeys to sit more than twenty years later. In the trial race Hutchings rode the black. It was beaten by the bay, and shipped to Chefoo.

This was *Black Satin*, who was among the ponies Cornabé took to Shanghai when he moved there in 1876. At the Shanghai Spring Meeting that year the pony won the French Challenge Cup, the Engineers' Challenge Cup, the Ladies' Purse, and on the last day, the Champions' Stakes, a truly fantastic performance which he repeated at the Autumn Meeting, winning again the French Challenge Cup and the Engineers' Challenge Cup, the Autumn Cup, and for the second time the Champions' Stakes, the greatest race in China, the supreme accolade for an owner.

After that meeting *Black Satin*, one of the great names in China racing, was bought by another great name, Paul Chater of Hongkong, the greatest racing man of his time. It goes to show that Chefoo ponies, given the chance, could prove to be quality material.

The Yingtze Races

Edward Bowra called Tientsin 'a dirty little hole'. What he would have said of Newchwang one trembles to think. The Treaty Port of Newchwang, in the Liaoning province of Manchuria, was by any standards a truly awful place.

It was the only Treaty Port not situated in China proper, Manchuria being beyond the Wall; and to make it simpler, the Treaty Port of Newchwang was nowhere near Newchwang.

This, however, was not entirely a misnomer. The inland town of Newchwang was still officially designated as the place of trade, which it had once been in the eighteenth century, when it was in fact the commercial main entrance to the whole of Manchuria for Chinese goods seaborne from the South. Due to the silting of the river Liao, on which Newchwang is to be found, the place of trade had had to be moved down river twice in fifty years, first to Tienchwang, then to Yingtze, which was where it was in 1860, and which was where the foreign settlement was. Newchwang was 30 miles further inland as the crow flies, though 80 miles by the incredibly winding river.

The first Yingtze Races, as they were correctly called, were held for three days in late September 1863, before there was even any racing in Peking, which says something for the energy and enthusiasm of the organizers. They, like the settlement itself, were German and British. Dreyer, Schöttler, Lauderdale, Barnes — such names appear in the programme. Dreyer presented the Challenge Cup, one mile, and Schöttler won the Handicap Stakes, half a mile. Germans seem to have owned the better ponies. Five entered for the Griffins' Plate; the last two bolted on entering the straight — not into a reed-marsh, one hopes, because this was likely.

Yingtze is situated 30 miles inland from the mouth of the river Liao, where, as with the Peiho, there is a difficult sandbar. The entire zone is utterly flat, without a single geographical feature. The mouth of the river, which is easy to miss, was marked by two huge buoys, visible from four miles distance. But once over the bar and up-river, Yingtze's anchorage, for a riverine port, was good, nine fathoms at low water. From this point the river began an amazing series of S-bends, with the peculiarity that the peninsulas so formed were reed-marshes, while the concave areas facing such peninsulas were high and dry. Yingtze was on the first of these parcels of dry land. It consisted of one street, with smaller cross-streets, and was a place of utter filth and squalor.

Apart from the few official buildings and the Trade Guild, which were of grey brick, the habitations were built of mud. Indeed the entire region consisted of mud. The foreign settlement, which would normally have been at a distance from the town, was near it, there being no alternative, built along the main road — the only road in this part of Manchuria — leading to Newchwang, ultimately to Mukden. The British Consul had the best residence, a former temple. The other houses were plain, to put it politely. There is no record of where the racecourse was, but the likelihood is that it too was along the main road, a device used also in Tientsin for a number of years, the verge of the road giving the alignment for the straight run in.

Yingtze's livelihood depended on the export of pulses and the manufacture of beancake, sold in the ports of South China. Another small but valuable export was ginseng, and later on pig bristles came to be a major trading item. Far and away the main import was opium, with sugar a very lame second. For four and a half months a year the river was icebound. For three months — December to February — the temperature was below zero Fahrenheit, rising just above zero in the afternoon. The three summer months were warm — 80°F in a cool room with venetian blinds — though not nearly so hot as at Chefoo. Races were held in May and September. Once, in 1875, they were held in late March and were 'wedged in between a rainfall and a snowstorm.'

Being utterly cut off from the world for four and a half months each winter, books were an essential. Very occasionally news was received by courier from Tientsin — 300 miles on horseback in rough conditions. A Cantonese cook was an absolute essential. Cantonese domestic servants commanded salaries four times higher than in Hongkong, and there was the feature that Cantonese anti-foreign sentiments took an unexpected new direction. Cantonese regarded Manchurians as the scum of the earth. Within the European home, where Cantonese and European confronted each other daily, it was a case of 'all men are brothers'.

It is a remarkable fact that the Yingtze Races were held at all. Even more remarkable, as the foregoing general description may suggest, is that these races were an accredited feature of the China race circuit. Whenever news of them was received in Shanghai, it was reported in full in the *North-China Herald*.

This being Manchuria, it can be taken as certain that the ponies were first-rate, probably better than any in China. The problem was the ice. This ruled out any possibility of entering Yingtze ponies in the Shanghai races. They would never have arrived in time for training for the Spring; they would never have got home after the Autumn. The Yingtze Races clashed with those of Chefoo, ruling them out as well. The Tientsin Spring Meeting clashed likewise. From the Tientsin Autumn Meeting the ponies would never have got home except by the 300-mile route used by couriers.

Added to this, no one ever went to Manchuria, which was regarded as quite close to the end of the world — a point few would dispute. Newchwang (Yingtze) people did sometimes race their ponies at Tientsin and Chefoo, but there is no indication that anyone ever brought a pony to them.

Where racing people were concerned, men and women, it was another matter. Newchwang people often attended the Chefoo races, and there was a specially friendly connexion with Tientsin, particularly among the twin German communities, both racing mad.

The most notable British figure in Newchwang was Henry A. Bush, who like Cornabé in Chefoo was a 'first in' man. Arriving as the agent for P. & O., he collected more agencies, went into the import-export business, owned a beancake factory, and expanded in the usual extraordinary way businesses did in China if well run. He was joined later by his two sons. Bush Bros. became a name inseparable from that of Newchwang. Harry, the younger son, opened the first British coal-mine in Manchuria, and solved the ice problem as far as the races were concerned. He kept two stables, one in Newchwang, the other in Tientsin, getting to and fro himself as best he could.[9]

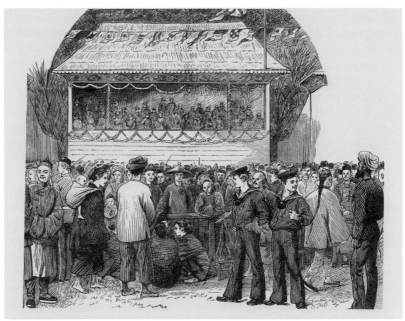

Above and on pp.94 and 101: The Hongkong Races, 1890. (By courtesy: Mansell Collection.)

Towards the end of the century, when the Powers divided China into spheres of influence, Russia demanded the lease of Port Arthur and Dairen, on the Liaotung peninsula to the

9. Harry Bush's finest pony was *Rinaldo*, who in May 1903 in Shanghai won the Griffins' Plate in a field of 25. Frank Dallas rode him, and did the three-quarter mile in 1 minute 29 and four-fifths seconds, the same speed as the record set by David Sassoon's *Hero*, of whom more later.

east of Yingtze, with the intention of constructing a railway linking these places with the Trans-Siberian system. The railway ran along much of the old Imperial road to Mukden. Manchuria became a Russian sphere of influence, and Newchwang (Yingtze) accomplished something of a metamorphosis. It became a bastion of reliable business and industry, a haven of security amid the reed-marshes, beyond which much was more Tartar than Russian.

Reporting the Yingtze races of 1899, the correspondent noted wearily that things were 'rather overcome by Russians all over the place, buying land and houses in the interior, and starting to mine coal, with complete disregard for the Treaty.'

The Russian headquarters were far to the north of Mukden, at Kirin (Chi-lin). Chinese, a minority people in Manchuria, began almost at once to migrate from the Russian zone, unable to pay the Russian taxes, which were exorbitant by Imperial standards and ruthlessly exacted. Hundreds streamed south to Yingtze, where the races, always popular, had record attendances, despite a cholera epidemic in the Chinese town.

A few months later the Europeans at Yingtze, Russians included, were to experience an epidemic more grave than cholera — the Boxers.

Tientsin to the Fore

IN 1864, a correspondent observed that 'Tientsin's attempts at the national sport cannot be compared with the magnificence and importance of the grand meetings in Shanghai and Hongkong.' Nonetheless, Tientsin was already on the look-out for the fastest pony in China.

At the Shanghai Autumn Meeting of 1872 Tientsin ponies and riders attended in force and had great success.

Tientsin riders seldom came to the Shanghai races in such force as this. One of the reasons so many of them came in 1872 and 1873 concerned conditions in the Tientsin region. Since late in 1868 the Nien-fei rebels had been plaguing the province. That autumn they were reported to be only 80 miles from Tientsin, and they were mounted, said to be capable of moving several thousand strong at a speed of 60 miles in a day. Without relays, this was a physical impossibility, but people believed it. The races were held beside the road to Taku, a lonely and exposed place several miles from the city. Needless to say, very few Chinese and no mandarins turned up.

By May 1870 things were slightly better. Both the senior mandarins, the Taotai and the head of the Imperial Arsenal, came and took tiffin. The Taotai was His Excellency Chunghow, very popular with foreigners — he later became an ambassador — and who always gave a Cup. Chunghow sometimes attended the Peking races as well. A large number of visitors came from Peking, Chefoo and Shanghai, but only a handful of Chinese.

Then, a month later, there were riots and a massacre in which 31 Europeans, all French, were murdered, their bodies so savagely mutilated that they were unrecognizable. The dead included 21 French nuns in charge of an orphanage, and all the Chinese orphans and other inmates, more than a hundred of them. French and British gunboats arrived to prevent further atrocities, the settlements under their protection.

A good deal of loose talk, mainly French, followed this outrage, to the effect that the authorities had known in advance that there would be riots and had done nothing to prevent them. Others felt the French had had it coming to them, the cause being 'the pretensions and secretiveness of the French missionaries, and the blind arrogance of the French Consul', who went to protest to Chunghow and was murdered as he came out.

Understandably, the atmosphere had been poisoned. Chunghow was replaced by an aloof mandarin with whom relations were confined strictly to business. This in fact is one of the only times in the history of racing under the Ch'ing dynasty when official patronage was withdrawn. The patronage had always been appreciated, and was much missed. In an indefinable way the races were not the same without it. They bore the air of a trespass. This was one of the reasons why, in 1872, so many Tientsin people went down to Shanghai. Another reason was that the racecourse had been almost completely inundated.

The withdrawal of patronage was to last several more years. Then, in 1878, a new Taotai was appointed who had different ideas, presented a Cup and attended the races. Things were back to normal. To emphasize the point, the Viceroy of Chihli made a donation of $200.

The Tientsin racing men — German, British, French, Austrian, Norwegian and Russian — took the purchase of griffins very seriously, endeavouring to establish reliable contacts with Mongolia. Whenever there were regional disturbances, as with the Nien-fei rebels, the quality of griffins dropped markedly. Batches would get through to Tientsin, but they were clearly rejects from earlier batches. It showed that somewhere, presumably beyond the Wall, some sort of selection was going on.

At last, in 1881, Moore, the manager of the Tientsin horse bazaar, went to Mongolia in person, a difficult and hazardous undertaking in those times, and made his own selection. This marks the beginning of the subscription system in Tientsin. Prospective purchasers subscribed in equal shares. Moore came back with 36 ponies, half for Tientsin, half for Shanghai. From the Tientsin batch he selected one for himself, and invited the 10 subscribers to decide which they thought were the 10 best ponies. These were then numbered and drawn by lot. The rest were kept in reserve, unsold.

The general feeling was that Moore had been pretty tough with the subscribers, though surely he had a right to be. After 35 years of racing China ponies, a European had at last reached the source of them, bringing back invaluable knowledge. From this time forward, with others following Moore's example every two or three years, there was a tenuous but direct contact with the Mongolian studs, as Hongkong rather grandly described them.

Hongkong, of course, being at the end of the receiving line, had had the subscription system long before this, from 1865, the ponies being obtained in Shanghai. They were raced as subscription griffins, and were generally regarded as inferior to owner-chosen griffins. When selected by dealers they may have been, though surely not when selected by an expert like Moore, who was looking for the best. The truth is that there is an air of prejudice on this subject, arising from the fact that in the South a subscription griffin was a relatively cheap buy.

Meanwhile the Tientsin racecourse shifted bewilderingly from place to place. Hanna's Course — Hanna was the manager of Dent's, and he found it — was wiped out irremediably in a flood. This was when they moved to the site beside the Taku road, the road giving the course a straight alignment of one-third of a mile. Yet somehow they were not satisfied with this; it seemed to be particularly exposed to dust-storms. Twice they moved again.

Predictably — except when the province was disturbed — Chinese always discovered in advance where the races were to be, and poured out of the city, on foot, on horses and donkeys, in sedans, in open chairs, and in those terrible carts, to watch them.

In 1873, however, the Race Club went too far — literally. Deciding that all previous sites had insurmountable drawbacks, they moved right out beyond the village of Se-low to the Treaty Joss House, where the Treaties of Tientsin, 1858, were signed. Pao Ma Chang in Peking was six miles out. This was nine miles, and proved too much even for Chinese. For once, there were none but foreigners at the foreign races — though there were a great many, from Newchwang, Chefoo, Peking and Shanghai.

They persisted in racing there, however, until 1876, in which year the rains came very late, dangerously near the Autumn Meeting, and were extremely heavy. The area was inundated, including the Treaty Joss House itself, and it looked for a moment as though there would be no races. Then it was discovered that the despised and forsaken site beside the Taku road was in perfect order. So back they went. The foreigners being returned to sanity — nearer town — the usual thousands once more poured forth to enjoy themselves.

Alarms and excursions of this kind continued until 1887, when the Tientsin Race Club acquired its permanent course. The land for this, and much of the development finance, was the gift of Gustav Detring, an Austrian who was Commissioner of the Tientsin Customs, and later Chairman of the Municipal Council, a remarkable man who made Tientsin his home. Associated with him in this, and in the development of the Country Club, which extended from the racecourse and embraced an area as large as a London park, was C. von Hanneken, the military architect and engineer employed by the Imperial Government to advise on its defences, and who among other things designed and built the defences of Port Arthur, making it ironically in due course so desirable a prize for the Russians.

Von Hanneken, a German, was a romantic personality, a legend among the Chinese. After the disastrous Sino-Japanese War of 1894–5 he was instrumental in raising and training the Newly-Created Army, which was his brainchild — China's first attempt to form an army on modern lines. His wife and Gustav Detring's wife were sisters. Thanks in great measure to these two remarkable men, the Tientsin Races came into their own. The course was a 1½-mile circuit, wide enough to start 14 horses abreast with ease, 18 without undue difficulty. Within it there was a training track of similar length. Within this there ran a canal, one of the many that were essential in keeping the earth dry in this exceptionally flat region. Inside the canal was a cinder track. Creeks surrounded the entire racecourse area.

The canal ran right round the course, draining it and ensuring that it did not flood. In exceptionally heavy inundations, naturally, it did, but nothing could prevent this.

As everywhere in the North, the course was a dirt track, turf in the North being an impossible problem. Yet in some ways it was the best of all the China racecourses. Since the land presented no obstacles of any kind, it was possible to design it from the outset as a classically correct course, if there can be said to be such a thing.

A Gentleman who Lost his Seat

THE following year the China coast received a visit from a person who described himself as 'an experienced racegoer in the United Kingdom and India', and who after attending a Shanghai race-meeting wrote to the newspapers with 'some good suggestions', as he put it — there was no false modesty in this important gentleman. Nonetheless, some of what he said is interesting. He tolerantly allowed that 'as all of you are personal friends, more or less' — that was well put — 'you cannot stick to hard and fast rules of professional racing.' But he pointed out that probable starters, with their riders' names, should be given to the Stewards the day before, and a proper card made up.

It is extraordinary to think that this was not being done in Shanghai. In Tientsin it had been the practice from the first day there was a printing press there. Also, the gentleman continued, the rider's name as well as the pony's number should go up on the telegraph board for the information of those in the grandstand — another strange omission. He conceded that the riders were good, but observed that the Starter was in a difficult position. Because he knew all the riders personally, he could not 'wield the authority of a

professional Starter.' This was undeniable, and was one of the reasons why visiting admirals and generals were often invited to be Judge. They gave an added authority to the Starter.

The august visitor proceeded thence to Tientsin, where he found much to disturb him. His first target was the ladies.

It should be explained that the Tientsin racebooks were about the best to be found anywhere. Of uniform size from year to year, allowing for them to be boxed or shelved, they were bound in calf leather with gold print, with an elegant pencil in imitation gold, and were always beautifully printed, usually at the press of the *Peking and Tientsin Times*.

Our visitor referred to

the ladies coming, each with a pretty book and pencil, but paying no attention to the races, so absorbed were they in their own affairs. The din of their conversation was at its loudest when the ponies were running! [he exclaimed in horror] Such would not be seen at Newmarket, or on the plains of India, or in Shanghai. And there were *children* rushing about the Grand Stand and being given wine *under twelve*! There was a notice which I shall take home as a memento. It reads: 'At the race tiffin today the centre table will be reserved for the children. Owners of stables and members of the Race Club are requested to take their tiffin with the Band.'

'Now, I am really fond of children . . .'— how often has one heard that before — but the visitor felt that if they were to be tolerated in the grandstand, chairs should be provided for them. 'I got up from mine only to find two fat little urchins packed into it by their mamma, and I was left standing!'

He was glad to see that ladies were *not* allowed in the judges' box. In Shanghai they were, a practice he thoroughly disapproved of — though he waited until reaching Tientsin before saying so. Being disappointed in the races — losing his seat seems to have disappointed him most — he went for a walk, and came upon the Astor House Hotel, which he found 'very good for a small country place like Tientsin, but one must obey rules.'

It is peculiar that a man so insistent on rules at a racecourse should object to them in a hotel. He signed himself A.H., which could be spelled out quite appropriately. No one has ever discovered who he was.

The Spore of Leprosy

THE next excitement at the Tientsin races concerned Chinese riders. In 1893 there was a serious shortage of jockeys, both there and in Peking. People were getting fat — this was the word used — and it was not surprising. Tientsin, transformed by the foreign presence, was by this time a very prosperous place, the most important commercial port in North China. Its city population had doubled, and was now over a million. In addition to the large foreign mining interests, it had become the main place of export for China's seemingly inexhaustible supplies of camel hair, wool, and mohair, brought across incredible distances from Tibet, Chinese Turkestan and Mongolia. Prosperity of this kind made for embonpoint. So did diplomatic life in Peking.

At a meeting of the Tientsin Race Club held in March that year, the continental element, led by Detring and his brother-in-law von Hanneken, proposed that there should in future be two races per meeting for Chinese riders. For a number of years Chinese had been racing in the Taotai's Cup, the Taotai insisting they must, otherwise he would not give a Cup; and the Taotai's Cup was invariably one of the best races.

The British element, utterly hostile to Detring's proposal, side-stepped the issue by proposing that weights be raised by 3 pounds. The British were the fat ones. This, however, would bring the Tientsin club out of uniformity with Shanghai, and met with protest from the lead-carrying continentals, who looked after their figures more carefully. A division produced deadlock, 18 for, 18 against. The chairman, McLeish, was a non-racing man. He declined to use his casting vote on an issue which was between racing men. He superbly observed, however, that uniformity of weights should not be a factor to the exclusion of gentlemen riders — indicating somewhat loudly what he thought the continentals were.

Michel and Dr Frazer, one from each side in the issue, both of them prominent owner-riders, then introduced a compromise motion: one Chinese race per meeting. 'This was carried by vote of the Chair after a meeting cyclonic in its temper.'

It caused a cyclone in the South of such dimensions that it even provoked the august *North-China Herald* to devote a leading article to the matter. This uttered the newspaper's complete condemnation of the Tientsin action. 'If there are not enough lightweights, raise the weights; but never let the professional element into sport — it is the spore of leprosy, which soon defies and ultimately destroys it.' The paper went on to point out that the Chinese mafoo was 'only too frequently a gambler and in desperate need of money', and consequently open to bribes. Assuming its loftiest stance — clearly fully supported by the Shanghai Race Club, which regarded itself as the supreme arbiter of the China races — the *Herald* stated that it was adopting an attitude towards Tientsin of 'vigilance and suspicious mistrust'. It was true, it conceded, that Tientsin had for years allowed Chinese to race in the Taotai's Cup. It was true that more Peking stables would enter if they could race Chinese jockeys. It was also true that in Chinese races there had been no complaints from anyone.

Indeed not. If you backed the winner in the Taotai's Cup in Tientsin, it was the nearest thing to a mark of your good judgment, because, as mentioned before, these were races with men of the right weight for the ponies.

The May meeting in Tientsin duly came off. The correspondent, who was a journalist, not a racing man, and thus saw the absurdity of the whole business, commented: 'The Chinese jockeys were closely scanned by critical and censorious eyes. The ponies were ridden as fair and square as the most exacting moralist could require.' Also, the Chinese races gave the European jockeys an after-tiffin rest.

But the British had got their teeth into this, and were not going to give up. At the next Race Club meeting they introduced a motion to the effect that there should be a reversion to former arrangements, Chinese being allowed to ride only in the Taotai's Cup. The Germans, Austrians and others were resolutely opposed to this, but the British packed the meeting, and the motion was carried. Weights were raised by 3 pounds. Tientsin returned to grace.

The *Herald* behaved like 'Auntie Times' of later years. While approving, it also admonished. It firmly pointed out that Chinese were allowed to race in the Taotai's Cup solely because the Taotai insisted on it, 'and while we fully recognize the ungraciousness of refusing a prize offered in a generous and urbane spirit, we must confess that not even under such auspices do we like the principle of Chinese riders.' Mafoos, the paper stated, were formed into guilds, and were subject to 'intimidation of which possibly few foreigners can form a conception, and which no Chinese can oppose.'

They were certainly right about their own mafoos in the South. Whether they were right about the North is doubtful. In any case, victory was to the fat, and the light carried more lead.

Improved Cultivation in Chefoo

CONCEALED behind the trees which flanked the landward side of the Chefoo racecourse, there was a village. Wondering eyes were occasionally seen peering through the foliage at the annual hullabaloo which descended on this quiet spot. The feeling grew in the village that they ought to be making something out of it.

It was Areia Preta all over again, except that here there were no 'gentry'. All in the village were illiterate, meaning they had no appeal to authority. Whatever they did, they would have to do it on their own.

In broiling August 1890 some of the Stewards and a party of workmen came out to fix the course for the training which was shortly to begin.

They found the entire racecourse planted with trees.

It has to be admitted that few literates could have composed so succinct a letter — written on sand, as it were.

The message was read. The villagers were contacted, and in October, after the trees had been removed and the races held, the Chefoo Race Club acquired the land on licence. Actually, the villagers were within their rights. By Chinese law and custom, a coastal village has prior right to the use of its foreshore.

A few years later, in October 1895, there was a real descent of Peking and Tientsin people to the Chefoo races. The genial Boyd Bredon, Sir Robert Hart's brother-in-law, had been appointed Commissioner of Customs at Chefoo. Boyd Bredon had one of the best stables in Peking, and he brought most of his ponies with him, including *Bayard*, *Bunyan* and *Bismarck*, all of them winners at Pao Ma Chang. The Chefoo races looked like being exceptional, with two of Shanghai's top jockeys coming up. Eminences from Peking included Count Cassini, the Russian Minister, and Sir Nicholas O'Conor, the British Minister. The Stewards included Boyd Bredon and the German, Austrian and Russian Consuls. The band of the American flagship played at the course. The Taotai and his suite were there. Chinese soldiers in their picturesque uniforms joined British sailors in lining the course. It was all very grand.

Boyd Bredon entered four ponies, all of which won races; he had eight wins in two days. Countess Margaret Cassini presented the Ladies' Purse, won by a very dashing young man on *Bunyan*. When *Bismarck*, C.R. Morling up, won the Champions, Boyd Bredon 'donned a tall white hat, and those who were quick enough signed congratulations on it.' For the off-day the United States Navy gave a magnificent Cup, there was a Sailors' Race, and Lady O'Conor gave the prizes.

So far so good. But the Tientsin visitors had a disconcerting experience. J.M. Dickinson of Tientsin was the Starter; J.S. Fearon, also of Tientsin at that time, was the Judge. Jaeger and several other Tientsin owners were there. All of them earlier in the year had sold their discarded ponies to Chefoo owners. This day all these ponies proved to be winners. Jaeger's *Rekrut*, now *Recruit* and owned by 'Hokee',[10] won the Chefoo Derby, $1\frac{1}{4}$ miles, in 3 minutes 1 second, and the others were scarcely less noteworthy. The Chefoo meeting ended in an unseemly struggle as the Tientsin owners desperately

---

10. Andrew Eckford of Cornabé, Eckford & Co.

bought back their ponies. Next year there was much excitement in Tientsin when the rejects returned as heroes. *Recruit* was once more *Rekrut*.

Actually, Sir Nicholas and Lady O'Conor's presence at that Chefoo meeting is of significance. The previous year, when they were there, the Stewards arranged a special tent for the Taotai and his retinue. They arrived after tiffin, and the bodyguards, spying the substantial remains of the tiffin, took control of the tiffin tent and whipped the lot, including all the wine. At the end of the day it was found that they had also stolen two of Sir Nicholas' racing ponies, who were never seen again.

Nothing could be said, of course. But one of the reasons Sir Nicholas attended the next year's meeting was almost certainly to show, without saying anything, that there was no ill-feeling. The Taotai must have learned of the misdemeanour, and this is the probable reason why, as a mark of esteem, he arranged for Chinese soldiers to line the course: diplomacy at its best.

All-China Records at Tientsin

IN Tientsin hitherto the Country Club had occupied the Grand Stand during the off-seasons. The Race Club had done so well financially that in 1896 they absorbed the Country Club, acquired corporate ownership of both institutions, and proceeded to develop the Country Club park into the finest demesne of its kind in China, all done from racing profits. The park was situated some three miles out from the foreign concessions, connected by an excellent road, the only good road leading out of Tientsin, and was among other things a paradise for children. The Country Club in its original form voted itself out of existence, its final act being a vote of thanks to Gustav Detring, who had masterminded the wholly admirable scheme.

Slimming seems to have come in that year. For the Spring Meeting of 1897 weights reverted to Shanghai levels. The *North-China Herald* did not know what to make of this. Was it a prelude to more sententious arguments about Chinese riders, over which such 'Homeric battles were fought', or were there more lightweights around? And why did Tientsin riders not bring their ponies down to race in Shanghai any more?

The reason they did not go to Shanghai was that they were doing very well on their own. That spring, the year of Queen Victoria's Diamond Jubilee, one of their best jockeys, Fritz Sommer, riding his own *Moribund* in the Peiho Stakes, three-quarters of a mile, came within one-fifth of a second of the all-China record of David Sassoon's *Hero*, of whom more anon. Sommer had a three-length lead, and at the very last moment let *Moribund* go easy. His time was $1\frac{1}{2}$ minutes.

Another fine achievement that day was that of a newcomer, James Watts, riding *Palo Alto*, a dun, making $1\frac{3}{4}$ miles in 3 minutes 47 seconds. This was an all-China record. *Palo Alto*'s owner was another of Tientsin's remarkable men, Colonel Johan Munthe, a Norwegian who came to China in 1887 to join the Imperial Maritime Customs. After a year he was detached for military advisory duties, became principal military advisor to Yuan Shih-k'ai, and his ADC when the latter was appointed Viceroy of Chihli. Munthe had close-cropped red hair and the longest handlebar moustache ever seen. It was black, and looked quite disconnected from his face, as if a swallow in flight had stopped there.[11]

It was at this meeting that *Stray Shot*, a grey, made his first appearance, 'indisputably the best animal on our racecourse at present or that ever has been. Older folk say he is the fastest animal ever to come to the coast from the plateaux.' Owned by J.M. Dickinson, he won the Champions, $1\frac{1}{4}$ miles, in an astounding 2 minutes $5\frac{1}{2}$ seconds, carrying 158 pounds, another all-China record, the second in two days.

As the *Peking and Tientsin Times* put it, 'Never since racing existed in the Port has such a Meeting been held; never have there been such fine ponies, such close finishes, or such phenomenal times.'

J.M. Dickinson was the main proprietor of William Forbes & Co., another of the firms which began as agent to a shipping company, and diversified and enlarged in the extraordinary way firms did. Forbes himself had been a popular figure in the early years of the Tientsin races, a frequent winner. His death in the prime of life was seen as a great loss to the racing fraternity, but was remedied the next year when his son returned to Tientsin after completing his education, and proved equally popular and successful on the course. The younger Dickinson was a tall, somewhat aloof bachelor.

11. After the Great War he married the widowed mother of Sir Alexander Grantham, Governor of Hongkong 1947–57.

Though a good horseman himself, whenever he knew he had a winner he would ask someone else to ride for him. Not a particularly sociable man, he was noted for his twice-yearly luncheon parties — coinciding with the racing seasons — at which each lady guest received a present of jewellery. A lesser-known feature: his head mafoo arranged the murder of a dishonest horse-dealer.

From the beginning, Tientsin racing men had been looking for the fastest pony in China. With *Stray Shot* they had him; and *Stray Shot* was an all-rounder, good equally as a stayer and as a sprinter. He was in fact Tientsin's finest sprinter.

Moribund, too, was exceptional. If only Fritz Sommer had given that final crack of the whip, and *Moribund* had surpassed *Hero*, who was considered the pony of all time, it would have created a sensation from one end of the China coast to the other. But of course how was Fritz Sommer to know he was so close to it?

Anyway, Tientsin had come into its own, being for the Races of the North what Shanghai was for the South, indisputably first-rate. And there are other indicative touches. One autumn the races were held very late. On the first day there was already frost on the ground, the course had to be strewn with straw, and it was observed that 'the creations of Worth et Cie. were ousted by the need for comfort,' meaning furs.

It was not only the ladies of Shanghai who bought their clothes from Paris. One way and another there was a good deal of money in that Grand Stand at Tientsin, and the Club had just laid out 20,000 taels to build another and larger one beside it.

The railway was now through to Peking, the first railway in China, bringing the two courses much closer. Racing ponies now travelled to and fro by rail. It made Shanghai seem even further away.

Pao Ma Chang

THE Peking races of May 1897 were marked by the sensational successes of the new British Minister, Sir Claude MacDonald, whose unremembered achievements include negotiating the lease of the New Territories of Hongkong. Sir Claude's ponies had names connected with the life of a diplomat. The three he entered on this occasion were *Attaché*, *Cypher*, and *Messenger*, and he invited three of the best Tientsin jockeys, Fritz Sommer, C.R. Morling and Hunt, to race them for him. Heads of diplomatic missions did not ride in races, even when fit enough, though of course like everyone else they rode whenever they could.

Between them, his ponies won 8 out of the 14 races, and the Mafoos' Race. In the Champions all three of them had to be entered, and *mirabile dictu* they came in first, second and third, Morling on *Attaché*, the champion, Hunt on *Messenger* second, Sommer on *Cypher* third. In many another country people would have said it was rigged. China was not like that. It is of note, moreover, that Sir Claude had selected his jockeys with a keen eye.

In succeeding meetings he figured less spectacularly, though always well. In May 1898 the races were attended on the second day by Prince Henry of Prussia, the first member of a European royal house to be received in Peking. On that occasion Sir Claude had three wins. The best performer that

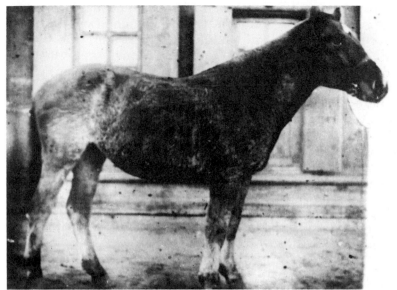

Diana, owned by Baron von Delwig, as she was when she first came down from the Mongolian plateaux in 1927. Actually griffins were more furry than this; but Diana had vermin in her fur, and had mange.

Diana, seen with her owner, as she was a few months later, when she raced and won often in Tientsin, 51 races, never unplaced. This is the only discoverable photographic testimony to the metamorphosis which occurred when a Mongolian horse came down and entered the China races. (Both pictures by courtesy: Andreas, Baron von Delwig, Salzhausen, West Germany.)

day was Gwynne's *Rumour*, a pony who had been turned down as a griffin, first in Tientsin, then in Peking, and who had been brought round late one night to Gwynne, who bought him. He won four races and the Champions.

By May 1899 a peculiar atmosphere had settled over Peking. While China's future was being argued out in the chancelleries of Europe, Peking was characterized by a total absence of activity. There was not even any gossip or rumour. The race-meeting was the quietest ever held. No heads of diplomatic missions were present, no mandarins.

A year later all was jubilation. 'The races were a grand success,' a correspondent reported; 'more entries, more ponies, more people than ever!' The French and the Belgians had a field day, winning 12 out of the 15 events. Sir Henry Blake, Governor of Hongkong, with his wife and daughter, made it to Pao Ma Chang, but evidently unfamiliar with the peculiarities of locomotion in the Peking region, got there too late.

In fact, as will already have been sensed, the Peking races had changed since last observed back in 1882. The crowds were large, but they were no longer on the enormous scale of those earlier days. Peking is politically one of the most sensitive of cities, with the speciality that it senses crisis long before crisis comes. A feeling was growing that the dynasty was ailing, and might be moving to its demise, which in China means only one thing — anarchy. China's humiliating defeat by Japan in the war of 1894–5 accentuated the *malaise*. The unprincipled behaviour of the Powers, their strength and evident superiority, reinforced the trend.

The foreigners in Peking, with the exception of men like Sir Robert Hart and others with long memories, were not aware of the falling away in popularity of the races. Because of continual changes of personnel, a diplomatic community has an exceptionally short memory. When thousands turned up at Pao Ma Chang it seemed splendid. They did not know there had once been tens of thousands.

Meanwhile in Tientsin another pace-setter had made his appearance: Gustav Detring's *Set*, a chestnut, who in May 1899 won the Maidens' Stakes, three-quarters of a mile, in $1\frac{1}{2}$ minutes less one-fifth of a second. This was one-fifth of a second faster than Fritz Sommer's *Moribund*, and the exact time of David Sassoon's *Hero* in Shanghai. In the Criterion Stakes, one mile, *Set* beat the record set by *Stray Shot*, and put himself into the all-China record class.

The Siege of the Legations

SOMEWHERE in the background of these meetings, both here and in Peking, were distant reports of the Boxer Rising, which had started two years earlier, in 1898, in Shantung, and spread to the metropolitan province of Chihli. No one knew much about the Boxers. They were apparently anti-Christian fanatics, given to massacres of Chinese Christian converts and the murder of missionaries. They claimed to be invulnerable to bullets, and this was widely believed by the Chinese populace.

In January 1900 an announcement by the Empress Dowager, the actual ruler of the country, the Emperor being a cipher, indicated that she did not regard the Boxers as rebels, but as loyal adherents to the Throne. She had in actuality decided to use the Boxers as her instrument for the total extermination of foreigners in China, although not even Sir Robert Hart, who understood the Imperial Court better than anyone else, could bring himself to believe her words meant what they implied. Neither did the diplomats.

On 9 June 1900 a Boxer mob set fire to the grandstand at Pao Ma Chang. It showed, as nothing else so aptly could, the danger in which all foreigners, not just missionaries, stood. The symbolism was clear. In Tientsin an urgent telegraph was received from the British Legation summoning immediate aid. An hour later telegraph contact with the Legations was lost. A force of 2,000 sailors and marines, under the command of Admiral Sir Edward Seymour, left by train for Peking. Eighteen days later, what remained of it struggled back to Tientsin by the river route — finished as a force.

On 17 June the foreign settlements in Tientsin, with a defending force of 2,400 men and only makeshift defences,[12] were attacked by 10,000 Imperial troops with modern armament, including heavy artillery. The situation became steadily more desperate. On 20 June young James Watts, whose all-China record on *Palo Alto* will be remembered, volunteered to ride to Taku to bring news of their peril to the naval forces known to be off the bar of the Peiho. It was to be the most famous ride of his life.

As Peter Fleming described it in *The Siege at Peking*:

12. The defences were erected using bales of wool, silk, cotton, sugar, rice and peanuts, the man in charge being the future President of the United States, Herbert Hoover, who was a mining engineer.

He was an excellent horseman and knew the country well. He set out at night, taking an escort of three Cossacks and one spare pony. They were twelve hours in the saddle. They charged at full gallop through villages and over the little hump-backed stone bridges where these danger-points could not be by-passed; Watts had one pony shot under him. They were favoured by a sea-mist as they approached the coast, and on the morning of 21 June Watts delivered to the naval authorities information in the light of which yet another relief expedition was mounted.

Five days after they set out, the Tientsin foreign settlements were relieved. James Watts was made a CMG.

For ten days not a word was heard from Peking. Then, on 29 June, a Chinese courier got through to Tientsin. He bore a message from Sir Robert Hart: 'Foreign community besieged in the Legations. Situation desperate. *MAKE HASTE*!!' The Siege of the Legations, one of the most dramatic events in modern history, and which excited the imagination of the world, had begun.

News of the Siege shook the chancelleries of Europe — and Japan. Within days troops were assembling in various countries, and within two weeks warships from many parts of the world were steaming to the mouth of the Peiho.

The military situation in the Legations was critical. Even with volunteer diplomats, Customs men and students added to the small contingent of guards, the defenders barely constituted a skeleton force, and they were subjected to merciless and near-continuous gunfire.

The besieged had about 150 ponies and a quantity of mules to serve as a source of fresh meat. Chinese living near the Legations had fled from their homes, in which a fair amount of horse fodder was found. An abandoned grainstore gave another good yield.

The staple diet of the Europeans during the Siege was pony-meat, rice and champagne. There was plenty of claret as well, but the ferocious heat of the Peking summer was the wrong season for it.

The foreign settlements at Tientsin having been reinforced, on the night of 13–14 July the walled city was taken by frontal attack. By morning much of it was in flames, and it was being looted with traditional thoroughness.

When news of this disaster reached Peking, it produced within hours a strange kind of truce with the Legations, during which the Empress Dowager had water-melons and other fruit sent in as gifts. The melons were taken doused in claret.

Meanwhile an International Relief Force, 20,000 strong, of whom 10,000 were Japanese, was assembling at Tientsin. By August, when the Force at last moved, there was a serious food shortage in the Legations. The last of the ponies were being killed. The best racing ponies had been kept until last, in the hope of sparing them. Saying goodbye to one's pony when the inevitable came was one of anyone's more miserable moments during the Siege; but the ponies themselves were by this time so emaciated that to kill and eat them was little worse than leaving them to starve slowly to death.

The Relief Force took 10 days to reach Peking. First to be in the Legation Quarter were the Rajputs and Sikhs, who got in through a sewer beneath the vast wall of the Tartar City. Above them, on the wall itself, American marines and Russian sailors overwhelmed the Chinese defenders of the Chien Mên, the normal entrance, and shortly afterwards the British commander of the expedition, General Gaselee, clattered in on horseback.

In the middle of that night the Empress Dowager, dressed as a peasant woman, left Peking with the Emperor and a few retainers in three common carts. The population of the capital had been reduced to a quarter of its size in the Boxers' orgy of slaughter. For it was the Chinese who suffered most. The streets through which the Empress Dowager passed were littered with corpses. It was raining heavily.

The flight, however, was officially described as an 'autumn tour of inspection'.

Thanksgivings of Various Kinds

IN Newchwang (Yingtze), at dawn the day after the Relief Force left Tientsin for Peking, the stockaded foreign settlement was attacked in a combined assault by Boxers and Chinese regulars. For seven hours battle raged, until at three in the afternoon a Russian gunboat opened fire on the town of Yingtze, while simultaneously Russian cavalry and infantry descended from all sides, and conducted an indiscriminate massacre of the Chinese population on a scale more extensive and thorough than could have been achieved even by the Boxers. From the lowliest mud hut in the smallest village every man, woman and child was dragged out and either sabred or bayoneted. For miles there was not a human being left. This, of course, settled the matter.

As soon as it was clearly over — the following day — young Britons and Germans went back thankfully to take their ponies out, made friends with sports-minded Russian officers, and within a week there was a pony paper hunt, the first of many, the Russians participating full-heartedly, obeying the English rules of these entertaining races. The first paper hunt was held before the Relief Force had even reached the Legations in Peking.

It leads one to wonder what took place in Peking and Tientsin at the successful conclusion of the campaign. Were there any paper hunts there, or preparations for an Autumn Meeting?

The reader is by now inured to the fact that it took a great deal to stop the races.

There were no races that autumn. The sad fact in Peking is that nearly all the ponies had been eaten. The Boxer Rising had completely upset communications with Mongolia and Manchuria. There would be no griffins until at least the spring, if then.

This must surely be the only instance in the world where races were brought to a stop by the owners and riders eating their horses.

In Tientsin no one had eaten theirs. Detring's *Set*, Dickinson's *Forget-me-not* and *Touch-me-not*, and all the other ponies who had survived the guns were in fine fettle, it appears. Yet somehow, as so often at war's end, people were foot-loose. No one felt like getting down to the brass tacks of organizing a race-meeting.

Shanghai solved it, without expecting to. The autumn griffins there were a very poor bunch, due to the disruption caused by the Boxers. In Hongkong it was even worse. There the position was so bad that the Jockey Club — there was at last a Jockey Club — had sent to Australia for subscription griffins, had dealt with unreliable agents, and had been thoroughly cheated. Of the 43 horses sent, 22 died on the voyage, and the remainder were considered unfit to train.

In gloom, thinking it would be a boring meeting, with only the old favourites and no griffins, the Shanghai Race Club sent out invitations all along the coast . . . and everybody came. In the largest gathering of Europeans there had ever been, representative of the entire foreign element throughout

China — missionaries excepted — the Shanghai Autumn Meeting of November 1900 became a spontaneous act of thanksgiving for the relief of the Legations and the return of peace.

The races themselves were run by Shanghai's old ponies, reinforced by cracks from Tientsin and Hongkong. Far from being dull, they proved exceptional, with particularly well-matched ponies. Dickinson's *Forget-me-not* and *Touch-me-not* had two wins each, as did Henry Morriss with *Blueberry* and *Nutberry*. *Fraser*, owned by Raymond Toeg, a Shanghai broker and a popular figure, always called 'Sir John' for reasons no one ever remembered, had two wins. *The Dealer*, owned by Duplex, evidently a group, was another exceptional pony, with several wins. A record $117,720 passed through the *pari mutuel*. With sweepstakes and lotteries added, a very large amount of money was circulating. The side-bets, in particular, were what really mattered — multiply by ten. The place seethed with naval and military personnel; for a large garrison had been stationed in Shanghai and another in Hankow, as a precaution in case the Boxer movement spread to the South.

Actually the meeting was dominated by the swaying fortunes of Detring's *Set*, for the North, and George Hutton Potts' *Desert King*, for the South. Hutton Potts was a new arrival in Shanghai. A Yorkshireman, educated at Harrow, he came to Hongkong aged 21, and for 15 years worked there for the American firm of Russell & Co. His 'King' stable, started in Hongkong, had made a big impact in Shanghai, to which he moved early in 1900 to set himself up as a broker. He, Henry Morriss and Raymond Toeg were the main contenders.

In the North–South contest, *Set* beat *Desert King* in the Military Cup and the Flyaway Plate; *Desert King* beat *Set* in the important Criterion Stakes. When it came to the Champions, all eyes were focused on these two, who led the field almost from the start in one of the most exciting Champions' races there had ever been. It was anyone's guess between the two, *The Dealer* a possible third, until the very last moment, when *The Dealer* made a magnificent dash, and passed both of them to the post. *Set* was second, *Desert King* third.

It need hardly be added that at this remarkable 1900 meeting, which was in fact a celebration, at least 10,000 Chinese attended every day. Shanghai Chinese, who had no regard whatever for either Peking or the Imperial Court, were almost as relieved as Europeans by the outcome of events.

The terrible year 1900 ended in a whirl of gaiety, even in Newchwang, where Cossacks danced at Christmas in their magnificent uniforms, while in Shanghai the latest creations from Paris swept past the tables in gentler forms of dance.

It is strange, though, and utterly in character, that the pivotal point of that year, giving the alarm without which the Diplomatic Corps in Peking would certainly have been wiped out before anyone even knew they were in danger, was the burning of the grandstand at Pao Ma Chang.

6. The Great Course

Presents for Gentlemen Riders

THE reader will have noted that however far the distance travelled in search of racecourses in China, and however remote the place, one was always conscious of Shanghai somewhere in the background. Shanghai was the heart of the matter where racing was concerned.

It is now time to retrace steps, and take a look at what had been happening there since the demise of the racehorse.

The Champions' Stakes, with forced entry for all winners, was first raced in November 1869, in Shanghai, and the idea quickly took on. Within a year or two all race-meetings throughout China had a Champions' race as their culminating major event.

The Shanghai Derby and St. Leger date from the previous year. The Derby was raced in the spring, the St. Leger in the autumn. Within ten years the Shanghai St. Leger had become — to use their own words — 'a very special race.' It was for griffins of the year, meaning the May and November griffins, and it was the only race in which the weight for inches scale did not apply. More money was laid out on it than on any other race in China. It was said to be possible for a winner to carry away 200,000 taels, which remembering the original 25-tael griffins gives an idea of racing's financial stature.

In 1875 a pony of the same star quality as *Black Satin* was entered. This was *Teen Kwang* (Heavenly Light), a grey who passed into folklore, his name being cited decades later, when no one could even remember for certain what colour he was. As a griffin, he won the Shanghai Derby of May 1875. At the November meeting following, he won everything he entered at a canter, including the St. Leger, 1¾ miles, in 4 minutes 2 seconds — again, at a canter. 'In this and the Spring Meeting he won himself a name unlikely to be eclipsed.' He was sold for $2,000 after the races, to a Hongkong owner.

Teen Kwang and *Black Satin*, two of the all-time greats among the China ponies, raced against each other only once, in Hongkong, for the German Cup, two miles, on 25 February 1876. *Black Satin*, at that time, was still owned by W.A. Cornabé, *Teen Kwang* by Messrs Paul and Brooks — Paul Chater and a man with whom he had a brief racing confederacy. As the *Hong Kong Daily Press* gave it:

Out of twenty-one entries only the above two came up, all the others retiring before such formidable competitors. *Black Satin* took the reins first, but *Teen Kwang* drew up on reaching the Grand Stand, and the two ran an almost neck and neck race until passing the Grand Stand the second time, when the excitement became intense. *Black Satin* got a slight advantage again, and coming up by the Black Rock, *Black Satin* had again overhauled his rival. Nearing the straight *Teen Kwang* showed slightly to the front, but the race appeared still far from certain. *Black Satin*, however, appeared used up before reaching the post, and *Teen Kwang* won by a length and a half. This was undoubtedly the best race of the meeting. Time: 4 minutes 38 seconds.

They ran again in the Champions, in which they were both beaten, *Teen Kwang* coming second, *Black Satin* fourth. This, however, was not a representative race. Due to the starting delays inseparable from amateur racing, the Champions on this occasion was run in near darkness. This frequently happened. It was the main reason why in Shanghai the Consolation Stakes and the Nil Desperandum were run *after* the Champions, to ensure that this race gave an authoritative result.

It does seem, however, that *Teen Kwang* was the faster of the two. *Black Satin*, in 1877 in Shanghai, won the Criterion Stakes, one mile, in 2 minutes 11 seconds. *Teen Kwang* won it the year before in 2 minutes 6½ seconds.

By November 1879, though, in the fourth year since Cornabé brought him down from Chefoo, *Black Satin*, 'a gallant and handsome little animal', had won 32 races, including 4 Champions, 4 Criterions, and 4 Ladies' Purses. In 26 of his wins he was ridden by the same jockey, and he

Going to the Shanghai Derby, 1879. (By courtesy: John Warner, Hongkong.)

was never in a Shanghai race in which he was not either the winner or second. As was rightly said of him, 'It would be difficult to find anything approaching a parallel to this extraordinary career in the annals of racing in the Far East, or indeed anywhere.' It is not certain how many wins *Black Satin* had in his career, but it was over forty, and was probably the highest of any pony.

Black Satin, by this time, was owned by Paul Chater of Hongkong. His 26-win rider was M.C. Nickels, a Shanghai commercial employee whom Chater engaged as his jockey and trainer. Descended from Armenian princes, Paul Chater was a man of discreet, princely munificence. Aged 33 at this time, he was already a millionaire. It is to be feared that it was he who started the practice of giving 'presents' to jockeys at the end of a meeting, though it cannot be proved, such matters being extremely private. Early in this century, however, at a time when a European employee of the type from which jockeys came earned $100 a month, Chater's 'present' to his jockey at the end of a meeting was liable to be $10,000, and if the jockey had to race for him in Hongkong he received in addition a first-class sea passage both ways, his hotel and other expenses in Hongkong, and an allowance.

To avoid such costly methods of retaining the services of a good jockey, a number of leading firms in Shanghai took to engaging young men to do nothing demanding in the office, but race and train their ponies for them, upholding the honour of the house flag and its racing colours.

The 'Strath' Stable

THE next star owner in the Shanghai racing firmament was John Macgregor, joint founder of the wines and spirits firm of Caldbeck, Macgregor & Co., which became the largest firm of its kind in the Far East. He entered the Shanghai races as a jockey in 1874, and in 1878 formed his own stable, which with *Strathavon* made a fairly sensational début. In a very warm November that year, 'the foliage in the surrounding country unusually green', *Strathavon*, a grey, won the Griffins' Plate in record time and the Shanghai Club Cup, and was at once seen to be one of the best ponies Shanghai had ever had. John Macgregor accepted an invitation to bring him to Foochow, where in January he won four races. In May he was back in Shanghai, where he won the Champions. After winning the Criterions that autumn, *Strathavon* passed to the Foochow branch manager of Caldbeck Macgregor. *Strathallan* took over in Shanghai, and more 'Straths' followed.

One of them, *Strathspey*, was purchased in the first year of the 'Strath' stable's existence by a Russian lady from Hankow, Eleanora Andraevna. She bought two ponies, in fact, and thus achieved the distinction of being the first lady owner in the China races. She did extremely well with them in the Hankow races, which at this time were almost completely dominated by Russian owners, whose tea bricks, incidentally, reached the samovars more smoothly after the Trans-Siberian Railway opened.

The 'Strath' stable was in existence for just over three years, after which John Macgregor returned to his firm's head office in London. It was said that 'Strath' ponies raced wherever there was a branch of Caldbeck Macgregor, which meant more or less everywhere, including Singapore and Penang.

Though brief, the Macgregor reign was significant. It is evident that he had great confidence in his judgment of ponies. It was noticeable how readily he sold winners which many another owner would have hung on to. On one occasion his friends laughed at him for spending so large a sum on a griffin which to them looked unimposing.

'I haven't made a mistake with that pony,' he replied to them. 'There is a little Arab blood in him.'

Those words were remembered, and were to be recalled.

Good Friday with the 'Heavies'

EMBONPOINT surfaced with gravity in 1883, in an unexpected way. This was not like Tientsin, where the issue lay between different national characteristics, and all the Britons were heavy. In Shanghai nearly all the riders were Britons — Continental owners with a good pony preferred a British jockey if they could get one — and the Britons were not all running to fat together. The Shanghai Racecourse by this time was an arena of money on a scale which not even Calcutta, capital of the Indian Empire and seat of the Viceroy, could equal. The 'presents' being given in Shanghai to young commercial employees who were good jockeys were on a scale sufficient to make any man watch his weight. As a result, at the last meeting, in which 24 riders took part, all of them Britons, 8 were on the heavy side, while 16 weighed 10 stone or less, and were clearly not going to put on any more.

The 'heavies', it need hardly be explained, were in addition the 'heavies' of the Race Club. Weights had already been raised once, not so long ago. Since an attempt to raise them again might meet with defeat, they decided that the meeting of the Club must be held at a time when the largest possible number of people were out of town, shooting game in the cotton fields, hunting wild boar, boating on West Lake, or whatever it might be. With perfect precision they settled for Good Friday.

Too perfect. When people got back and discovered what had taken place, there was an outburst. It was held that in any case decisions made at a meeting conducted on Good Friday were null and void. Another meeting was called. It was attended by over a hundred members, a large number for the Race Club. The proposal was to raise the weights by 4 pounds.

Objectors held that weights were already heavy. There was always a welter race, and it was unfair that ponies, with penalties added, should have to carry what were almost welter weights, 'all for the benefit of three riders who are too heavy,' as one member put it with splendid exaggeration, 'giving them an unfair advantage over 15 or 20 others. Live weight is much easier than lead!' he proclaimed. 'Quite a number of riders already need 2 stone in dead weight,' said another.

The basic height for racing ponies had by this time reached 13 hands 2 inches. Since 1874 China ponies of up to 14 hands had been allowed to race, though 14-hand ponies were very rare.

H. de Courcy Forbes, in the chair, stressed that the rule being proposed 'will allow many more people to race, and has been in force in Hongkong for many years.' It was important, he said, that all races in China should have the same scale of weights. Hongkong's example had already been followed by Amoy. Shanghai should do likewise, and 'drive the big, high ponies out of the running. Small ponies carry weights much better than large ones. *Prejudice* [a small pony] won in

Hongkong carrying 12 stone, and the Hongkong races this year were the most glorious ever seen in China,' he concluded with a flourish.

'The Hongkong races were all won by three or four men,' someone muttered.

Nevertheless, when it came to the vote, the 'heavies' had it: 61 for, 44 against.

Tell it not in Gath, but de Courcy Forbes uttered what he must surely have known was not true. *Prejudice* won in Hongkong carrying 10 stone 12 pounds, not 12 stone as he had said.

One is left somewhat aghast by this meeting, with its odd mixture of exaggeration, hyperbole, and nonsense. Certainly

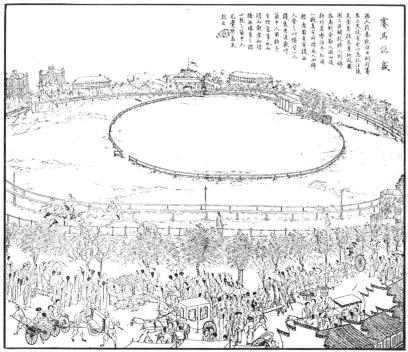

The Shanghai Racecourse, as shown in the Hua Pao, Shanghai, 1884. The text accompanying the illustration reads, in part: 'Horse Racing Spectacular. The Europeans regularly hold races on three good days in spring and three in autumn. They lay heavy bets, regardless of loss. Before the racing begins, the jockeys wear bright colours of fine cloth, the horses dressed with metallic bits, bridle and reins. When the red flag flicks, so the jockeys start abreast. Whoever is the winner, thousands of people cheer for him. Jockeys enjoy it as the most joyful event in their lives, while spectators, packed up like walls, without committing themselves to win or loss, are even more excited.' (The innuendo here, of course, is that Chinese do not bet.) The Hua Pao, China's first newspaper, was produced by the foreign-language interpreters at the Taotai's office in Shanghai. When it first came out, the North-China Herald described it as the most beautiful newspaper they had ever seen. (By courtesy: Yim Shui-yuen, Esq., Hongkong.)

to find Shanghai, which never gave a damn for what happened in Hongkong, following Hongkong's lead is choice. The 'heavies', of course, were prepared to use any argument in order to have their way; and it is undeniable that there were quite a number of men, some of them present at the meeting, who wanted to race but could not because of the weights.

The strangest feature of the meeting, however, is the wish to oust the 'big, high ponies.' This is the first clear enunciation of a prejudice which became so ingrained in the Shanghai races as to amount to a fixation. One would have thought that a big, high pony would have been a preferable ride for a big, high Briton. Not so, evidently. The prejudice is rendered even more curious by the fact that in speed and stamina there was nothing to choose between a big, high pony and a small one. This is of detailed record, an extraordinary feature of the China pony. A griffin of 12 hands 3 inches was still quite liable to win the Derby. *Strathaird* did precisely that in 1880.

There it was, however; and it became more marked as time went on. This is one underlying difference between the races of Shanghai and Hongkong. In Hongkong there was always a hankering to go back to Australian horses, the obstacle being that since so few riders could afford it, there was the risk of the races being delivered into the hands of one or two stables, the entire spirit of the thing lost.

The Sassoon Saga

EVEN without Australian horses, however, the Shanghai races were to be delivered — or very nearly so — into the hands of one stable, in the most extraordinary episode in the China races, an episode lasting eight years.

The Jardine stable had not been doing well in Shanghai, where their ponies were frequently unplaced. In the outports they did better, and Jardine Matheson personnel were always prominent in racing events, the Ewo Cup — the company's Chinese name — being a feature of the races at several places, with Jardine men themselves racing for it.

In 1886 the owners of the Jardine stable in Shanghai sold the premises to David Sassoon as part of a larger land deal. David Sassoon's grandfather, of the same name, was born in Baghdad in 1792, son of the head of the Jewish community in Mesopotamia, who bore the title of Nassi, or Prince, of the Captivity. David Sassoon left Baghdad and in 1832 established himself in Bombay, where his main interest was the opium business. His sons grew up to be so completely English it was impossible to believe they were not descended from a family resident in England for generations. They achieved, apparently without effort, a cultural metamorphosis.

After the Treaty of Nanking some of the brothers — there were eight — came to China with a view to commanding the opium trade at both ends. As Jardine Matheson steadily withdrew from opium, and dissociated themselves from it, so did the Sassoons between them achieve the mastery of what was by this time a legitimate trade in China.

David Sassoon of Shanghai was still in his early thirties. Lithe and slim, he had a long, narrow face, serious-looking; he seldom smiled. Modest of manner, almost diffident, yet in whatever he touched he had an unquenchable urge to be first and best. When he turned his hand to racing, his urge was not just to win, but to sweep the board. He was a superb rider, a good judge of a horse, and money was no object.

Hongkong during these years was getting its own back on Shanghai. The top pony in the Hongkong Stable, as it was called at the Shanghai races, was Paul Chater's *Piccadilly*, a grey, who in November 1883 won the St. Leger, $1\frac{3}{4}$ miles, in 3 minutes $52\frac{1}{2}$ seconds, the fastest ever in this race.

The Autumn Meeting of 1884 was held in cold, damp, foggy and rather windy weather, and once again the Hongkong Stable had a great success, with five winning ponies, including Chater's *Piccadilly* and *Sunlight*. On the third day Hongkong ponies won five out of the eight races, and in May they again had a great time. On the third day, in gusty weather, with clouds of dust, they won three out of the eight races, and *Piccadilly* won the Champions.

David Sassoon attended this meeting. He had almost certainly resolved to enter, but was holding his hand. He had to be absolutely sure before committing himself. In the autumn he again attended. *Councillor* won the Criterion Stakes and the Champions. *Red Gauntlet* won several races. David Sassoon bought both ponies.

Though no one realized it, the scene was being set for something never before experienced in the China races.

Quite a number of interesting things were taking place at this time. With Shantung mafoos now working in Shanghai, people had at last awakened to the significance of the Mafoos' Race. In former days the grandstand began to empty before this race was even run. It was now designated the Mafoo Champions' Race, and was watched with keen interest. Equally so the Mafoo Steeplechase: formerly farcical, it was now a serious matter. Victorians naturally could not bring themselves to contemplate even the possibility that Chinese could do anything as well as they themselves could. The steeplechase of 1885 was described as 'a good race', however, which in Victorian terminology is an admission that Chinese were very able riders.

Chinese, in fact, were infiltrating the proceedings. Respectable Chinese, as they were called, had always been allowed into the enclosure on payment. For the men at the gate it was simple. One followed the old Chinese adage: 'Judge a man by his silk.' Along the approaches to the racecourse Chinese shows, booths and stalls did a thriving business, and there were two incredible Stands, known as the 'Grand' and the 'Little Grand', perilous edifices crammed with Chinese — crazy-looking erections which somehow never fell down. It was clear that in the course of time there would be a Chinese grandstand and club.

The introduction of the *pari mutuel* in 1888, in a tent in the enclosure, was heaven-sent for 'respectable' Chinese — a new way of betting. The European attitude to the *pari mutuel* was that it would be 'extremely popular with those who like to put $5 on, just to have an interest in the ponies.' With Chinese participating as well, however, the tent had to be taken down at the end of its first day, and replaced by another one twice the size.

At a Race Club meeting held in March 1886 James Dunn, a popular rider, rose to ask, 'What is a professional jockey?' He gave as a provisional answer 'one who rides for pay', and admitted to doing this himself. It was the first time the ticklish matter of 'presents' had been aired.

For the Stewards this was critical. If they gave a faulty answer it could wreck racing in Shanghai, and could have detrimental effects on the races elsewhere — though other places were less afflicted by the problem, and in some, such as Peking and Chefoo, it does not seem to have existed at all.

As so often in Shanghai at critical moments, everybody behaved with admirable calm. The embarrassment Dunn had caused was offset by his honesty. The Stewards did not answer his question directly, thus evading a definition of a professional jockey. They simply said that the races were a sporting event, and were to be entered in the spirit of sport.

'Most racing men make a business of the sport,' the *Herald* sighed afterwards, and this was undeniable. Though amateur, racing was business. In a businessman's world it could hardly be anything else. 'Gentlemen knights of the field keep discreet books, and lay about the field in well-bred whispers,' but at least it had to be remembered that 'the seamy side of racing is absent at the Shanghai meetings.' 'Glorious uncertainty' — a phrase used again and again from the earliest years of the griffins — prevailed, and there was 'no sharp practice, on the turf, in the enclosures, or in the stables.' Admittedly there had been a foul at the last meeting, 'but *Cheapside* has a reputation for boring his neighbour.' All were agreed it was the pony's fault, not the rider's.

So it was business as usual.

In May 1886 David Sassoon entered for the first time — 16 ponies. His principal rival was Raymond Toeg — 'Sir John' — who like Sassoon himself hailed originally from Baghdad. Each had two wins on the first day, Sassoon riding *Councillor* and *Red Gauntlet*. On the second day Toeg's *Euphrates* won the Derby. On the third day Sassoon won three out of the seven races, and himself rode *Councillor* to win the Champions. First and best: in one shot he had done it.

The effect of it was flattening. By the second day it was observed that people were more interested in the tiffin than in the actual races. A correspondent rightly queried whether this was not

due to there being one enormous stable, whose owner is said not even to know how many ponies he has in training, who entered sixteen ponies, and won eleven of the twenty-three races, who can afford to buy up at whatever price every old pony with a record, and every promising griffin, and has influence enough to call on every prominent jockey to ride for him.

Actually, the correspondent went on, it had to be admitted that the (unnamed, of course) owner was 'raising the quality of the sport by entering ponies in the highest possible condition.' Nevertheless, he called on the three one-horse owners who had won in the Maidens to hang on. 'Let them refuse to sell, and the big man is powerless.'

It is to be feared they sold. Few would turn down money such as Sassoon was prepared to offer.

That year he bought *Piccadilly* from Paul Chater. *Piccadilly* was the greatest pony of the day, Chater the biggest man in racing. If the transaction was made *viva voce* between the two men, it would have been nice to be a fly on the wall. As it is, we are left for ever to wonder who got the better of whom. Chater had raced *Piccadilly* for four years, and may have felt the pony had done enough. It is of note that *Piccadilly*, after joining the Sassoon stable, did not do much. This, in any event, is the most prestigious purchase ever made in the China races, between two of the wealthiest and most extraordinary men who ever figured in them.

The Tiffin Crisis

TIFFIN was mentioned earlier. The Race Club tiffins were invariably sumptuous, 'a sort of three-day wedding breakfast without the responsibilities.' They were expensive. $1,000 of Club money was spent on tiffin at each meeting, which considering the cheapness of food and drink in Shanghai is a pretty startling figure.

Early in 1887 a member formally proposed lowering the cost of tiffin. There was no panic, naturally. There was just a very large meeting, larger even than the one about weights. To interfere with tiffin was tantamount to desecrating the altar at High Mass.

The Chairman agreed with the proposer that the cost of tiffin was extravagant, but . . . In fact, the word 'but' hovered in the air throughout the ensuing debate, rendered awkward by the fact that no one could quite come round to admitting that he disliked being short of champagne. Wainewright, the magistrate, solved it neatly by pointing out that 'the main pleasure of the ladies coming to the races is getting something to eat.' This was a cardinal point. Without the ladies . . . Vote was taken. The motion was defeated by 100 votes to 4.

The mood that spring was serious. Goods imported or dealt with were now 5 per cent lower in sterling value, silver having fluctuated adversely. 5,600,000 piece goods had passed through the port, compared with 4,000,000 the year before; but the profit had gone.

'Never mind,' someone commented. 'Tiffin has been preserved, and the big stable won't win all.'

The Shanghai Paper Hunt Club, as shown in the Hua Pao, sets forth, 1884. The commentator took it to be a military exercise, which was what it looked liked to Chinese eyes. (By courtesy: Yim Shui-yuen, Esq.)

The Leviathan Stable

DAVID Sassoon this time entered 48 ponies, and in fact had surprisingly few wins. On the third day, however, he had a sensational win. The Chau Shang-kiuk Cup had to be won twice in succession by the same horse and owner. Sassoon had won the race at the last meeting. The Cup had been contested 24 times, never carried away. It was in a sense the most valuable Cup to be had. When he won it the second time, himself riding *Fontenoy*, he received an ovation.

That autumn he entered 39 ponies, and had 5 wins, the highest number of anyone. Just before the races started, he offered 1,500 taels to buy *La-de-dah*, but the owner, 'Choufleur', refused to sell, and won three races, including the St. Leger. In the best contested race of the day *La-de-dah* came first, *Tycoon* second, owned by Hormusjee Mody of Hongkong, Sassoon's *Encounter* third, himself riding.

In 1888 the name 'Leviathan Stable' was coined, and was used openly in the newspapers. On the first day Sassoon had four wins in succession, the last four of the day, with a cream pony, *Harbinger*, and three greys.

It was at this meeting, and from Sassoon's whites, creams and greys, that the curious belief arose — widely held at one time — that ponies of these colours were faster than others. There was nothing about it in the racing columns. It was all in conversation. But Mongolia came to know about it — this is the mysterious East. Whites, creams and greys were carefully selected for export to China, and the price went up.

Sassoon was wary of griffins. He preferred to buy other people's sure winners. It was one of the reasons why he was so resented. The mark of the true sportsman, it was held, was to train and race griffins in the 'glorious uncertainty'. Another indicative feature about him: he only once allowed a pony of his to enter the Mafoo Champions' Race. It won, one need hardly add.

With *Dolores*, however, whom he almost certainly bought from someone else after she had been trained, he won the Derby of May 1888, and himself riding *Bullion* went on to win the Ladies' Purse. This meant a speech. Sassoon was not given to moving about much in society. Very few even knew what his voice sounded like. He was undoubtedly a man of dash, however, and one expected him to show it.

To everyone's surprise, in accepting the Purse he was visibly too overwhelmed to say more than a few words. The diffidence which was part of his character had surfaced at the least likely moment.

On the first day in November it was noted that interest in the races was not so great as before, owing to the 'paralyzing presence' of the Leviathan Stable. 'No one denies one owner's right to monopolize the meeting if he can;' but there was no financial black cloud over Shanghai at the time to account for the lack of interest. There was fine weather too, but little excitement. Sassoon's *Eureka*, the favourite, won the Maiden Stakes in silence, and went on to win the St. Leger similarly. Yet later, when Sassoon himself rode *El Dorado* to a win he was loudly cheered, and at the end of the last day they were saying it was one of the best meetings enjoyed for years, with very popular wins.

The fact is, the Europeans were of divided mind where David Sassoon was concerned. They were backing his ponies to the hilt in the *pari mutuel* and with the gentlemen bookmakers, and they were making money. Yet somehow they could not bring themselves to believe he was a true sportsman.

Chinese reaction, of course, was entirely different. A winner is what every Chinese wishes to be. The bigger the winner, the greater the admiration he excites. Sour grapes were in the Grand Stand, not around the course. It is noticeable that in the year Sassoon entered, the Chinese round the course stood four deep, the year after they were six deep, and the year after that they were uncountable. A third perilous Stand went up too, for Chinese ladies only, at the Loong-fei Gate — all part of the instinctive Chinese desire to watch a winner.

An interesting test occurred for the Europeans and David Sassoon after that meeting, when for the first time ever a Horse Show was held at the racecourse for horses and ponies. The distinguished panel of judges, drawn from Peking and several of the Treaty Ports, included names well known in China, among them Boyd Bredon and C. Vincent Smith.

The Champion Prize for ponies went to David Sassoon's *El Dorado*, described as 'the best specimen of a China pony exhibited.'

It was no use arguing about David Sassoon. He knew what he was doing. He had the best stable, he was the best rider, and he was the best judge of a horse. He also almost certainly had direct contact with Mongolia, through a trusted agent, presumably Chinese, though he could equally have been Russian, even at this early date. It is not possible to state with certainty anything concerned with contacts with Mongolia which bypassed the Horse Bazaar, because these were kept a close secret. The indications are there, however; and it will be agreed that it would have been entirely in character.

In the Criterion Stakes of May 1889 he had an all-time win: *Eureka* first, *Fontenoy* second, *Fair Sport* third. He won 5 out of 8 races on the first day, 3 out of 9 on the second, 4 out of 8 on the third, and risking a griffin for once, won the Derby with *Zephyr*, who in the autumn won the St. Leger as well. His main rival now was J.D. Humphreys, whose interests were in real estate, and who had a fine stable. Hormusjee Mody was taking increased interest in the Shanghai races, and was another rival. Mody's best pony, *Pao Hsing*, was a grey, contributing to the colour myth.

'The Leviathan stable throws a wet blanket over the meeting,' the *Herald* commented in May 1890. Out of 90 entries for the Shanghai Stakes, only three came to the post when it was known that *Zephyr* was entered. Riding *Unicorn* in the Derby, Sassoon found he had started alone, drew the pony up at the Loong-fei Gate, and walked back. This irritated the Grand Stand more than anything he had done so far. It seemed so contemptuous on his part. In the Champions, however, *Zephyr*, who had never been beaten, was outrun by J.D. Humphreys' *Vaticinator*. Amid transports of enthusiasm in the Grand Stand, Humphreys and his jockey were several times carried round shoulder-high.

On the first day that autumn, four successive Sassoon wins were received in absolute silence in the Grand Stand. The Chinese crowds were enormous, naturally, cheering their heads off as the ponies passed. In retrospect the silence in the Grand Stand is doubly strange, because one of the ponies they were watching for the first time was *Hero*, the skewbald wonder-pony, the greatest pace-setter in the China races to date, who at that meeting won the St. Leger and the Champions.

Hero won the Champions again in the spring and autumn of the following year, making three wins in succession, and established himself as the supreme pony of the China races, the point of comparison for all other ponies, the fastest and best ever. From 1891 onwards it was every owner's unspoken ambition to have a pony who could exceed *Hero* in performance; and this remained so until the 1920s, when the wonder-pony of an entire century of racing arrived in Peking.

The Grand Stand behaved as usual: silence for a Sassoon win, tumultuous enthusiasm for a Sassoon defeat. In May 1891, on the second day, *El Dorado* was beaten by Chantrey's white *Autocrat*, and this was considered a moral for the Sassoon stable — as if he minded — because the *pari mutuel* closed with 148 on *El Dorado*, 34 on *Volcano*, and only 21 on *Autocrat*, the winner. Of the 96 entries for the Shanghai Stakes, only 5 came out against *Hero*.

There was a sensation in May 1892 when *Hero* was defeated by Henry Sylva's *Majestic*. David Sassoon bought *Majestic*.

Hormusjee Mody of Hongkong had now become a serious rival. He won the Derby with *Royalist*, an exceptionally fine animal, a dun who for many years held the all-China record for the $1\frac{1}{4}$-mile. Of the 28 races run at that meeting, Sassoon won 9, Hormusjee Mody 7.

The ease with which David Sassoon bought winners from other owners is incredible. He even bought a winner from Henry Morriss, who heaven knows did not need the money. Only Hormusjee Mody eluded him — and 'eluded' is the right word, because Mody was difficult to find. He was one of those people who leave before anyone else, and though capable of taking hair-raising risks on the Hongkong stock exchange — his nickname was Napoleon of the Rialto — he was very much a man of hearth and home, which was Buxey Lodge in Conduit Road, Hongkong, a kind of citadel which not even David Sassoon seems to have succeeded in penetrating.

Majestic won the Criterions that November. Silence. Sassoon's purchase of *Majestic* was particularly disliked. It was felt to have been arrogant. However, when *Hero*, kept in reserve for the first two days, won the Shanghai Stakes, there were the biggest cheers for the Leviathan Stable yet, especially because *Hero* had galloped at top speed right round the course before the race could even be started.

There was a better division of wins that year. People were trying harder. Sassoon was in fact elevating the quality of racing.

When *Majestic* again won the Criterions in May 1893, there was an outcry reflected in the press next morning. Why not race him against *Hero*, and give everyone some fun? So on the second day Sassoon did just that, and it settled the matter. *Hero* came first, Hormusjee Mody's *Torchlight* second, *Majestic* third.

When electing a horse to win, Sassoon sprang no surprises. If the public had their money on his elected winner, they must not be disappointed; and he himself would usually ride the non-elected pony. In 1892 *Hero* and *Lightning* took all, and both were in the Champions, Sassoon on *Lightning*. 'Mr Sassoon had elected *Hero* to win, and win he did, despite *Lightning* running rings round him from start to finish.'

Somehow, whatever David Sassoon did, they were never satisfied.

Frank Dallas rode *Hero* on this and many other occasions. The younger son of Barnes Dallas, who had come to join his elder brother Grant Dallas, when the latter left Jardine's to go into business on his own, and who was longtime Clerk of the Course, Frank and his elder brother George were born beside the racecourse, and were brought up in the stable. Racing was their life. George was the buyer and trainer, Frank the jockey. George ran a livery stables. He spoke pidgin English and the Shanghai dialect — nothing much else. Frank seems to have had some kind of job with Jardine Matheson, though if this was so, it was probably because it was cheaper to employ him full-time than to hire him when needed to race their ponies.[13] He raced everywhere, as required. The Hankow races would not have been the same without him. Wherever he went, rumour of his coming doubled the excitement.

David Sassoon liked to race with Frank Dallas, and must have paid him large sums for doing so. Even when not electing a horse to win, he had a tendency to give Frank the better pony, letting the win go to him. There is an appealing side to David Sassoon's character. As he aged and mellowed, this side came to predominate.

In the Champions of May 1893, Frank Dallas rode *Hero*, with David Sassoon on *Blackberry*, the pony he bought from Henry Morriss. *Blackberry* was the favourite, and a number of Club members had the impression that Sassoon was reining him in. *Hero* won.

As Sassoon rode in, there were expressions of disgust, which he overheard. Next morning, the Stewards received a letter from him demanding that they ask the members who had uttered these expressions either to substantiate them or withdraw them in writing. A special meeting was held, of which no report was given. The offending members dutifully wrote, withdrawing anything they had said.

A year later, when Sassoon attended a Club meeting, they took their revenge. In the printed list of those who attended the meeting, his name was put at the bottom. At moments such as this the Shanghai Race Club does not shine.

In the Flyaway Plate of November 1893, seven furlongs, Frank Dallas won on Sassoon's *Mighty* in a record 1 minute $48\frac{1}{2}$ seconds, with Sassoon himself second on *Blackberry*. *Hero* won the Champions for the sixth time, a success never achieved before or after.

Hero had one interesting characteristic. He refused to face the Starter unless accompanied to the post by his stable companion *Dolores*, the former Derby winner, who no longer raced. *Dolores* became known to the public as '*Hero*'s Amah'.

In 1894 a totalizator was installed, acquired from Australia.

13. The Jardine Matheson records, otherwise very extensive, tail off at this point for about twenty years, for reasons unknown. Frank Dallas' son Norman was employed by Jardine's, and the likelihood is that he was following in his father's footsteps.

Hero was not entered, and there was 'increased interest'. There were not quite so many Sassoon wins as usual, and — one could almost have sworn it — it was described as 'the grandest race meeting ever held in China.'

Then, as mysteriously and unexpectedly as he had entered, David Sassoon withdrew. No one had any idea of his intentions until he asked Henry Morriss if he would like to have *Blackberry* back. The Sassoon ponies were quietly sold to individuals. When autumn came the name Sassoon was not to be seen on the race cards. 'WITHDRAWAL OF LEVIATHAN STABLE', ran the headline.

He had gone. *Hero* too had gone, *Dolores* as well. *Blackberry*, once more owned by Henry Morriss, at last won the Champions. Many ex-Sassoon ponies won for their new owners; and as was noted with relief, the nine races on the first day were won by eight owners.

Sassoon had in fact revolutionized racing in Shanghai. It had become professional, not in the racing sense, but in the sense that unless owner, trainer, rider and pony came up to professional standards there was no point in entering.

They were happier without him, though.

7. A Tour of the Racing Circuit

THE OVERLAND GRIFFIN

MY LONG YOU BUY, TEN DOLLAR TLUE
ONE MOON MY PAY HE' PLENTY CHOW
MY SAVEE HE B'LONG MA LOO
MY TALKEE ALL SAME LLAMA MIAU

NOTE —
    FOR TEN DOLLAR I'LL SURELY BUY HIM
        FROM YOU
    AND FEED HIM UP FOR A MONTH (ONE MOON)
  I KNOW HE'S NO MORE THAN A CARRIAGE
        PONY (OR A HACK — MA LOO) LIT. ROAD PONY
  BUT ILL TELL THEM HE'S A RACER
      FROM THE NORTH (LLAMA MIAU)

The Jockey Club's Non-riding Knights

PAUL Chater arrived in Hongkong in 1864, aged 18. The following February he went to the races at Happy Valley, and he attended every annual race-meeting held there throughout the ensuing 61 years.

An Armenian Christian, descended from a princely family resident for several generations in India, he was born in Calcutta in 1846, lost both parents when young, and was brought up in straitened circumstances. He came to Hongkong as a clerk in the Bank of Hindustan, China and Japan. Three years later he left the bank, and set himself up as an exchange and bullion broker. Ten years after that he was a millionaire.

The keynote to Paul Chater's life is that he loved Hongkong. Brought up as an impoverished member of the small, narrow Armenian community of Calcutta, he found in Hongkong his real home, and he contributed enormously to it. The development of the port of Hongkong at the foot of the Kowloon peninsula, a revolutionary idea at the time; the reclamation which created Central District; the acquisition of the New Territories; the construction of Nathan Road, 80 feet wide heading straight to nowhere, and originally called Nathan's Folly; all these and much more were Chater's ideas, and he was central to their execution. As a Member of Legislative Council, and later as a life Member of the Governor's Executive Council, for 42 years he was at the hub of public affairs. As the *South China Morning Post* put it in their obituary of him, 'a biography of Sir Paul Chater would be a history of Hongkong.'

He was the epitome of beneficence. With his high, broad forehead and wide-spaced, friendly eyes, he radiated kindliness. Everything he did in his long life was for the public benefit as well as his own. It is a mark of his eminence that in order to explain the changes and improvements in the Hongkong races it is first necessary to explain about the man himself. He presided over a racing revolution similar to that wrought by David Sassoon in Shanghai, though less drastic. Chater never did anything drastic. He simply contrived to make things happen.

He first entered the races in 1872, with two subscription griffins, one of which, *Last of the Mohicans*, came second in the Subscription Challenge Cup. The next meeting, 1873, was the occasion when Shanghai made a clean sweep of the Happy Valley races. In Foochow or Amoy this would not have mattered much. In Hongkong it did. The earlier rivalry between Shanghai and Hongkong had settled itself by this time. Shanghai was one of the largest and most important cities in Asia, while Hongkong, though very considerable as a port, as a town was just a small place with some 170,000 inhabitants. Nevertheless, there was something special about Hongkong. It was a British possession, which the Treaty Ports were not. However insignificant it might be in comparison with Shanghai, for Shanghai to have a clean sweep of wins was somewhat humiliating.

Chater was 27 that year. A number of his ponies were placed. In his third year of racing, 1874, he at last had a win. *Flyaway* took the Celestial Cup.

There it was, however. Hongkong was not getting good griffins. Owners were entirely dependent on a purchasing agent in Shanghai. Though seemingly reliable, on one occasion he sent down 42 griffins, of which only 12 were any good. The answer was to send someone to Tientsin to buy for Hongkong direct; but as Hongkong had no race club and the races were run without any organizational staff, this was not a viable proposition.

Indeed, that race-meetings were held regularly in Hongkong for forty years without a race club is extraordinary. It says much for the zest and enthusiasm which lay behind the races. It says even more for the fact that racing in Hongkong was a Jardine affair. They even owned the licence for the course.

Exactly how *Teen Kwang* was bought is uncertain. This, however, is what altered the face of the Hongkong races. *Teen Kwang*, it will be recalled, was bought at the end of the Shanghai Autumn Meeting of 1875 for $2,000 by a Hongkong owner. Three months later he is found racing in Hongkong for Messrs Paul and Brooks. On that occasion W.A. Cornabé brought *Black Satin* down, and, as we have seen, the two champion ponies ran what was, in effect, their match race.

This, for the Hongkong racing public, was exceptional. Here they saw the two greatest and fastest ponies in China running together, and one of them was, by purchase, a bona fide Hongkong pony. The fact that one was black and the other a light grey meant they could be distinguished with exceptional clarity. That they did an entire circuit of the Happy Valley racecourse neck and neck made it one of the most memorable races ever.

That was in February 1876. In November, after the Shanghai meeting, Paul Chater bought *Black Satin*. He now

*Sir Paul Chater, 'the greatest man Hongkong has known', for 34 years
Chairman of the Board of Stewards, in the full-dress uniform of the
French Legion of Honour, with his CMG insignia attached to it.*

owned the two best ponies in China. Having started as a broker
with only modest capital, he was now much better off than
when he bought his first subscription griffins. Moreover, he
had learned an important lesson. The clue was to have a
Shanghai stable, which he opened that year with *Black Satin*
as his prize entry, and a reliable agent — his jockey Nickels
presumably — to buy griffins for him, to be sent down to his
Hongkong stable.

The Jardine stable in Hongkong — 'Mr John Peel' and 'Mr
St. Andrew' — followed suit. A connexion was developing
during these years between Chater and Jardine Matheson. It
led to the joint formation of some of Hongkong's most notable
concerns, including the Hongkong & Kowloon Wharf &
Godown Co. and Hongkong Land Investment & Agency Ltd.
— Hongkong Land, as it is called today. The net outcome
was that Hongkong shortly had two stables capable of
challenging all comers, and the effect at Happy Valley was
sensational. The Shanghai owners and riders no longer came
down for easy wins. They came down on their mettle and

brought their best. Without doing anything noticeably — this was part of Paul Chater's genius, never to be particularly noticeable when he was doing anything important — he had raised the quality of racing at Happy Valley. This went hand in hand with the amusing fact that his main adversary was the Jardine stable — men with whom he was associated in business — thus creating a rivalry different from that earlier one between the Dents and the Jardines. This was a truly friendly rivalry, and it set its stamp on the Hongkong races. But then that was typical of Sir Paul Chater.

From 1877 to 1884 Chater's ponies reigned supreme at Happy Valley, with the Jardine stable in fine form, particularly during the taipanship of John Bell-Irving, who was a keen and experienced racing man.

Chater's ponies won the Hongkong Champions three years in succession, 1882–4. In 1882, with *Tajmahal, Sunlight*, and *Shamrock* he had first, second and third in that race. In 1884 he had 9 wins in 3 days, the Jardine stable 7 wins between them. The weather that year was dreadful — gloomy, wet and misty — and the Champions, which Chater won with *Rose*, was run in the dark.

Tajmahal, incidentally, cost only 35 taels at the Shanghai griffins auction. *Teen Kwang* was originally bought for 65 taels. Both ponies must have made thousands. *Teen Kwang* was

At the Hongkong Races, 1876. (By courtesy: John Warner, Esq., Hongkong.)

withdrawn not long after his famous race with *Black Satin*. Though Paul Chater was not a rider, he was a real pony-fancier. The suspicion is that he was fond of *Teen Kwang*, his first major acquisition in racing, and may have thought the pony had brought him luck. In any case, he never wished to risk him being anything but a winner.[14] As was seen when he sold *Piccadilly* to David Sassoon, Chater's judgment of ponies was exceptionally shrewd, specially for a non-rider.

Then there were his twice-yearly steamship sailings to Shanghai to watch his wonder-winner *Black Satin* and other ponies from his stable there. *Black Satin's* triumphs were well known in Hongkong. In 1882, when Paul Chater was seen in the Happy Valley grandstand, the regimental band played Piron's *Black Satin Polka*. It is a small point, but worth noting. Even at this early stage in his career, he was on the way to becoming what he later was, Hongkong's first citizen.

In the autumn of 1884, at a meeting of what was usually called simply the Race Fund — meaning the subscribers to the previous meeting — and which was held at the City Hall, it was decided to place 'racing in Hongkong on a more stable footing by the formation of a Jockey Club.'

This belated development was the culmination of events stemming from the 1876 race between *Teen Kwang* and *Black Satin*, and was a measure of the *élan* that Chater had given to racing.

Among those elected to the first Board of Stewards were (Sir) Thomas Jackson, head of the Hongkong and Shanghai Banking Corporation, and a Member of Legislative Council, whose fine statue dignifies Statue Square to this day; Frederick Sassoon, another Member of Legislative Council; John Bell-Irving, shortly to be appointed likewise; two other members of the Court of Directors of 'The Bank'; and the Chairman of the Hongkong & Whampoa Dock Co., who at that juncture was a German. There was always at least one German on the governing body of the Jockey Club.

Paul Chater was among the 34 men who attended the meeting at which the Club was formed, and who as subscribers to the 1884 meeting automatically became Jockey Club members. David Sassoon was there as well, just about to enter the races for the first time. Most surprising of all, Chater had

14. I first heard the story that Sir Paul Chater had a pony who he felt had brought him luck — not just on the racecourse — in 1949, from Portuguese friends who had known Sir Paul personally. They could not remember the pony's name. Since doing the research for this book I have come to the conclusion it must have been *Teen Kwang*.

somehow persuaded Hormusjee Mody to be present, presumably because automatic membership of the Jockey Club would save him the trouble of applying later on. Mody never attended meetings unless it was absolutely unavoidable.

Hormusjee Mody, a Parsi from Bombay, came to Hongkong in 1860, four years before Chater, and first worked in a Hindu bank which was in fact an opium agency. Two years later he formed his own opium firm, which held out until the telegraph was installed, when Mody realized — as Jardine's did too — that the opium business as then run was finished. Mody gave it up, and joined Chater in one of the most successful brokerage undertakings in Hongkong history. Chater interested Mody in racing, with results already noted in Shanghai. The two of them were an extraordinary combination, Chater essentially outgoing and steady, Mody mercurial and elusive. Both married Europeans. Lady Chater was Swedish; Lady Mody was French. Mody over the years built up the finest collection of European works of art there has ever been in Hongkong; it included a Goya — one of Goya's greatest portraits, in fact — works of Chardin and Greuze among many others, and an entire set of Sèvres from the largest man-sized urn to the smallest coffee cup.[15]

Chater had given Mody a lifelong interest in racing. Years later Mody reciprocated by suggesting that Chater take an interest in art. Chater knew he was no match for Mody in such matters, and engaged the architect James Orange — Messrs Lee and Orange — to advise him, the outcome being the Chater Collection of China coast pictures which he bequeathed to the people of Hongkong. He then suggested to Mody that he take up an idea put forward by the *China Mail* to combine the medical and technical colleges and form a university, which in 1908 Mody did, publicly offering $150,000 for the construction of university buildings, an offer which was eventually taken up, and which led to the foundation of the University of Hong Kong.

These were two of the great racing men of their time, and they demonstrate the quality of the people who were drawn to the China races. When Sir Hormusjee Mody died in 1911, without living to see the completion of his great gift of the university buildings, his place was taken by a third great racing man, Sir Ellis Kadoorie,[16] yet another Jew from Baghdad, who

15. Virtually the entire Mody Collection, including all the finest items, are at present in a private collection in Manila.

16. Bachelor brother of Sir Elly Kadoorie, and uncle of Lord Kadoorie.

by his numerous benefactions and sound advice as a member of the Court of the University steered that institution securely through its early years.

It is an interesting reflexion that Happy Valley should have owed so much to three knights, an Armenian, a Parsi, and a Jew, none of them European, and none of them riders. Sir Paul Chater was made a CMG in 1897, and knighted in 1902. Sir Hormusjee Mody was knighted in 1910, Sir Ellis Kadoorie in 1917.

Left: Sir Hormusjee Mody, 'Napoleon of the Rialto', who gave the University of Hongkong its gracious buildings.
Right: Sir Ellis Kadoorie, great public benefactor in the field of education in Shanghai and Hongkong. A feature of his box at Happy Valley was that the gentlemen of the Press were always invited to lunch there — the curries were said to have been beyond compare.

If the weather for the Race Fund's last meeting in 1884 was dreadful, for the Jockey Club's first meeting it was ghastly. There was incessant rain for a week before the meeting. It was decided not to postpone, however. The first day started in wet gloom. Adding to the gloom, there was no music. Indeed, it was difficult to think how any band could have played in such weather. In the afternoon, just when it looked as if it was going to clear up, some warships entered port, and the customary salutes of guns were fired. Down came the rain again, and it rained all night. The nullah flooded as never before. At one stage the entire racecourse was under water, and in the process it was covered by thousands of tons of mud, sand, and forest débris, rendering it totally unusable.

The Jockey Club had come into being in excellent financial condition. The cost of restoring the racecourse put it severely in the red. This, however, was not the entire story. Too much was being spent on the Race Ball, for example, too much on prize money. A member blandly suggested an appeal to Hongkong's 'many millionaires' for help.

This was the kind of muddle, with priorities wrong, which Paul Chater, who was a born financial organizer, simply could not abide. It led to the next step he took, of great importance to the Jockey Club. It was useless to pretend that Hormusjee Mody, his partner, would have anything to do with Jockey Club management. He would never attend the meetings, to begin with. But he might race, might he not? Chater made over his entire stable to Mody, and himself became a Steward, in which position, unencumbered by a stable, he could keep a watchful eye on the Club's direction and finances. None was better qualified to do so.

Mody — 'Mr Buxey' — raced for the first time in 1886, and had four wins on the first day. Next year the pattern completed itself. With Mody racing, Chater was the Judge, and he was Judge every succeeding year until Sir Hormusjee Mody's death in 1911, after which Chater returned to racing, this time as 'Sir Paul'. In 1892 he was elected Chairman of the Board of Stewards, and remained so for 34 years, until his death in 1926. The partnership between Chater and Mody was in every way extraordinary, in that it extended into so many areas of both their lives.

David Sassoon at Happy Valley

MEANWHILE the David Sassoon saga had started in Shanghai. It extended to Hongkong, naturally, the Sassoons being evenly spread; but here there were good adversaries. The first three years that David Sassoon raced in Hongkong were the years when John Bell-Irving won the Champions three years in succession with different ponies.

In 1891 Sassoon brought the unbeaten *Zephyr* down, and in one race Mody's *Skipjack* beat him to second place, a win which in Shanghai would have caused a sensation, but which in Hongkong was taken as all in the day's work. That apart, *Zephyr* won as usual: the Lusitano Cup on the first day, the Exchange Plate and the Flyaway Stakes on the second, the Challenge Cup and the Champions on the third.

Next year the incomparable *Hero* came. The Champions that year gives the clearest impression ever of the wonder-pony. His main rivals were *Talisman*, owned by the formidably black-bearded James Johnstone Keswick, the Jardine taipan, and *Porpoise*, owned by 'Mr Darius'. Sassoon himself rode *Hero*, with *Lightning*, also from his stable, ridden by the Australian jockey he usually engaged when in Hongkong. This is how the *Hongkong Telegraph* correspondent described the race.

Mr Sassoon declared to win with *Hero*. The favourite got a bad start, *Lightning* taking the lead, with *Porpoise* and *Talisman* next. Mr Sassoon quickly overhauled the last two, and at the village was racing at the girths of his second string. This order was maintained until the last two furlongs, when the undefeated champion came along in the best style, though without any encouragement, and won as he liked by a length, his stable companion being second, and *Porpoise* and *Talisman* at wide distances in the rear. Time: 3 minutes 23 seconds.

That simple description of the win conveys *Hero* as no other description quite did; and though the correspondent says nothing of this, one realizes from his words what a perfect rider David Sassoon must have been. *Hero's* bad start, one suspects, was partly due to *Dolores* not being there, though of course the Hongkong public probably did not know about 'Hero's Amah'.

The last time Sassoon raced in Hongkong was in February 1893, when he brought *Majestic*, who did splendidly on the first two days. On the third day, however, the barometer fell, and there was fine, misty rain, the weather 'in the last degree mournful and depressing', as the Hongkong spring sometimes can be. It was not only the humans who felt it. Its effect on the best ponies was terrible. Everything that could possibly go wrong went wrong. Outsiders won everything. The climax came in the Champions, in which Sassoon, riding *Majestic*, came in ninth.

Small wonder he never came again.

An interesting feature concerning David Sassoon at the Hongkong races is that he aroused none of the resentment evinced for him by the *habitués* of the Shanghai Grand Stand.

From the description of Hongkong in its early days, given in a former chapter, one would have expected it to be the other way round: that Hongkong would have resented him, and Shanghai hailed him. It was not so. The Hongkong public were delighted to see *Zephyr* and *Hero*, and did not in the least begrudge their owner his numerous wins. The Jockey Club in fact had a special reason for being pleased. In 1888 Sassoon entered such a large number of ponies that it visibly improved the Club's financial position.

Racing Righteously

I N 1890 a question was asked in Parliament about gambling in Hongkong. Questions in Parliament were the bane of the Hongkong Secretariat's existence. It behoved the local authorities to bestir themselves in applying with more vigour the provisions of the Gambling Ordinance, one of the strangest pieces of legislation ever introduced in Hongkong, meaningless in terms of Chinese life, and all but totally unenforceable. All the same, when the Government bestirred itself, trouble could be created for many people.

At a Jockey Club meeting in January 1891 a member pointed out that the Stewards were liable to six months' imprisonment for participating in the profits of the tote. He must have been like the man who tried to interfere with the Shanghai tiffin. In this case, however, it was not a matter for the members to vote upon. There was this law, and the man was technically right.

The Annual Meeting was held as usual. It was the year *Zephyr* raced. In December, however, a new Governor arrived.

Sir William Robinson was one of Hongkong's more faceless Governors — there were quite a few. He began his career as a clerk in the Colonial Office, and was a Colonial Office man, meaning he toed the line, one of Victorian righteousness, a feature of which was that gambling was evil. In circumstances unrecorded, the Chairman of the Jockey Club was given to understand that the new Governor would be pleased to attend the February meeting, but that of course there would be no gambling. Facilities for betting, he was assured, would be removed.

There followed the most depressing race-meeting ever held in Happy Valley, and the most sparsely attended. The weather contributed to the gloom. Cloud hung low over the hills; it was damp and sombre. A ragged line of Chinese occupied a small part of the rail, and stared vacantly into space — no *pari mutuel*, no tote. Most Chinese

simply came and emphatically recorded their protest by leaving the scene almost as soon as they had reached it.

In the enclosure, too, there was absolutely no excitement. The tote was not there, many people seemed to think that even the private sweep was punishable, and there was comparatively little speculation on any event. The meeting indeed was a model of morality. It was after the worthy Bishop's own heart. Had there been no ponies, as one dissatisfied gentleman remarked, it would have been perfect.

This was the welcome Happy Valley gave to *Hero*.

On the second day people arrived to find a notice had been set up, framed in a deep black border. It read:

DIED. The Hongkong Races, aged 50, from an overdose of grandmotherly legislation. The funeral will take place at Happy Valley tomorrow at 5 o'clock. *Resurgam*.

The Governor, with Lady Robinson and their daughter, arrived well before the first race and stayed to the end. They did the same on the following two days, plainly to demonstrate how enjoyable racing was when it was righteous, the sport of kings with no exchequer, horses racing in the kingdom of heaven.

This 'dead-and-alive burlesque', as the *Hongkong Telegraph* termed it, prevailed for two years, when after what must have been a great deal of negotiation, discussion and persuasion, the tote and *pari mutuel* were restored. Chinese knew nothing about this, and on the first day in February 1894 there was the usual small and dismal attendance. Word quickly passed back into town, and towards the end of the day the Valley began to fill up. Next day there were the usual thousands.

Rising and Dwindling Ports and Races

THE Foochow races had meanwhile changed greatly for the better. By 1877 people were becoming tired of the Tartar Camp venue for the races, and — the recurring Victorian problem — very few ladies were coming, because of the 'wearisome journey' getting there. Even a male visitor was heard to remark that it was not an excursion he would care to undertake twice.

At last, in 1882, a new racecourse and recreation ground was acquired, and was dubbed very satisfactory. In dry weather it was still a dusty journey to get there, but once arrived at the broad expanse of green, the dust was forgotten. There were three Stands, one for Club members and their guests, and two for Chinese, both in excellent positions, one set apart for mandarins, the other for the compradore class, meaning well-to-do businessmen. Foochow being the provincial capital, seat of the Viceroy of Fukien and Chekiang, more mandarins were to be seen at the Foochow races than anywhere else.

That year little *Strathaird*, who won the 1880 Shanghai Derby for John Macgregor, won the Champions both in Foochow and Amoy. They were getting good ponies, too. One year they had 10 subscription griffins, and 7 of them turned out to be winners.

That this standard of racing was achieved at this time is

The Amoy Races, 1905. (By courtesy: John Warner, Esq., Hongkong.)

particularly noteworthy, because Foochow as a Treaty Port was in fact dwindling into insignificance. Its commercial bastion had from the beginning been tea. The development of Assam and Ceylon tea — cheaper, equally good, and costing less to freight to Britain — dealt the China tea export trade a blow from which it never recovered. As early as 1875 the largest British tea firm in Foochow folded up, and others followed. The prevalence of racing depended to some extent on the size of a community, but equally on the degree of commercial prosperity. This was soon reflected in Foochow. At the April meeting of 1891 the races were entirely between Foochow and Amoy stables. There were no visitors. Another feature: over a period of twenty years they only once had a band.

Kiukiang — again, a tea port — was even worse afflicted. Its tea, not being of the same high quality as 'the fragrant Bohea', had even less chance of competing against Indian and Ceylon tea. There was still a Kiukiang Cup at the Hankow Races, but there is no record of any further racing in Kiukiang itself.

Amoy, with a more diverse commerce, fared better, and in 1894 produced two prominent figures in the China races, 'Mr Dryasdust' and F.B. Marshall, who became one of the most popular owners of his time. 'Mr Dryasdust' was H.P. White, known to his friends as 'Shiney', who in later life succeeded Sir Paul Chater as Chairman of the Hong Kong Jockey Club. Shiney White began his career in Formosan tea, from which he joined the Lapraik shipping and mercantile empire, in due course becoming chairman. He entered the Amoy races in January 1894 with *Shawnee*. The previous month David Sassoon had visited Foochow, and in a rare moment rode *Shawnee* to win the Hongkong Cup. This was the last time he ever raced in China as a jockey, riding for Shiney White.

January 1894 at Amoy was described as the best meeting in memory. *Shawnee* had several wins, F.B. Marshall riding. Frank Dallas was there, riding for a German owner, and taking three of the best Cups. Owner-riders from Foochow, Swatow and Formosa came to compete in the big race of the meeting, the Douglas Challenge Cup. This was a bequest of John Lapraik, owner of the Douglas Steamship Co., whose efficient and comfortable ships kept Amoy and Swatow in touch with the outside world — in other words, Hongkong. Owner-riders from Formosa were always encouraged to come to the Amoy races. Swatow had been a Treaty Port since 1860, but there was not a patch of flat land there for racing. Instead, Swatow people raced at Amoy and in Hongkong.

Shiney White's next winner was *Shiney Villiam*, who in 1896 won everything he entered at Amoy, including the Champions, and went on to a fine career in Shanghai and Hongkong. Next came a real wonder, *Sinbad*, who won the Amoy Champions of 1897, the Foochow Cup at Happy Valley in 1898, and in 1901, when practically everyone one can think of in the races in the South was either competing or present, won the Hongkong Champions, beating *Set* by 4 lengths — something no one had ever seen before — and Mody's *New Rose* by 10 lengths, about the most decisive Champions' win ever.

Throughout these years F.B. Marshall was invariably Shiney White's jockey. In 1905 he formed his own stable, based originally in Amoy. By 1908, with his 'Tree' series — *Pine Tree*, *Nutmeg Tree*, *Rubber Tree*, all winners at Happy Valley that year — he was carrying away prize after prize, and put himself in the top rank of owners, which at that date meant Hormusjee Mody, George Hutton Potts, Ellis Kadoorie, Henry Morriss, and Raymond Toeg, with leeway allowed for the Jardine pseudonyms.

These years were the heyday of the Amoy races, largely because there were now two stables capable of challenging all comers. At the 1907 races the Taotai was so delighted that

Group picture taken after the Taotai's Cup, Amoy, 1901. The Taotai of Amoy, with two other mandarins, is seated central. (By courtesy: Donald Cumming, Esq., Inkpen, Berkshire.)

on the third day, after the Champions had been run, he insisted on there being another race, and presented an additional Cup.

On this pleasant note, strange to relate, the Amoy races disappear from view. Though races were still held there, they were no longer reported in the Shanghai and Hongkong newspapers. The truth is that Amoy and Swatow were dwindling in importance as Treaty Ports. Both were old and well-organized Chinese commercial centres where there were few opportunities for Europeans other than to provide services, mainly shipping and banking, for Chinese international trade. Newchwang began in the same way, but there a European like Henry A. Bush could break in. In Amoy it was more difficult, doubly so in Swatow. Chinese had more experience and acumen.

Now, for a moment, to the Canton races.

Canton's refusal to respect the terms of the Treaty of Nanking, to permit foreigners to move about in peace in the city, and allow them a place of residence more amenable than the intolerably cramped foreign enclave of the eighteenth century, was the underlying cause of the Second Chinese War of 1856–60.

When, as an outcome of that war, diplomatic missions were at last allowed in Peking, Canton was under foreign military control, which was not withdrawn until it seemed certain that Canton, once open, would remain so.

Thus Canton, technically a Treaty Port since 1843, did not really become one until twenty years later. The foreign settlement was on Shameen, an artificial islet secured against the river by stone walls, and created by silt scooped up from the river — Shameen means Sand Surface. It lay alongside what were in those times the outskirts of the city, from which it was separated by a canal — really a broad ditch.

Racing started while the city was under Anglo-French military government. An account of 1865 describes the arrangements:

A racecourse is formed annually upon the site of paddy-fields leased for the purpose after the harvest, and pony races are held in January. The unpretending 'family-party-like' Races at Canton are considered among the most pleasant meetings in China.

The most probable venue of these meetings was somewhere out in the fields towards White Cloud Mountain, some three miles from the city. After the resumption of Chinese civil government, all went well for a time. In December 1870, however, an attempt to combine a race-meeting with an excursion by boat to a beauty spot some twenty miles up-river led to an ugly incident, in which the Europeans were pelted with stones, and had to escape under guard to their boats.

After this they cast their eyes across the river from Shameen to the garden island of Ho-nam, lying immediately opposite on the other side. Ho-nam, occupied by the very wealthy, was a Chinese version of a garden suburb. Though it did not bode well for wide open spaces, it did mean more personal safety.

The first recorded meeting was held there in December 1874. Once again rice-fields were used after harvest. There was a small area of fields surrounding a hill. This provided a 950-yard circuit with the hill in the middle. At a given moment in any race the ponies and riders disappeared, and there was much excitement to see which were the first to reappear on the other side. The French were prominent in these races, as is attested by the many winning ponies with French names.

Nothing much is heard of racing in Canton after this. With Hongkong only 90 miles away by river it may be assumed the Canton races died a natural death. Their interest is that they show how different conditions were in Canton from anywhere else in China where racing was introduced.

The Ningpo races, which started with such éclat, died a similar natural death, with Shanghai only 120 miles away. Ningpo was another Treaty Port which was dwindling. It had not taken Ningpo merchants long to see that business could be conducted more profitably in Shanghai, to which many moved and established their headquarters, their Ningpo offices becoming subsidiary. To a peculiar extent the China races rose and fell with the degree of commercial prosperity.

Another instance of this concerns Chefoo, which in its charming country way had witnessed some of the most colourful and successful race-meetings ever held in China. In 1898 Tsingtao, on the opposite, southern side of the Shantung peninsula, became a German possession and was declared a free port. In its first six years under German auspices the volume and value of Tsingtao's trade rose from 2,000,000 taels a year to 30,800,000 taels a year. Though foreign firms hung on in Chefoo, and Consuls and Customs alike declared it had an assured future, this was in fact a body-blow. Chefoo

Tsingtao, the Beach City, seen in the 1920s. On the left, the residence of the Japanese Consul-General and, prior to 1922, of the Japanese Governor. (By courtesy: Charles E. Wolnizer, Esq.)

might be in the right place strategically; Tsingtao was in the right place economically, and it was this that mattered.

A race-meeting in the usual fine style was held at Chefoo in September 1905, after Japan's shattering defeat of the Imperial Russian Navy at the Battle of Tsushima, which took place on 27 May that year. Thereafter a different political climate prevailed. The hostility which Germany had aroused, particularly in Japan, by seizing Tsingtao and its hinterland, had cast a sterner light on naval movements. Gone were the days when superb naval vessels rode at anchor in ceremonial array off the Chefoo racecourse.

Racing continued, though there were fewer visiting Tientsin jockeys, and none from Shanghai. Tsingtao — the Beach City, as it came to be called — had become a favourite resort for Shanghailanders. Chefoo was dwindling, and racing dwindled with it.

The last announcement from Chefoo came in October 1924, saying that a golf course was to be laid in the middle of the racecourse, in conjunction with a reorganization of the Race Club. It was the death-knell of racing in Chefoo. Whether a golf course was laid down there, so far out of town, is uncertain. The Race Club was never reorganized. European children brought up in Chefoo in the 1930s, all of them riding ponies and knowing the area well, had no idea that there had ever been any races there.

The only people who would know today would be the great-grandchildren of those who in that village — if one could find it — had told them how once the forefathers went out and planted those trees.

The Germans developed Tsingtao in their own distinctive way, many of the buildings displaying features of German provincial architecture. As an old hand looking back on it said, 'With its red-tiled roofs, it was like a little German town.' This apart, it was a Treaty Port in all but name, a thriving and important one, a main port for the export of coal. Jardine Matheson and most of the principal firms had branches there. There was an English newspaper, and — trust the Germans — an excellent band. With a healthy climate, it was not long before it started becoming a resort, particularly for people from Shanghai.

The inaugural race-meeting was held on 18 October 1905, and was an all-German affair conducted strictly on English lines. It had many of the usual features, a 1½-mile Derby and a Champions' race. The Commissioner of Customs sponsored a race, as did the compradores. The largest field was 10, the average 6.

Tsingtao had the only turf course in North China. The Germans were of divided mind on the matter, but decided to risk it, and a turf course it remained throughout the duration of its life, though as Baron von Delwig observed, the Tsingtao Race Club was arguing the merits of converting to a dirt track up to the last meeting ever held.

It was also proudly stated of Tsingtao that it was the only place in China where races could be held in summer. This was so, but the summer months consist of alternating bouts of rain and fine weather, and the course was nearly always heavy. There is no instance of a record ever being set at the Tsingtao summer races.

While men of nationalities other than German raced during these years, management of the races was exclusively German. Thus when, with the Great War raging in Europe, Japanese forces seized Tsingtao on 31 October 1914 and interned all the Germans, racing came to an end.

The Japanese take-over met with full Allied approval. Japanese administration in Tsingtao was efficient and sensible, and care was taken not to damage anything connected with the prevailing culture. Thus the imposing German Club on the sea-front survived intact with its magnificent furnishings and library — it would have made marvellous loot — as did the racecourse, which no one was allowed to build on or interfere with.

As an outcome of the Washington Conference of 1922, Tsingtao was retroceded to China and came under a special administration — once again a Treaty Port in all but name. A Japanese-sponsored race club of sorts, which had existed for some years, had become semi-defunct 'through lack of experience and organization.' An attempt was now made to resuscitate it, clearly with a view to maintaining Japanese prime social sponsorship in the absence of political primacy.

Here, for the first time in these pages we meet the Chinese gentleman rider, the mere mention of whom is enough to indicate what had been taking place socially in China during these years of foreign racing.

At this point a group of Chinese gentlemen riders weighed in. Bringing together the principal nationalities concerned — Japanese, German, British — the Tsingtao International Recreation Club was formed, with the American Consul as Patron. The Chinese acted with typical *sagesse*. The governing body of the Club was neatly divided fifty-fifty between Chinese and the rest. It meant that should the rest ever be divided among themselves, Chinese would be in control. As will be seen, this is precisely what happened.

The Tsingtao races were part of a varied and colourful scene. The Beach City had entered its palmiest days. Most prominent Shanghai people, including a number who figured at the races, had resort residences there, some of them the size of small palaces. Life was smart, stylish and relaxed, with all-night ballroom dancing at the Edgewater Hotel throughout the summer. People went there to swim, gamble, dance, and have illicit liaisons. Leading Hongkong owners had their ponies shipped there in summer to enjoy the cooler climate and sea bathing. Considering that the return sea voyage is a distance of some 2,800 miles, and it was an annual affair, one is obliged to admit that these ponies rated high on the scale of pampered animals.

Newchwang after 1900 steadily rose in commercial importance, expanded and became more up-to-date. After 1905, when the Japanese threw the Russians out of much of Manchuria, the Yingtze Race Club had Japanese members and owner-riders in addition to Europeans of several nationalities. Though for climatic reasons Newchwang remained off the main China race circuit, its race-meetings enjoyed status, enhanced by economic prosperity.

Mukden had a Japanese Race Club in 1923. While Westerners could race there and train their ponies at the course, management was exclusively Japanese. This was the first instance of Japanese organizing races successfully outside their own country. There were one or two Japanese racing enthusiasts in China. Matsumoto of Shanghai once won the Champions to immense public acclaim. In Tsingtao a Japanese club had been attempted, and as noted, it became moribund. The same had happened in a number of other places in Manchuria. Mukden was exceptional in being a success. Japanese and Europeans thus raced at Mukden and Newchwang, more Japanese at the former, more Europeans at the latter.

A sensational incident occurred at the Mukden Race Club in July 1925 when a force of Chinese police invaded the course and tried to stop the races on the grounds that gambling was illegal in China. The third race was about to start, jockeys mounted, when a posse of about twenty police dashed out and seized the ponies' reins. The ponies were too strong for them. Goodness knows what kind of start it was, but off they went. The police in fact lost face so badly that no more was heard about illegal gambling.

Peking carried on as usual, except for the four years of the Great War, when racing was brought to a stop by the impossible situation that all the belligerents had their diplomatic representatives there, and all normally supported the races. The Allies could in fact have conducted races successfully on their own, but wisely decided against such an affront.

Peking lay off the main race circuit by virtue of its diplomatic rather than commercial atmosphere, its connexion with the circuit being exclusively with Tientsin. This relationship had been facilitated since 1908, when the Peking–Hankow railway was completed. The railway had a branch line to Tientsin, and there was a station less than two miles from Pao Ma Chang. This meant that Tientsin owners and riders could bring their ponies by rail direct from Tientsin to the Peking racecourse. In addition, on Friday evenings and Saturday mornings during the racing season trains from Peking made

As seen by Georges Sapajou at the Peking races, 1921:

Top left: D.L. Newbigging, father of the present Taipan of Jardine Matheson.

Top right: Sir Eric Mieville, at the start of the distinguished career which led to his becoming Private Secretary to King George VI. In 1921 he was Private Secretary to the British Minister in Peking.

Left: Colonel Weatherbe D'Arcy, who owned the first pack of foxhounds in China, in Peking. He later brought them down to Hongkong, where they hunted in the New Territories.

unscheduled stops at Pao Ma Chang for racegoers. It was all very civilized and pleasant.

'There was not much money in that Club,' Baron von Delwig observed, 'but it was a charming place, and on race days one saw there a most elegant and interesting public, both foreign and Chinese.'

By 1920, with Peking and Newchwang in separate positions for different reasons, major racing had narrowed down to Tientsin, Shanghai, Hankow and Hongkong. This does not imply there was less racing. On the contrary, there was more. In Tientsin, Shanghai and Hankow there were additional clubs and courses where Chinese gentlemen riders raced and where riders from European clubs were welcome. The Extra Meeting came into being. From 1917 Shanghai even had races on New Year's Day, and despite the freezing weather, the city under snow, these races were extremely well attended.

In the 1920s the racing cities of China went racing mad. Bearing Tsingtao in mind, with its summer racing, there were race-meetings in one place or another in China every week of the year. Moreover, it was logistically possible to attend a meeting every week of the year. Some of the more sought-after jockeys seem nearly to have succeeded in doing this without trying.

The scale of it was extraordinary. To quote Baron von Delwig on the subject of Tientsin:

There were usually about 25 race days in the spring, and just as many in the autumn, usually ten races a day. Thus in theory an amateur rider in China had a chance to ride in 500 races a year, and in practice many did ride in 250 races a year. At the outbreak of war there were several jockeys who had ridden in over 2,000 races with an average of 8–10% wins and over 20% places in addition to that.

In the good old days — say from 1923 to 1930 — the official four days of the Spring and Autumn Meetings were a holiday for the whole town. All offices and banks would close in the afternoon, and all the foreign community and a great deal of the Chinese population would drive in an unending column to the Race Course, women wearing their new spring dresses and hats, and Chinese wearing their smartest silk robes. Large lunch parties would be arranged with lots of champagne, and gold and silver trophies displayed on the lunch tables.

The Schleswig Cup, Tientsin, 1920. About the largest and heaviest Cup ever presented in the China races, it was given by the Danish community in Tientsin as a gesture of thanks to the British for lending support to the restoration of Schleswig-Holstein to Denmark, from Germany. As it chanced, the winner in the race was a British owner with a Danish jockey. (By courtesy: Maurice Lister, Esq., Bourne End, Buckinghamshire.)

8. Revolutions and Innovations

Previous page: The ladies came, 'each with a pretty book and pencil.' A visiting gentleman was furious that the ladies paid no attention to the actual races. This is one of the books they held. The pencil is missing. It is the year of the Revolution, the overthrow of the Manchu dynasty. (By courtesy: Michael Boycott, Esq., Cranleigh, Surrey.)

Lady Owners

BEFORE going further, a word about the ladies.
There are recurring Victorian references to there being
ladies in the grandstand, and lady visitors at the races. It will
be remembered, too, how in the Shanghai tiffin crisis the
magistrate Wainewright saved the situation by pointing out
that ladies enjoyed the tiffin. The racing correspondents of
those times invariably began their coverage with a description
of the weather, followed by an observation on the number of
ladies in the grandstand: one of approval if there were many,
one of disappointment if there were few. The success of a
meeting was judged in part by the number of ladies present.

The fact is that only a few Victorian ladies in China were
interested in the races. In a male-dominated society, which
Victorian society in China was, with men living almost
permanently in the atmosphere of a men's sports club, to
expect women to take an interest in racing was taking things
too far. There was that imposing Race Club at Shanghai, too.
The only provisions it made for ladies were the toilets.

Husbands expected their wives to come to the races, and in
their smartest dresses, which in the China climate were very
uncomfortable. Many a European woman of those times, when
on her own at home, lived permanently in a night-dress.[17] To
persuade wives to attend the first and second days of a meeting
was difficult. Out of a sense of duty, and with a sigh, they
might go on the third day. At Happy Valley, to make sure
they did, the third day, normally Champions' Day, was
changed to Ladies' Day.

Hongkong in fact fared better than most places in this
respect during Victorian times. With its European-style houses
scattered on the side of a steep mountain, Hongkong was
never a very neighbourly place. Since wives left behind were
apt to be lonely, they went to the races with their husbands
more readily. Tientsin, as has been seen, met the situation by
making the races a family affair. This was due to the important
continental influence in the Race Club. Hankow was similar.
Russian ladies in particular needed no luring to go to the
races. Elsewhere Victorian ladies simply had to make the best
of the situation and patiently tolerate their sporting husbands.

The one place where there was no difficulty was Peking.
The wives of the diplomats, many of them aristocrats, came

17. Considered more seemly by Chinese, in that it revealed less bare flesh.

from societies where women traditionally took part in equestrian activities. In addition, in Peking all the women rode ponies, which was not the case in the Treaty Ports.

Attitudes began to change in the 1890s, Shanghai in the lead as usual, as it dawned on ladies that the races were a heaven-sent opportunity to show off their latest and finest clothes. The press took this up at once, punctuating their racing reports with descriptions of any eye-catching toilettes or colour schemes. No names, of course. As with the pseudonyms, you had to guess if you did not see the lady yourself. But this did the trick. Never again was it necessary to mention whether or not there were many ladies in the grandstand.

In Edwardian times women became prominent in the paper hunts, riding side-saddle and looking extremely elegant. The first lady owner at the Shanghai races was Isabel Moller in 1920. She won the Jessfield Cup with *Safetylight* at the November meeting that year, with her husband Eric Moller, wealthy shipowner and industrialist, and a magnificent rider and judge of a pony, riding as her jockey. This, obviously, was a courtesy ownership. Eric Moller, for many years a top jockey, had by this time leased the Sassoon stable premises off Bubbling Well Road, and started the 'Light' series, which in the course of time was to achieve the most sensational of all wins in South China.

The Hong Kong Jockey Club acted likewise, changing its rules to admit lady owners. The first, in February 1921, included Lady Chater and Mrs John Johnstone, whose *Irish Stew* won the Valley Stakes, her husband riding. John Johnstone at the time was head of Jardine's in Shanghai, and later became the taipan. One of the best and most successful riders in a century of racing, he rode with style — virtually everyone used the same word about him. Once again, he was a relative, a great-grandson of Jean Jardine. With the exception of the Jardine brothers in Hongkong's early days, he was the outstanding Jardine rider, and the only Jardine taipan actually to ride in races. He did not own many racing ponies and generally rode for others — all the leading owners, in fact. Indeed, possessed of great stamina, he thought nothing of riding in consecutive races at Happy Valley, sometimes for the best part of an entire day.

These again were courtesy ownerships. The first lady to own and train her own ponies in Shanghai was Ada Law. Daughter of a Glasgow engineer and his Edinburgh-born wife,

Shanghai Spring Races, 1907. (By courtesy: The Hongkong and Shanghai Banking Corporation.)

Mimi Hayim leading in Comedy King, Shanghai Derby, 1920. This was the first year lady owners were admitted to the Shanghai Race Club. Mimi Hayim certainly lent weight to the proceedings. The Hayim family took over from their relatives, the Benjamins, in the brokerage firm of Benjamin and Potts.

who came from Scotland to Hongkong to marry him — they shortly afterwards moved to Shanghai — Ada Law had been riding there since the age of 4. She entered the races the moment it became possible, and as an owner-trainer was a tough challenge to the men. Next in was Billie Coutts, whose family had been associated with the Shanghai Race Club since its earliest days. She entered as an owner-trainer in 1924 and had two wins on her first day. Both ladies were notably successful with their winners.

Remembering Eleanora Andraevna of Hankow, the first lady owner in China some forty years before, one appreciates just how far ahead of her time she was, as indeed was the Hankow Race Club.

The Starting Gate

IN 1896 the Calcutta Turf Club introduced Victor Carandini's starting machine at their Hurdle Races. It was found to be highly satisfactory. When, it was asked in Hongkong, would they have this machine in the Far East? Calcutta, seat of the Viceroy of India, tended to be ahead of the rest of Asia where innovations were concerned.

Racing in Calcutta was basically an Indian Army affair. Riders there, when told to race with a starting machine, did so. Not in Shanghai, where a starting gate was first introduced in November 1902.

To begin with, some of the Stewards didn't like the damned thing anyway. In the first race one pony ran through the gate and broke the lower piece of webbing. In the second race the ponies waited for a second or two after the gate flew up, before starting. In the Maidens, the third race, the 26 entrants got off to an excellent start save for *Tarquin*, of the Jardine stable, who was frightened by the noise of the gate, turned tail, and galloped off in the opposite direction. Mercifully his jockey managed to rein him in before there was a disaster. At the end of this race a number of riders complained about the gate. The Stewards vacillated, then ordered that it be removed.

In May 1903 the gate was tried again, the Stewards still undecided about it. In November it was tried for the third time, and with the ponies more accustomed to it, it seemed there to stay.

Not so. Starting in this fashion was too organized. Opposition to the starting gate continued doggedly until at last it was removed entirely, to be replaced by tape-starting. The truth is that most of the riders prided themselves on their skill at getting away at a disorderly start.

The End of the Empire

THE Russo-Japanese War of 1904–5, in which for the first time a European power was defeated by an Asiatic one and when in India the slogan 'Asia for the Asiatics' was born, had no effect on the Shanghai races, where people were more concerned about whether the motor car would oust the horse. As was said at the time, no one on the China coast could claim *not* to be interested in horses. The war brought the Newchwang races to a temporary halt until after March 1905, when with the Russians in full retreat up the railway line, racing was promptly resumed.

Six years later, on 10 October 1911, the revolution which Dr Sun Yat-sen had for many years striven to inspire, broke out in a totally unforeseen manner. Three soldiers in the garrison at Wuchang, one of the three cities which combine to make the joint city of Wuhan, were disciplined and shot — unjustly, it was held. A revolt of the troops took place which rapidly turned into an irresistible anti-Manchu uprising. The issue was never in doubt. Manchu authority collapsed. The Imperial Government was paralyzed.

The Chinese then turned on each other. In a situation so confused it has never been fully explained, amid mass slaughter and appalling butchery, the Chinese city of Hankow was totally destroyed. The adjacent foreign concessions were not touched, but it certainly brought the Hankow races to a standstill.

In Shanghai, 600 miles away, things proceeded in their usual amusing fashion. A racing correspondent, describing the November meeting of 1911 — held less than four weeks after the revolution started — wrote, 'The stirring events of the past few days seemed to have little influence on the community's interest in its sports; and the nine-star banner of revolt flying over the Chinese Race Club was the only indication of an upheaval in the Empire.'

The unified Empire of China was founded in the year 221 BC. After 2,131 years it had come to an end. This did not interfere with the Shanghai races.

Not on the first day, at any rate. John Johnstone, riding for F.B. Marshall, who was a Steward, won four races for him in succession. *Willow Tree, Persimmon Tree, Cypress Tree,* and *Cherry Tree* won the Criterion Stakes, the Fah Wah Stakes, the St. Leger, and the Autumn Cup respectively. As if this was not enough, John Johnstone went on to win the Eclipse Stakes on the Ewo (Jardine) pony *Drumlithie.*

Some time in the night news was received of a massacre in Nanking. This was in fact the massacre in the Chinese city of Hankow. Immediate news reaching Shanghai from any part of China was notoriously inaccurate.

The next day was very cold. Chinese had the news well before Europeans. The second and third days of the race-meeting were among the most poorly attended ever, and the least enthusiastic on record.

Some days later it was learned that republican forces were on their way to take over Shanghai. It was known by this time that at Hankow the military had been under the strictest orders not to interfere with the foreign concessions. Nevertheless, as a precaution, settlement police were sent to take control of the main Shanghai railway station, which was in Chapei, outside the foreign zone. The republicans in due course arrived, taking over the walled city in complete order, without resistance. The police were withdrawn from Chapei. Next day the streets of the settlement were hung with thousands of nine-star banners, creating a glowing spectacle. Shanghai, in fact, was entirely republican in sympathy.

The years that followed were marked by Yuan Shih-k'ai's misjudged designs to have himself declared Emperor, his subsequent death, the rise of the warlords, the struggles of the Kuomintang to establish itself in the South, and its short-lived alliance with Russian communism. All this and much else had little effect on life in the Treaty Ports, or on the races.

For most of the period the situation in China was so confused and varying that few people in the Treaty Ports had much idea of what was happening, and often could not understand even the little they knew or read about. Contributing to this detachment, the China coast experienced boom conditions much of the time, notably during the Great War years. Shanghai, in particular, witnessed a boom for an unprecedented 20 years, from 1913 to 1933, the most dazzling years in its history, though it continued to dazzle till the end.

By contrast with the conditions of life for the great mass of China's population — conditions which sank during these times to levels almost humanly unbearable — Shanghai became ever more strikingly different, until Europeans coming from the interior usually confessed they found the place quite unreal. Inevitably, in such a setting, the China races, with their *orgueil*, their display of wealth, and their rich patrons — Chinese and European alike — intent only on enjoying themselves, appear in a harsher, more unkindly light. It has simply to be borne in mind that the setting was not of these Europeans' making, nor of the Shanghai Chinese for that matter. The fall of a dynasty, as mentioned earlier, means anarchy — rural anarchy, which is the worst of all. This time,

George Hutton Potts, old Harrovian, who raced as an owner in China for more than forty years. This cartoon was made of him circa 1928, and is signed by the most prominent members of the Shanghai Race Club. He headed the Macao Jockey Club from its start in 1930 to his death in 1937.

moreover, it was not just a dynasty which had fallen, but over two thousand years of a system of government.

There would be no more Taotais in the grandstand, no more mandarins in the weighing room, no more blindfold British sailors with Chinese desperately yelling instructions to keep them on course, no more viceroys with mouths full of toffee. It had all gone; and what would come next no one could say. So — one raced. One carried on.

Chinese Race Clubs

IN the very last days of the Chinese Empire, about a fortnight before the Revolution broke out, the newly-formed International Recreation Club held its first race-meeting at Kiangwan (Chiangwan) at a new racecourse in the Chinese outskirts of Shanghai, some three miles north of the foreign settlement boundary.

On the Chinese side the prime mover in the formation of this Club was the Ningpo millionaire merchant and banker Chu Pao-san, a great and wise public benefactor and keen racing enthusiast. An outstanding man, he served three successive terms as Chairman of the Chinese General Chamber of Commerce — never an easy seat to hold, and one of much consequence. He had a tremendous following. When he died in 1926 his funeral procession was watched by tens of thousands, even the rooftops being covered with people.

The stimulus for the formation of the Kiangwan club was undoubtedly Chinese dissatisfaction with the Shanghai Race Club's disinclination to admit them as members. There was the likelihood, therefore, of Kiangwan being a rival club, one which could easily drain away Chinese public support for the Shanghai races, which without that support would be only a modest affair.

By a strange fortuity the other principal proponent of the idea was Hsü Ling-yün, another millionaire, who was the Shanghai compradore of Jardine's. Inevitably the boss, John Johnstone, top jockey of the day, learned of what was afoot, and suggested that they go into it together, making it an international club. A little-known feature of the Jardine taipans is that they were the leaders in promoting anything sensible which made for more understanding between the British and

John Johnstone, head of Jardine's and a top jockey in Shanghai, saddling. Sketch done in the 1920s by Juel Madsen.

Mrs Hickling, a prominent member of the Shanghai Paper Hunt Club, and John Johnstone's sister. She took all the jumps side-saddle. Sketch by Juel Madsen.

T.U. Yih, catalyst figure in the affairs of the International Recreation Club, Kiangwan, and in the revival of racing in Macao, 1927. A man of impeccable taste, with a gift for good organization. Sketch by Juel Madsen, done in the 1920s.

the Chinese. This dates from the rise to maturity of English-speaking, Western-educated Chinese, and John Johnstone, in associating himself with the Kiangwan idea, was the first to give expression to it. Hsü Ling-yün and Chu Pao-san had the wit to see the wisdom of the suggestion. With their combined forces, Kiangwan would enjoy immense prestige.

It would also, from the Shanghai Race Club's point of view, avert a financial disaster.

With men like John Johnstone weighing in, the Britons, whose initial attitude to the Kiangwan venture was far from favourable, changed their minds. The course was excellent, there was a comfortable grandstand, and at the first meeting an attendance of over 5,000. Soon practically everyone from the Shanghai Race Club was to be seen at Kiangwan. The early meetings were called gymkhanas. This brought in the paper hunt crowd. There were open steeplechases and a Paper Hunters' Cup. Leading European jockeys rode for Chinese owners. Chinese jockeys rode for European owners. Over the years the Club had a succession of extremely able Secretaries. Kiangwan from the start was first-class.

In Hankow, as soon as the dust had settled after the atrocious massacre, and the Chinese city was being rebuilt, Chinese racing fanciers got together and took matters a stage further by forming the Chinese Race Club.

They secured a fine piece of land, laid out a superb course, and raced strictly to the rules, with once again first-rate organization. In no time at all the Kiangwan top riders were on their way to Hankow as fast as the fastest river steamer could take them. European residents of Hankow were welcome to race at the Chinese Race Club as visitors, and most of them did. The two clubs co-ordinated to prevent their dates clashing.

The two new clubs, Kiangwan international and Hankow Chinese, were a tremendous success. It was impossible to say after this that Chinese were incapable of organizing anything properly, as was usually said.

Kiangwan in its early years presented the public with something which was unique and delightful. Most of the owner-riders were young, all of them were 'son of', and all of them were doing well in their own right. There was Harry Morriss and his brother Hayley, sons of the Mohawk Chief, founder of the *Herald* and the *Daily News*; Chuck Burkill, whose father headed A.R. Burkill & Sons, one of the largest British firms in China; the Ezra brothers, grandsons of the fabulous Isaac Ezra, whose family moved from opium into urban development so ahead of its time and on such a scale that the Municipal Council looked upon it as a public service; and J.A.S. Alves, scion of one of the first Portuguese families to settle in Shanghai. Then there were the Chinese, C.T. Chu, first Chinese star owner-rider and descendant of Chu Pao-san; and S.P. Ma, T.L. and H.F. Hu, and T.N. and T.U. Yih, all of them sons of the great merchant families, many of them from Ningpo, who helped create international Shanghai and who were the cream of Chinese society there. Among the non-owners in these early days were one of the best Portuguese jockeys, Dalgarno, and above all the Chinese superstar J. Liou — Liou Hsin-teh — who had European and Chinese owners tumbling over each other trying to get him to ride for them, both in Shanghai and Hankow.

Of the Chinese in Kiangwan's early days, the most significant was T.U. Yih, who gradually emerged as the mainstay of the Club. He was joined after a few years by Ed Sheng and his brother Henry — again, sons of a vintage Shanghai family and a highly successful racing partnership.

It was often thought that Chinese were interested in the races only because they themselves were inveterate gamblers. This was wide of the mark. First and foremost, a whole crowd of Chinese from prominent families wanted to ride in English-style races, and had wanted to for a number of years, riding their own ponies. This is the overriding factor that brought the Chinese clubs into being — no different from anywhere else, love of horses and racing. As for the spectators, betting came into it, as was seen when Sir William Robinson brought it to a stop; but this was not the whole story. Though betting on horse-races depends undeniably on luck, it is also a skill, and it was thus that Chinese saw it. The Chinese who went to the races were far more discerning than most Europeans gave them credit for. As one of the characters in Ann Bridge's novel of the Peking races, *The Ginger Griffin*, says:

'There's very little the Chinese don't know about horse-racing — they're all as mad on it as Yorkshiremen.'

It will be remembered how at the Happy Valley races Chinese swarmed all over the Black Rock. 'This,' as an observant European pointed out, 'showed racing judgment, for the Rock is the place where many races are lost or won (or very nearly) so that those who choose the Rock have an excellent view of the manoeuvring for position. It is an excellent place of vantage, too, from which to see the race from end to end.'

Chinese gentlemen riders weighed in at the same time in Tientsin, where in due course there was an additional club at Nan Kai, near the future University. There was another one at Nan Yuan, within comfortable distance of Peking. At both clubs Europeans raced determinedly with their Chinese counterparts. Eventually Tientsin, Shanghai and Hankow all had three race clubs and courses.

Another Shanghai innovation of this period occurred in 1912, when the Town Band converted itself into the Shanghai Municipal Orchestra, with an international body of musicians recruited from all over Europe. In the early days of the races, unless a flagship was in port there was no music, and there were frequent complaints on the subject. In 1878 the French at last produced a band. This shamed the Municipal Council into activity. Next year the Town Band came into being, with a French conductor, the musician element mainly Portuguese. Shanghai, with one of the finest orchestras in the world, became widely admired for its symphony concerts. It is of note that this stemmed from the need to provide music at the races, which the brass, woodwind and timpani of the Municipal Orchestra continued to do.

The Shanghai Horse Bazaar, around 1913. A great centre of innocent devilry. The Revolution is over, the Manchu dynasty abolished, and Chinese men have cut off their queues. (By courtesy: B.B.C. Hulton Picture Library.)

When the Great War broke out, there was much heart-searching in Shanghai on whether racing should be suspended, or should continue but without betting. The dilemma was at its most acute in Shanghai because whatever the Race Club there decided to do, all the other clubs would follow suit. Where the turf and its rules were concerned, it was a case of what Shanghai does today, all the rest would do tomorrow, or as soon as the first steamer reached them with the news. After much public and private discussion, the Race Club decided to carry on as usual, but make part of the profits of each meeting over to war charities and to specific war projects, which came to include a series of scout aircraft and Red Cross field ambulances, all marked 'Shanghai Race Club' with the series number. This was the beginning of a system of making over racing profits to the public weal which many years later, in Hongkong, reached dramatic proportions.

In Tientsin the Great War produced another impossible situation, similar to that of Peking, because of the strong German element in the Tientsin Race Club. Racing continued, and the Germans wisely dropped out. The Japanese seizure of Tsingtao, and the general approval this met, had given the Germans a clear indication of which way the wind of opinion was blowing on the China coast. The Shanghai Municipal

Council elections of January 1916 gave an even clearer one, when Baron Yoshiaki Fujimura polled 1,016 votes, the highest of anyone, against the German candidate's 131 votes.

At the end of the war the Hong Kong Jockey Club, with Sir Paul Chater as Chairman, gave the lead to the whole of the China coast by ruling that German former members be welcomed back and reinstated. This aroused a great deal of ill-feeling at the time, though it did not last. For most Germans in China the Great War was the very last thing they ever wished to see happen. German commerce in China never recovered from it.

Tragedy at Happy Valley

IN those times the entire west side of the Happy Valley racecourse, from the village at the top end to the monument at the Valley entrance, was lined by a long row of private matshed stands. A few of these on the stables' side were on the Jockey Club's meagre piece of land. The great majority were on Crown land which the Government would not part with, since it exacted licence fees for the annual hire of this land, with further fees for permission to erect matshed structures on it. The Jockey Club was extremely careful to ensure that all matshed structures on its property were properly constructed and safe. The Government, as it turned out, was not so careful.

Towards evening on Tuesday, 26 February 1918, the *Hongkong Telegraph*, always the most welcome newspaper at this season, because being an evening paper it was first out with the race results, appeared with a gaunt and dreadful headline, placed central and boxed, making it look like the obituary it indeed was: 'TERRIBLE CALAMITY AT RACE COURSE'. In a few lines of bold print — all there was time for before the news was rushed out to the streets — it gave the bare facts.

The Derby had already been run, and the ponies were going round to take their places in the China Stakes, when a section of matsheds beside the course 'collapsed like a pack of cards, and fire was seen.' In a few seconds the large stand, holding an estimated 3,000 spectators, was an inferno. It was feared that many hundreds of people had perished.

In this gaunt manner the public learned of one of the worst disasters in racing history. It was the Chinese New Year festive season, and thousands of Chinese had taken their wives and small children with them to the races. Soon the streets were thronged with anxious people of every colour and nationality struggling down to Happy Valley for word or sight of their relatives.

It had begun as an ideal race day. For Europeans the only cloud in the sky was anxiety for distant relatives fighting in the Great War, and sorrow for those lost. This apart, these were boom times for everyone, with plenty of money around, pleasant weather, and a general mood of optimism. Sir Ellis Kadoorie had just won the Derby with *Tytam Chief*, and as one of the best-liked and most esteemed men at Happy Valley he was roundly cheered as he led his jockey in to weigh. Twenty-five minutes later, with terrible suddenness, the holocaust occurred.

The matshed concerned stood some distance down the valley from the grandstand, on Crown land. It was a large, long, three-storey Stand which at the time held upward of 3,000 spectators, nearly all of them Chinese, with a handful of their Portuguese and Japanese friends, 31 of whom were accounted for among the missing presumed dead. The matshed had been put up annually for years by the same contractor; there had never been anything wrong with it. At the rear of the Stand, at ground level and under shelter in case of rain, the cooks prepared snacks and brewed tea on open charcoal fires in chatties, as they had done annually for years.

A section-holding element in the matshed construction was either shifted by someone (perhaps in order to see better in the throng), or worked itself loose, or was not properly held in place — the subsequent Commission of Inquiry was unable to determine which of these it was. The rear of the Stand collapsed like a house of cards, right on top of the cooking fires. Flames rose immediately. Spectators in the second and third storeys at the rear fell into a raging inferno from which, with more of the structure continuously falling, escape was impossible. Hundreds were burned alive; hundreds more were trampled to death in the stampede to escape.

The first casualty count gave 1,000 killed and injured. A subsequent count gave 600 killed, 400 injured. The round figures speak for themselves. No one ever knew how many perished.

The Commission of Inquiry learned that the Stand had been inspected by an officer of the Public Works Department. Pursuance of this matter, however, revealed that the Buildings Ordinance made no reference to matshed construction. Thus unless the inspector was an expert in this form of construction — highly unlikely — without guidelines his inspection was worthless. The Director of Public Works was severely criticized by name for his inattention to this omission in the ordinance. The Captain Superintendent of Police was criticized similarly for his inattention to safety precautions. All told, a sorry tale, in which, amid the general shock and mourning, the Government of Hongkong cut a poor figure.

High in the hills overlooking nearby Sookunpoo a Chinese shrine was erected as an assurance to the spirits of the uncoffined and unknown dead that they were not forgotten. The shrine is still there. It has always been both a memorial and a warning.

Chinese Members of the Hong Kong Jockey Club

UNQUESTIONABLY the most remarkable innovation of the period was the decision to open the doors of the Hong Kong Jockey Club to Chinese members. Since nothing was put into writing concerning the reasons for this decision, it becomes necessary to explain, for the first time, how it came about, because in the heyday of the British Empire it was totally extraordinary.

The innovation arose from the so-called General Strike of 1925. This was organized from Canton by Lenin's sinister political appointee, Mikhail Borodin. It was financed from Moscow, and was an attempt to bring British control of Hongkong to an end. By late May that year, over half the working population of Hongkong had gone 'on strike', downed tools, and left by train for Canton.

The Russian idea was so to reduce the Chinese population of Hongkong that the British, left entirely on their own and unable to run the place, would fold up their tents and go away. Simplistic to a degree almost unimaginable, it nonetheless nearly succeeded. By June that year Hongkong was crippled, the waterfront deserted and silent; and all the time, with every train, more and more Chinese were leaving.

The Government of Hongkong had called for volunteers to man essential services. The response had been excellent. By mid-June, however, it was becoming clear that this was not enough. Hongkong was dangerously near collapse.

The news from Canton in the morning papers of 24 June 1925 was particularly grave, indicating a deepening of the crisis. Dr Ts'o Seen-wan, an eccentric but forceful lawyer, an authoritarian, lost his patience with things in general, a not infrequent occurrence, and decided something must be done. He crossed over from his home in Kowloon, commandeered an office in the City Hall — it was dangerous to argue with him — and publicly called for Chinese volunteers to man essential services and take on any other work needed.

The Government had not asked for Chinese volunteers. Unsure of itself, with a Governor who was politically out of his depth, the Government had feared that Chinese response would be negative.

Reaction to Dr Ts'o Seen-wan's call was positive and immediate. Within hours his City Hall office was awash with applicants. Within three days he had 500 volunteers, and in the ensuing weeks their numbers rose to 3,000. Many of them were from old and deeply established families — vintage stock.

Borodin in Canton saw he had failed. The Chinese who really mattered were not going to leave Hongkong. Conditions in Canton meanwhile, with such an overflow of population, were becoming chaotic; there was a serious food shortage. In August a trickle of Chinese began to return to the Colony. Six months passed before things were back to normal, but as all could see, the Chinese volunteers had saved the situation.

The Government expressed its appreciation. Dr Ts'o was awarded an OBE. This, however, paled into insignificance when set beside an act of thanks more esteemed and valued than any other could have been. At a meeting held in 1926 the Jockey Club changed its rules, and Chinese were admitted as members. Not even the Jockey Club realized the significance of its action. The prestige value went far beyond dollars and cents.

At the February race-meeting of 1927 Ho Kom-tong, compradore of Jardine Matheson, and Yung Hing-lun, related to the compradore of the Chartered Bank, made their first appearance as owners. Ho Kom-tong entered seven ponies, and won the Valley Stakes with *Kom Tong Hall*. Two years

Happy Valley, February 1927, the first day on which Chinese attended as members of the Jockey Club; in rain, which in China means a good omen, or money. (By courtesy: G.F. Gardner, Esq.)

later he won the Derby with *President Hall*. Four of the leading Chinese owner-riders at the Kiangwan races brought their ponies down and raced at the 1927 meeting, which they were able to do as visitors, Kiangwan being a recognized club. A new social era had begun.

It is strange that Hongkong — narrow, stuffy Hongkong, which many people from the Treaty Ports found socially unbearable — should have had the only European race club in China which admitted Chinese members. None of the other clubs ever did.[18]

Here one senses the influence of Sir Paul Chater. It would have been characteristic of him, after the long and anxious ordeal of the so-called General Strike, to wish to see the Jockey Club make this gesture, and it is safe to say he would have had the Jardine taipan solidly with him.

The Club meeting at which the decision was taken to admit Chinese members was the last at which Sir Paul Chater presided as Chairman.

He died in May 1926, aged 82, 'the greatest man Hongkong has known,' as was said at his memorial service. This was held appropriately at St. Andrew's, Kowloon, the church he built and gave to the community.

18. The largest stable in pre-war Hongkong was that of Eu Tong-sen, the Malayan tin, rubber and medicine multi-millionaire, who preferred to live in Hongkong, in castles, of which he built three. His stable ran to 23 ponies, beating even Sir Paul Chater, whose maximum was 18.

The Parade Ring

A NOTHER innovation concerning Chinese occurred in the autumn of that same year in Shanghai, where at the Kiangwan races Chinese owner-riders in the International Recreation Club insisted on the introduction of a parade ring, in which all jockeys must walk their ponies prior to a race. Incredible as it may seem, this had never been done before.

Kiangwan having given the lead, and it being from all angles the correct way to introduce the ponies and their riders, the august Shanghai Race Club — 'what Shanghai does today . . .' — was with extreme reluctance obliged to follow suit. It caused a great deal of fuss. In the matter of the starting gate the Stewards' conservatism has already been observed. In the case of the parade ring, having with considerable difficulty overcome the problems posed by the Stewards' conservatism, the organizing staff next had to contend with the jockeys — most of them rich, some of them millionaires, and none of them noticeably responsive to discipline. There was a danger of this being the starting gate all over again. When the parade ring was introduced, a very firm notice appeared, reminding all jockeys that it was COMPULSORY — heavily underlined — to walk their ponies before any race they entered. The Shanghai Race Club was unquestionably the most extraordinary racing organization there has ever been.

To glance ahead for a moment, another example — indeed a rather more serious one — of the Stewards' conservatism is to be had from around the year 1930. By this date the club and grandstand, the extravaganza of 1862, was visibly falling to bits. To build a new replacement was essential. To convince the conservative element of this, however, proved almost impossible. They loved their club. They loved it just as it was.

Stewards and members with progressive ideas were up against a peculiar form of opposition. One afternoon a huge section of plaster crashed down from the ceiling of one of the main rooms, narrowly missing one of the progressives. Proceeding at a decent speed to safer ground, he turned back as he heard the door open. In walked one of the conservative Stewards. He strode right through the room and into the next without noticing the fallen plaster.

Anyway, to return, the Chinese at the Kiangwan races having determined how things were going to be, the Europeans at the Shanghai Race Club had a parade ring.

The Chinese Jockey Club at Yangtzepoo

THE next innovation concerned the Chinese Jockey Club of Shanghai, the first announcement of which was made in November 1924. Organized entirely by Chinese big business, it began with a subscribed capital of an astounding $1,200,000. Land was purchased at Yangtzepoo, some miles north of Shanghai, off the main road to Woosung. A magnificent course was laid down, a fine grandstand erected.

The promoters of this new club were a group of extremely wealthy and influential men who, because they were regarded in vintage Shanghai society as *nouveau riche*, would never, however wealthy, gain membership to the International Recreation Club at Kiangwan, which was an élite club. Faced with this opposition, which on the part of the Chinese élite was well grounded, the excluded resolved to produce something bigger and better — the terms in which they naturally thought.

The course was unusual. It was in the shape of a long oblong with curved ends, having more than a half-mile straight on each side. For sprint races it was ideal, probably unique. Who, however, was going to organize and manage the races? None of the Chinese plutocrats who had set up this enormous thing had the faintest idea about racing. They were in it simply for money, it was thought. They were, but not simply.

The Chinese Race Club at Hankow had begun in somewhat the same way, and had produced all the same dubious British reactions as were now being voiced anew over Yangtzepoo. In British eyes the Chinese were doing it all the wrong way round. In true sport one thought first of the horses, then of a track, and then of money. The Chinese approach was the opposite: money first, which paid for a track, and after that the horses.

The promoters duly asked for European advice on organization and management; a committee was formed with a number of European (British) members, whereupon the Chinese Jockey Club 'jumped immediately into public favour' — British public. It slowly dawned on the European members, however, that the promoters' aim was to hold race-meetings that would coincide with those of the Shanghai Race Club, with the intention of attracting Chinese — and their money — away from that club to theirs. Their real aim was to break Kiangwan, but the European members may not have realized this. In any case, they quietly resigned.

Nothing more was heard for some months. Then, early in March 1926, various Europeans prominent in the racing world received an ominous-sounding invitation to a dinner to be given by the Stewards of the Chinese Jockey Club. With misgivings they went, only to discover with surprise and relief that their host was Ed Sheng, and that the Kiangwan Chinese racing men had taken over the organization of the new club. All was well. The first race-meeting, held later in the month on a Sunday — itself an innovation — was an unqualified success, without any hitch in the arrangements and drawing a crowd of over 5,000, despite the fairly long distance out. In fact, traffic congestion was to be a feature of the Yangtzepoo races.

No Britons rode at the first meeting — they did later — but two of the Shanghai Race Club's top jockeys, Vic Haimovitch and Charlie Encarnação, had several wins, riding for Chinese owners. J. Liou, most popular of all the jockeys, rode on this occasion for Ed Sheng.

Bolshevism, Massacres, and Excellent Racing

IN July 1926 the Southern Army advanced north from Canton by several routes — it was said to be 100,000 strong — to suppress the warlords and unite China by force, political endeavours having failed. In September a large force invested Hankow, where under Borodin's direction what amounted to a Bolshevik régime was set up. Thousands of refugees streamed into the foreign concessions; the volunteers were called out, the concessions barricaded. The settlement at Kiukiang was fired, looted and severely damaged. Clearly the same would befall the Hankow settlement. The Kuomintang government had moved its capital from Canton to Hankow. Under orders from Whitehall, the British Consul-General negotiated an agreement with the Kuomintang. Hankow ceased to be a Treaty Port, as did Kiukiang.

It is pleasant to record that even under Bolshevism the Hankow races proceeded as usual. The Hankow races had peculiar national phases, when for several years in succession one or other of the nationalities seemed to win nearly everything. In the days of Eleanora Andraevna a Russian phase was in progress. It was preceded and followed by a British phase. At the turn of the century a French phase set in, dominated by Elie Bouchard, the outstanding figure of his time, with interests in coal-mines and machinery imports. Under Bolshevism the flag of France flew splendidly, its principal upholder being Madame A.V. Labis, who for years was undisputed queen of the Hankow course with her 'Bois' stable. At the autumn races of 1926 she entered *Prince des Bois, Beauté des Bois*, and *Brigand des Bois*, all winners. As a gesture to her English friends, one of her ponies was *Robin des Bois*, the French name for Robin Hood. It was all but impossible to beat Madame Labis' ponies, and a great feather in the cap for anyone who did. Of all the lady owners in the China races, she was far and away the most successful.

Another winner at this meeting was Jack Liddell, riding his own *Punch*. Liddell Bros., hydraulic packers, was a huge firm with an establishment at every port. John Liddell, the father, a notable figure at the Shanghai races, was one of the Shanghai Municipal Council's ablest chairmen. His son in due course held the same office. It was an almost exact modern parallel with being the Doge of Venice.

In the Shanghai races Jack Liddell frequently found himself riding against ponies owned and trained by Billie Coutts. He and she both rode in paper hunts. Billie Coutts, a slim, *svelte* creature, a superb horsewoman with a mind like a rapier, who ordered men about all her life, never did a day's work, shopped annually in Paris and was about the best-dressed woman on the China coast, was not exactly the easiest person to marry. Nevertheless, Billie Liddell she became, and remained so to the end, long after the marriage had dissolved itself.

They were right to carry on racing in Hankow, moreover. Bolshevism did not last. In March 1927 Chiang Kai-shek shifted the Kuomintang capital to Nanking, and seeing his great drive for unity degenerating into mob rule, decided to rid himself of his communist left-wing. As Maurice Collis described it in *Wayfoong*:

Soon afterwards a rising inspired by Communists caught him unawares. He suppressed the rising and went on to take strong measures to eliminate the Communist party. In this purge he had the assistance of the Chinese financiers of Shanghai and the secret societies in their pay. Communist leaders of trade unions and worker councils were arrested and executed. Members of underground organizations were massacred. Public mass executions continued for days, carried out often with savage brutality. Tens of thousands of persons perished in this holocaust. The future Communist leaders Chou En-lai and Mao Tse-tung were among those proscribed but [who] managed to escape. Borodin fled the country.

Believe it or not, an Extra Meeting at the Shanghai Race Club was cancelled during the holocaust. The reason given for this was that they wanted to avoid a possible international headline: 'Britons Race in Shanghai under Protection of Canton Troops.' Britons one and all preferred the warlord Chang Tso-lin in Peking to Chiang Kai-shek with all his talk about the evils of foreign imperialism.

Kiangwan decided to go ahead with their races. The *Herald* advised them not to, and cautioned people against going. Kiangwan paid no attention, and people went. It was an excellent meeting.

It brought the Shanghai Race Club to its senses. If Kiangwan, outside the settlement, could carry on, so could they. The settlement was guarded by a very large international force, British, American, Japanese, French and others. The British contingent alone numbered 20,000, the largest British force ever sent to China. It was decided to go ahead with the Spring Meeting. The decision was 'widely approved'; there was 'very good racing' and 'the place was very full.' Fred Elias made his début as a winner riding his own *Firefly*. Norman Dallas, son of George Dallas, won the Champions on his father's *New Zealand*. Public executions continued as usual.

The British force in Shanghai was code-named Shaforce, and the commanding general presented the Shaforce Challenge Cup. The Stewards, deeming that this should hold a place of highest honour, made it the prize for the Champions, which from then until the end was raced as the Shaforce Challenge Cup and Champions' Stakes.

The importance of the secret societies has been indicated in the quotation from Maurice Collis given earlier. A small, little-known, and extraordinary fact is that it was Tu Yueh-sen, head of the most formidable of all secret societies, the Green Circle, and himself more powerful in his own way than all the warlords put together, who sorted out the muddle in the Chinese Jockey Club at Yangtzepoo, enabling the Kiangwan racing men to take over the management and organization. Just as the Chairman of the Municipal Council was like the Doge, so too was it with the inner politics of Shanghai. They were Venetian.

Burkill's Words of Truth in 1927

BETWEEN 1911 and 1926 the Chinese came into their own in the China races, with their own or international race clubs in Hankow, Shanghai, Tsingtao and Tientsin, and as members of the Hong Kong Jockey Club. Before, they had seemed a remote people. It had been inconceivable that there could ever be a field of action in which they could combine completely with people from another continent and, as it were, speak the same language. Yet racing achieved this, to a far greater extent than in anything else, even business, in which the methods of the two continents were so different. In the races, and only in the races, was there a combined identity of action. When one thinks of them competing against each other, actually on the turf, riding, in the heat of the moment — jockeying for position, as the saying goes — it is not a little remarkable that the races created goodwill, not ill. Men were hot at the end, but not their tempers.

In addition, there was the outstanding organizational ability Chinese showed in their race clubs — a feature which took Britons completely by surprise — and the clean running. Chinese had learned from observation of what was in fact about the cleanest racing to be found anywhere in the world. This was what they wanted, and what they insisted on. There was nothing to choose between the Chinese and the European race clubs in this respect.

At the end of the November meeting in Shanghai in 1927, towards the end of the most tumultuous and ghastly year since the fall of the Empire, years which had seen nothing but the rise and fall of warlords and pseudo-governments and internecine strife, there were speeches, the Naval Commander-in-Chief, Admiral Tyrwhitt, and the General in command of Shaforce, General Duncan, both presenting Cups.

The Chairman of the Stewards was Bertie Burkill, older brother of Chuck, both of them in their day top jockeys, as had been their father before them. A.R. Burkill & Sons was yet another of those amazing firms which effortlessly expanded into seeming infinity, yet with good management held together. They began as silk exporters, from which they moved steadily into general import-export business, real estate investment and management, shipping, a chemical works, cotton-seed (edible) oil mills, general insurance, rubber plantations in Sumatra, and so on. In short, if a member of the Burkill family opened his mouth on the subject of organization, what he said was probably worthy of note.

The General was thanked in terms of deepest cordiality for the Shaforce Cup, the Admiral for the Navy Cup. Burkill then came to the Chinese Cup, presented by Chinese friends of the Club. Chiang Kai-shek had not yet established himself to the extent of not seeming to be yet another warlord.

'Factions come and factions go, and generals rise and fall,' said Burkill, 'but it seems that our Chinese friends always will remain with us; and I have come to believe, so well do we get on together, that if the three race clubs had the power to rule this country, they would do it very well.'

There was laughter, faintly derisive.

He did not go on for a second or two.

Suddenly they burst out cheering. He had touched the nerve of political truth. China since the fall of the Empire had become the prey of self-seeking brigands, who from their very faces can be seen to this day in their proud photographs to have had not even a fraction of the intellect and ability needed to control such a vast and complicated country as China.

What China needed at that moment — in 1927 — was the organization, efficiency, and expertise of young Chinese businessmen such as those who ran the races at Kiangwan and Yangtzepoo. There you had racing to strict Newmarket rules — just what China needed politically — with no one making illicit gains. If it could be done in racing, it could be done in the government. There was all the talent there; it would certainly have moved in . . . and the Republic never touched it until it was too late.

9. Off-circuit

Previous page: Honan Race Club, 1924. By Georges Sapajou, Russian-born cartoonist on the North-China Herald, Shanghai. About the new Race Club the correspondent commented, 'The scheme is doing more to cement friendship with our Chinese friends than columns of newspaper articles.'

Wooden Spoons

WHEN the Kailan Mining Administration, a combination of Chinese and British mining interests, was formed in 1912, the first executive head of it was Major Edward Nathan, RE. He was already a prominent figure at the Tientsin races, owning a stable with a steady record of successes. Within months, and with his encouragement, racing started at T'angshan — spelt Tongshan in those days — the Kailan Mining Administration's largest arena of operations, and which became one of China's major industrial cities.

Though the Tongshan races were not on the official China race circuit, for a number of years they were popular in the North. Tongshan was the halfway point on the railway between Tientsin and Pei-tai-ho, the seaside resort patronized by foreigners of all nationalities from Peking and Tientsin. Most of the leading Tientsin owners raced at Tongshan. During the Great War so too did diplomats and others from Peking, when Pao Ma Chang was closed.

In 1924, under joint Chinese and British auspices, the Honan Race Club was formed, again in a mining area. The correspondent of the *North-China Daily News* observed, 'The scheme is doing more to cement friendship with our Chinese friends than columns of newspaper articles.' This prompted the gifted Russian cartoonist Georges Sapajou to depict two robed Chinese and a portly English racing gentleman being introduced to each other by a horse.

The Honan Race Club's course was at Chiao-tso, north of the Yellow River, within striking distance of the Lifêng mines and the Peking–Hankow railway. It was comparatively easy for Tientsin owners to bring their ponies to Chiao-tso, and quite a number did. Numerous Chinese owners and riders participated, as did people from the mines and from Lifêng itself. The omnipresent Jardine Matheson usually ran an Ewo Cup. This was for Jardine personnel only, enjoyable for those who raced, a hazard for those who did not, because all Jardine men were expected to enter for the race. Those who did not own a racing pony had to borrow one, and the last rider in received a wooden spoon with a bowl large enough to hold a pint of whisky. The English schoolboy tradition dies hard.

Strange as it may seem, however, the souvenir value of such of those wooden spoons as survive today renders them almost as valuable as the surviving silver Cups.

Chungking

THE most intriguing of the off-circuit races were those of Chungking, where a Club was formed which held its first race-meeting in November 1923. Szechuan, the largest and most populous of the provinces of China, entirely surrounded by high mountains, is almost another country. In those times, for all practical purposes, there was only one entrance to it: by river steamer up through the Yangtze gorges to Chungking, its largest city. Szechuan, though prosperous, was so remote that very little news came out of it.

However, press reports of the founding of the Honan Race Club prompted someone in Chungking to send an account of their own races to the *Herald* in Shanghai.

Szechuan was famous for its ponies — in Szechuan, that is to say. They were almost certainly of the same type as the River ponies encountered earlier at Hankow and Kiukiang. Their main breeding grounds were far away in Chinese Turkestan. So great was the demand for horses in China, particularly by farmers, that it was worth bringing the animals across thousands of miles, for sale in the land which cannot breed them. They were narrow little creatures, with a curious shape which had developed from being used — not bred — in mountains, over a period of many centuries, and they were designed for nimbleness rather than speed.

Chungking is a dramatic place. The seasonal rise and fall of the Yangtze there is spectacular, while the city itself, at the confluence of two rivers, must surely be the hilliest of all large cities in the world. Here the so-called Szechuan pony came into its own. Unlike almost any other horse, it could walk down steps.

Most residents in Chungking keep a pony or two each to carry them up and down the hills and over the everlasting steps which are such a feature of the fantastic geography of the place. That our local ponies are capable of climbing up and down the most intricate and impossible flights of steps is a commonplace of our daily life. It always remained to be demonstrated that our ponies could be trained to flat racing.

The difficulty was to find some flat plane on which to race them. In Chungking there is hardly 50 yards of flat going to be found anywhere. The only level stretches to be found near the city are the shingle banks which lie exposed in the bed of the Yangtze during autumn, winter and spring. But shingle and small boulders are impossible to race on, even to the cat-like ponies of Szechuan. We have gazed upon the shingle banks for years, and often idly speculated on the project of removing the pebbles and boulders and laying down a track of sand, ashes and lime; but where was the money to come from? However, in November last, the rising tide of local energy, fed by a controversy over the respective speeds of well-known ponies, burst its old banks. We actually raised a guarantee fund and constructed a half-mile course.

To the unbounded delight of all, the track proved a great success and the ponies took to the rails like ducks to water.

The first meeting covered the entire costs and left a credit balance.

Needless to say, this handsome result has been made possible by the interest taken by our Chinese friends. We have found, as was found by the Honan Race Club, that there is no finer common meeting ground for Chinese and foreigners than a race course.

For instance, soon after the Chungking Race Club came into active existence, the city was captured for the second time last year by our old friend Yang Sen [a crypto-warlord], a busy man whom we did not see a great deal of in the ordinary way. No sooner had he returned and been informed of our Race Club than he signified his wish to attend our next meeting and to enter his own ponies and, what is more, his intention to ride them himself. Our next meeting was held on Boxing Day, and the General's bodyguard duly arrived early on the course; but at the last moment General Yang himself, to the great disappointment of all, was prevented from attending by the inopportune arrival of another General. [Another crypto-warlord, evidently a doubtful ally. This was a very peculiar period.] His bodyguard, however, made themselves very useful by patrolling the course and lending an official air to our meeting, which duly impressed the large crowd of Chinese in attendance.

One Chinese gentleman jockey rode, however — he is the compradore of a well-known foreign hong. He had the misfortune to come a very spectacular cropper in the second race, to the intense delight of the native populace; and the chance of his repeating this performance will be sufficient alone to ensure an enormous crowd at our next meeting.

Remarkably good racing and large fields were noted. British and American sailors clubbed together to form a stable, and it headed the list of winners. Stoker P.O. Northcote of HMS *Teal* was discovered to be a star jockey, and won the Champions. 'Meanwhile we are seeing more of our Chinese friends socially, and they are equally benefiting with us in an added interest in life.'

The Boxing Day meeting was marked by the mishaps of the Chairman of the Stewards, who won the fourth race and was disqualified on a protest, the Judge being the Commissioner of Customs. This was difficult to dispute. As will have been realized, Commissioners of Customs sat on the left hand of the Almighty — left being senior to right in China.

In the next race, the Champions, the Chairman's own ponies not having qualified, he was riding our German shopkeeper's pony *Hans*, a dark horse, little known on the course. In the home straight *Hans* was leading the field by a length or two when in some unaccountable fashion a lump of earth went into its rider's mouth and he involuntarily swerved aside into the tiger country and was not even placed.

The community had a journal called *Babylon of Babylon*, entirely written in biblical language. On this occasion it noted that after his disqualification from a win,

Greybeard waxed bitter and cried have ye no camels which belay not the binnacle nor trim the periwig [meaning a griffin] and they answered him saying yea verily, here is a camel of the Philistines called Hans· whose periwig hath never been trimmed and is like unto Samson before he was shorn. So Greybeard mounted again and sped upon the course and overtook his adversaries and was winning hands down when a lump of mud struck him in the gullet so that he swerved aside into the wilderness, and the dromedaries of Midian and the riders thereof passed by him and he was left with nothing but the hump.

For sweet it is to shake the dust of Babylon from off the feet, but take heed that ye swallow it not!

The Chungking Race Club held one-day meetings, bunched fairly close together — roughly three a month — during a strictly defined seasonal period. When spring showed signs of merging into summer, it behoved to stop, and quickly. Within days, even hours, the racecourse would be under water. Not just under water, either. Under between 18 and 30 feet of it. And, if the snows melted quickly, surging, tumultuous, terrible water, as the Great River, cascading down from heights nearly Himalayan, hurled its millions of tons of melted snow down its thousand miles to the sea.

Yet, come late October, there were the shingle banks once more; ashes and lime were ordered, labour laid on. Next month they were racing again.

Solely on account of these races, by the way, the average price of ponies in Chungking rose from 60 taels to 200 taels.

It has to be acknowledged, too, that General Yang Sen seems to have been a warlord with a fair amount of common sense.

10. Crossing Borders and Breeds

A Special Race in Mongolia

R OY Davis, born in Melbourne, came to China in 1903, aged 12. His father managed a chain of hotels in North China, and the boy and his mother had come to join him, living in one of the hotels, in Tientsin.

According to the rules, no one under the age of 18 was permitted to race. In Roy Davis' case the Tientsin Race Club made an exception. At 16 he raced for the first time, and won. There was much family excitement next morning when the *Peking and Tientsin Times* opened its racing page in bold print: 'The baby of the course has won his first race on his first time out, and on his own pony.'

That was 1907. By 1914 he had a business of his own. With a long history of surgery as a child, he was turned down for military service. He was in his office one afternoon in the summer of 1918 when an unusual-looking European, a man he had never seen before, came in to inquire whether he would be interested in buying racing ponies from him. Having dealt with a number of horse dealers, Roy Davis had scant faith in them. Moreover, the dealers at this time were either Chinese or Russian, and this man was clearly not Russian. It made Davis doubly suspicious.

His visitor apparently lived in Inner Mongolia, and he certainly seemed to know what he was talking about. Roy Davis was interested but, to test the man, decided to lay down stringent conditions. He himself would come to Mongolia, he said, if this was acceptable, and his visitor would arrange for a race of animals there, with the stipulation that all animals entered in the race would be saleable to him, if wanted. He would present the winners with reasonable prizes in cash. Furthermore, he would bring two of his own race ponies from Tientsin, and two grooms, and these would ride in the special race (no monkey-business while the animals were racing).

'Certainly,' came the reply. A race could be arranged in about six weeks' time, and would represent some worthwhile contenders. Moreover, an important Mongol race was to be held fairly soon about a hundred miles from where he lived, and he could probably get the winning horse to run in the special race.

The ease with which the visitor treated these matters made Roy Davis — he was 27 — more and more intrigued, and determined to go ahead with the proposal.

The legendary Frans August Larson, Duke of Mongolia, who acquired Bengal from the far western side of Outer Mongolia.

He had no means of knowing, but the man seated before him was a living legend, the most fabled person ever to be connected with the China races, Frans August Larson, a Swedish missionary who was a Duke of Mongolia.

Larson had been sent to Mongolia in the 1890s by the Swedish Mission to interest the people in Christianity and sell Swedish Bibles. On arrival he discovered that the great majority of Mongols could not read even their own written language; his mission was hopeless. By being generally helpful, however, he won enormous respect among the people, and settled in Inner Mongolia with his American wife.

A year or two later, in the late 1890s, the Chinese Imperial Government decided to build a railway across Mongolia into Europe, to speed their exports of tea and other products. This was one of a number of ill-thought-out schemes set afoot by the dying dynasty in a desperate effort to modernize China. Negotiations with the Mongols were consequently put in hand, and as the only educated person capable of speaking both Mongol and Chinese, Larson was invited by both sides to be the interpreter.

The negotiations went on for two years, at the end of which the Mongols decided they did not want a railway. The reason they gave was that no news could be so important that it could not be carried on a pony's back and, by way of three different mounts daily, cover a hundred miles. This being unarguable, the Chinese went home, thanking Larson for his services. The Mongols, on the other hand, were so thankful to him (for getting rid of the Chinese) that they made him a Duke.

Apart from the Living Buddha, who was never seen by the people, the Dukes were the rulers of the country, each Duke being the complete ruler of the territory awarded him, and of necessity the owner of that territory, enabling him to breed the country's only real product, Mongolian ponies. As the only power in his territory, he meted out such punishments as he chose on any ill-doer committing an offence on his land. Since ponies were the land's sole product, apart from a little farming here and there, the only real offence that was punishable was pony-stealing. For any intruder passing by with an animal which was branded with someone else's marking, and for which he could not account, the regular punishment was the severing of his left arm below the elbow. As Roy Davis related,

Larson never punished anyone, but I have seen a few of the unfortunates so treated by others. The most rigorous punishment affordable could be the severance of both arms below the elbow.

Larson's land was awarded to him in Inner Mongolia, which of course is the part adjoining China, and which, apart from being, to my knowledge, tree-free, was just a series of beautiful undulations covered with magnificent wild, hip-deep grass cum hay. Larson was taken to a rocky outbreak and then told, 'The land so far as you can see in all directions, plus a day's walk further in all directions, is yours.' And so, and automatically, pony breeding became a 'must' for him.

In August 1918, therefore, Roy Davis set forth by train from Tientsin with two race ponies, two mafoos, his cook, and his Pekinese, whose name was Guts. With one change of train they reached the railhead at Kalgan, main point of entry in the Great Wall. The ascent to the plateau, which at this point gives the impression of being a mountain, was by a narrow, rocky and very dangerous road which wound its way up the edge, ever with a sheer drop on one side. A few years after this it was made motorable, and became in some ways even more dangerous. Coming down by car, one hired an ox and attached it to the car by means of a pole underneath the ox's tail fastened to the car by a very strong rope. The ox provided an extra brake, since if the car's brakes failed it meant certain disaster.

How China ever obtained any horses at all is a marvel, when one comes to think of it.

Having arrived on the plateau, some 6,000 feet up, he hired a Peking cart: in Mongolia this was travelling in style. From there it was four days and three nights to Duke Larson's territory. 'All went well, the weather was beautiful, and I entered Mongolia for the first time.'

Larson's homestead was built mainly of mud, and was fairly weatherproof during the long winter months, which are among the coldest of any inhabited region on the globe. Climate undoubtedly contributes to the wonder of the Mongolian horse, who in terms of endurance has no equal. Sir Ernest Shackleton took China ponies with him on his first expedition to Antarctica.

'Everything is in order,' Larson reported when the procession and cart drew up. The special race would take place in about ten days' time.

Various problems had to be dealt with. Since all the ponies lived entirely off grass they were pot-bellied, and had to be starved for five or six days to slender them down for the race. They were given ample water, but otherwise stood tied to an overhead railing during this time.

Then there was the question of the length of the race. Racing was the major sport of Mongolia, along with wrestling. Endurance as well as speed was basic to the sport. A normal length for a race was 30 miles in a straight direction. Useless to explain that in China the longest race was two miles; no one would have credited such an absurdity. After long and complicated discussions they were finally persuaded to make it a short gallop of 10 miles — in a straight line, of course.

Mongolia was indeed a far country. There was no currency. When people had sold their ponies for silver taels, they hastened down into China to buy goods, mostly clothes and foodstuffs. The only wool in Mongolia was on the animals; when it left them it was turned into Peking carpets. There was no cloth, though there was an infinity of skins. These, when sewn together, made tents which, with a fire inside, were warm and strong enough for human habitation through the rigorous winters.

Society was polyandrous, wives having several husbands and making their own choice when acquiring an additional one. Prospective husbands could be taken on approval, discarded if unsatisfactory. Villages were in the centre of pony-breeding grounds. Each village had a priest, and no animal could be slaughtered without his absolution. Thus Buddhism, a vegetarian religion, met the challenge of a country where without meat there would be no human life. Nothing important in life, including the races, was done without a priest's sanction and blessing. In many families the eldest son became by tradition a priest.

The normal food was mutton from the Mongolian sheep, which is half-goat, similar to those of Barbary. Dried horse dung, cut into bricks, served as fuel. There were no trees or forests because the Mongolians disliked shadows, feeling that only dishonest people would wish to walk beneath them.

The date of the big Mongol race was now known at Duke Larson's, the winner of it already committed to the special race. Calculating that the winning pony would take three days to cover the hundred miles to Duke Larson's territory — the travelling speed of a Mongolian horse is about thirty miles a day — and allowing for two days' rest on arrival, the date of the special race was fixed.

A point Roy Davis had overlooked was that while his two grooms, who were to ride in the race, were grown men, their competitors were to be Mongol boys and girls about 15 years old, much lighter than the grooms, some of them not even riding with wooden saddles, but bareback.

Anyway, the winner of the big race duly arrived.

I must say I was quite impressed. Although only about 13.1 hands, he was beautifully built, and of course very much down to racing weight. My final instruction to my two grooms was not to try to win the race, but just stay up with the leaders.

At daylight, off rode the competitors to some ten miles distant, and all we could do was just wait. As the country was undulating, our first indication that the race was on came when we saw some dust on the downward slope on the horizon. Finally, after quite a long wait, the leaders appeared, comprising maybe ten ponies in a bunch, with the others separated by possibly fifty or sixty yards. Down the slope they galloped, one falling, his leg having caught a marmot hole. I suppose at that time the animals were three-quarters of a mile in the distance when, separating itself from the second batch, some thirty yards on the right side, came an animal which, by the time they reached the bottom of the slope, was even with the front runners. As they came racing up the final slope, that one moved to the lead quite easily, and by the time they reached us was a winner by some twenty or thirty yards.

This, of course, was the animal who had come from the other race; and you can be mighty sure that my first job was to make sure

*Roy Davis, Tientsin, 1918. He rode the wonder-
pony Bengal to 41 wins out of 42 entries, almost
certainly a world record.*

there could be no substitution, by separating him from the others.
The first fifteen or so others to arrive were also put separately.

Both of my ponies, which were much heavier, even bigger but
with heavier riders, didn't arrive till near the very last of the second
bunch.

He bought the winner and five others. After a few days'
rest they set off on their return journey to Tientsin.

They all got home safely. The prize pony, mentally lined
up for the Shanghai St. Leger, had an accident and never
raced, but the other ponies fully justified themselves, winning
many races in Tientsin and Peking. Quite soon Roy Davis and
Duke Larson entered into a partnership in Mongolian pony
breeding and bartering. The Mongols having no currency,
the business on Davis' side involved bringing in from China
clothing and foodstuffs, and bartering these for precious furs,
ordinary furs, wool and mohair, for sale in Tientsin. Duke
Larson was pony dealer, breeder, and salesman.

We generally tried to keep a fairly large stock of ponies, including
a majority of mares for breeding purposes. Apart from the better
type, which was good for racing, and which we bought wherever
we found them, there was a large demand from Chinese farmers
for mares, which we traded to them.

With only two or three exceptions in the course of a century, all ponies in the China races were geldings. It being impossible to breed horses in China, it was pointless to send anything other than geldings, besides which a Mongolian gelding grows taller than average and commanded a higher price. The better-quality furs, by the way, were brought down in Ford cars and on dromedaries.

The Crossbreed Crisis

BEING himself an owner and a top jockey in Tientsin and Peking, as well as having, through his partnership with Duke Larson, a direct interest in breeding, Roy Davis was inevitably involved in the next racing complication, noted in an earlier chapter: the campaign to 'drive the big, high ponies out of the running.' As he himself recounted it:

Whereas in my earlier days a Mongol pony was just that, it soon became apparent to breeders that the faster the pony, the better the price. Actually, a Mongol pony hardly ever reached more than 13.1 hands. About this time — between 1915 and 1925 — cross-breeding between imported stallions and Mongol mares commenced. Ordinary European stallions being unable to stand the climate, and there being a lack of accommodation for these animals, more or less all such breeding fell into the hands of Russians. The Russians living around or near the city of Harbin handled most of the breeding, and it was soon discovered that the Arab produced the trimmer and faster mixture.

One is reminded of John Macgregor's shrewd remark made many years earlier, in 1880, 'There is a little Arab blood in him.' History does not relate which pony this was; but the fact that his friends laughed at him lends weight to the suspicion that he was referring to his little Derby winner *Strathaird*, who stood only 12 hands 3 inches. A point to be remembered about cross-breeding between Arab stallions and Mongol mares is that it did not necessarily produce larger and faster horses. Often it produced horses which were larger but no faster, or else horses which were faster but no larger.

Amid all the fervour that surrounded the subject of cross-breeding, that point was often overlooked. Crossbred ponies were undoubtedly better animals in general, and their behaviour was noticeably better; but whether a mare produced a winner was just as unpredictable as usual. Moreover, the greatest of all China ponies, to whom we shall come in a moment, showed no signs of cross-breeding whatever.

The main places of Russian activity in horse breeding were around Harbin, the principal city of North Manchuria, and around Hailar in Inner Mongolia, some 700 miles north-west of Harbin, not all that far from the Siberian border. There was the advantage that both Hailar and Harbin were on the railway connecting with China.

Where pure-bred Mongol ponies were concerned — though by this time the word 'pure' had lost some of its validity — Duke Larson's territory was comparatively near. Using the railway between Kalgan and Tientsin, warlords permitting, the journey could be done in about a fortnight. The best China ponies came from much further away, from Outer Mongolia, on the plains in the region of San Beiss. These plains, some 6,000 feet above sea level, extend along about a quarter of the 850-mile trade route from Manchouli, on the Siberian border, to Urga (since renamed Ulan Bator), capital of Outer Mongolia. The plains lie on both sides of the Kerulen river, which flows east into the Dalai Nor and never reaches the sea. One reason why the animals from this region are of such exceptional quality is that the soil contains a fair quantity of lime, affecting grass and water. The first person to point this out was Henry (Harry) Morriss of Shanghai, son of the Mohawk Chief and owner of the *Herald* and the *Daily News*. By 1923 Harry Morriss had made the journey to San Beiss five times to buy ponies, his 'Field' stable — *Warrenfield, Castlefield, Petersfield* — reigning supreme at the Shanghai races in consequence.

San Beiss had been known of indirectly for a long time. Throughout the two Mongolias it had a reputation, which was enhanced by the demand for racing ponies. Harry Morriss seems to have been the first racing man actually to go there — a daunting journey, 400 miles beyond Duke Larson's territory as the crow flies, though much further than this on the ground. The quickest way of getting there was to take a ship from Shanghai to Dairen, from there the South Manchurian railway to Harbin, the Chinese Eastern railway to Manchouli, and then the old trade route to Urga. This, after 200 miles or so, brought one into the San Beiss country, and was (just) motorable, depending on the season, and on knowing the right people. High summer — perfect in Mongolia — was the only possible season for the fastidious. It had the advantage of being the off-season for the races in China.

As Roy Davis explained:

Between those years 1915 to 1925 the word crossbreed became more and more frequently used, and larger animals were being produced. Because of their longer legs etc., they were becoming quite prominent in the racing even down as far as Shanghai. This mixed breed was increasing fairly rapidly, and it was easier for the wealthy sportsmen to outbid the ordinary pony owner.

The crossbreed crisis — there is no other word for it — came to a head in Tientsin, when J.M. Dickinson

sent his grooms up-country, probably to or near Harbin, and brought down some 20-odd quite outstanding and beautiful animals, such being on average two or three inches taller at the wither than the normal Mongol pony.

Although this word crossbreed had been disturbing our racing for some time, when his mob arrived there was such an outcry amongst the racing community that the Stewards of the Tientsin Race Club decided to call a meeting of us voting members to decide what to do about the acceptance of such ponies, as from one year ahead.

The meeting was packed. As Davis recalled it, Dickinson appealed to the sportsmanship of members. He pointed out that despite having a fairly large stable he had not had a Champions' win for twenty years; yet now that he owned ponies which could prove themselves champions, measures were set afoot to debar them. Was this sporting?

Davis replied in the same coin, asking whether it was sporting of Dickinson to bring in ponies so superior to those presently being raced that they belonged in a different class. He then moved that 'any animals altogether superior to our own' be barred, not next year, as the Stewards had in mind, but now. The motion was carried overwhelmingly.

Setting aside the 'us and them' aspect, at the root of this strange business lay the question of purity of stock.

Yet what had become of purity? There had been the injection of chargers when the Second Chinese War ended in 1860. There had been another injection of chargers after the Siege of the Legations in 1900, another after the Russo-

Japanese War of 1904–5. There had been an even larger one, from Russia, after the Bolshevik Revolution of 1917, from which many Russians and others fled to the Far East on horseback. Cross-breeding had now become a business — mainly Russian. It enjoyed the approval and support of some of the wealthier owners, such as Harry Morriss and J.M. Dickinson and, as in due course transpired, every Chinese owner.

However, the Tientsin Race Club in its wisdom appointed a committee to inspect *all* ponies. As a result, all of Dickinson's mob except two were barred. The absurdity of the affair is revealed in the matter of these two. Dickinson, known for his generosity in helping others in difficulties, was much respected. His admirers combined to pressure the committee into giving him a fair chance by allowing two of his splendid animals to pass as acceptable. Already they had broken their own rules.

As earlier related, Shanghai had the same prejudice. Each year the Shanghai Race Club placed with Duke Larson an order for subscription griffins. In 1925 the order was for 120 animals. Larson was taken ill, and Roy Davis had to make the delivery. Warlords had taken over several of the northern provinces; the railway between Kalgan and Tientsin was inoperable. The mob had to be driven down from Mongolia the whole way to Tientsin.

They suffered considerably by way of insufficient feeding, as the drive from Kalgan is mostly mountainous, and the available grass is extremely limited. The result was that when they did arrive in Tientsin they were wasted. There was certainly no time, if the animals were to reach Shanghai by the contracted date, to fatten them up. As the journey was by way of dockages at both Chefoo and Tsingtao, I cabled ahead to have large deliveries of fresh grass to be waiting at both places.

The animals, though very thin, were delivered to the Shanghai Horse Bazaar on time.

An ominous three weeks passed with no payment. Roy Davis was then summoned before the Stewards. The animals were not only very thin, he was told, but they were crossbreeds, and the Club had decided to reject the lot.

Davis, pretty shaken — this was worse than Tientsin — stressed the grave blow to his business, and requested reconsideration. Twenty minutes later he was called in again. Their decision was unchanged. He then pointed out that the animals had already been branded with the Race Club brand, and drew their attention to the contract, in which the Club based their price for each pony on its withers, with a 5-tael increase for every inch above 13 hands 1 inch. Surely, he said, the Stewards, fully informed concerning the Mongolian pony and its size, must know that when buying ponies and raising the price by 5 taels per inch, anything so tall would have to be of mixed breed.

This time he was out of the room only five minutes. The animals were accepted. He was paid next morning. But of course the Club having caught itself out, it was clear that efforts would be redoubled to keep the crossbreed out.

Meanwhile the argument raged on the subject 'What is a China pony?' Zoologists, anatomists, veterinary surgeons, all kinds of people addressed themselves learnedly to this intricate subject. Diagrams were produced showing the exact dimensional proportions of a real China pony, pinpointing the means of detecting a crossbreed. It was very strange, and became more and more esoteric.

Hongkong did not pay much attention. There they had always preferred larger animals anyway, and there was the strong Chinese-owner influence in the Jockey Club, solidly in support of crossbreeds, the stronger and bigger the better. It was principally in Shanghai and Tientsin that the murky argument was pursued.

In the midst of all the argument, Harry Morriss drew attention — though without actually saying so — to the fatuity of it. Harry Morriss was a shy, withdrawn person who seldom mentioned anything personal, and never indulged in confidences. Virtually the only subject he would wax expansive on was his horses — and his violin; he was a very good amateur player. Keenly interested in breeding, he shortly after this founded his own stud at Cheveley, near Newmarket, today still very much a going concern, run by his grandson. `

Harry Morriss pointed out that over the previous eight to ten years — since around 1913 — the change in the breed of the Mongol pony had been extraordinarily pronounced. (This was a fact, actually, which none of the scientific pony experts seem to have noticed.) On each of the five occasions when he went to San Beiss, he said, he noticed an increase in the number of foreign stallions running about in the Mongol-owned mob. The year 1922 witnessed the most remarkable increase, owing to the numbers of Russian-owned herds that had migrated southward and eastward, Mongol owners being

Harry Morriss, shy, retiring, top owner, good violinist, owner of the North-China Herald and North-China Daily News, and winner of the Epsom Derby, 1925, with Manna, Steve Donoghue riding. Sketch of Harry Morriss by Juel Madsen, Shanghai.

quick to buy stallions from the Russians as a means of improving their own stock.

Here, from a most unusual angle, can be observed a major historical event, one which took place so quietly and in so remote a region that scarcely anyone noticed it until it was accomplished. For years it had been Czarist Russia's aim to detach the Outer Provinces from China and annex them if possible — in any case, detach them. The Soviet Union pursued in this matter a policy identical to that of the Czars, though more ruthlessly. What Harry Morriss saw in 1922 — he was well aware of it — was the Soviet Union detaching Outer Mongolia from China by means of artificially organized migrations of horses, a piece of Russian cunning which has gone all but totally unnoticed in history. Next year, 1923, 'all the fine old Mongol squires and llamas whose ponies have made history on the Shanghai turf' were summarily shot by the Soviet Russians. The export of ponies from Outer Mongolia was declared contraband. The entire vast land passed from Chinese to Russian control. As Harry Morriss wrily observed, when the Shanghai dealers resumed trade with San Beiss, they would find that in the homeland of the Mongol pony they were no longer dealing with Mongols.

Characteristically, it was a Chinese, William Hu of the promiment racing family, who first publicly put forward the idea in Shanghai that no crossbreed should be thrown out on that account, but that there should be special races for them. That was January 1924. The Shanghai Race Club being what it was, nothing immediately happened. It eventually did, however. One is left to regret — an expression shared in Hongkong — that the crossbreeds were not regarded as ordinary China ponies and allowed to race generally. In the circumstances, however, in view of the utter opposition to crossbreeds entertained by a large majority of the European racing fraternity, William Hu was right, though it led to endless complications of definition, classification, insoluble borderline cases, most of it based on sheer unreality, as Harry Morriss quietly pointed out.

Shortly after this, in May, the most devastating of all comments on the subject issued from Tientsin. It ran:

One or two decades hence, when the last of the pure China pony tribe is pensioned off by the last Municipal Council to make way for the latest motor water-sprinkler, the evolution which spelled his well-earned retirement may be chronicled by a keenly observing historian as having commenced with the Tientsin Spring Meeting in 1924. It will be written that back in those good old days an attempt was made by amateur racing men to legislate against evolution — Darwin and Huxley notwithstanding — in an effort to maintain a useful but worn-out strain of animal because the racing men of those times wished to indulge themselves in the Sport of Kings at the price of peasants.

The *Herald* was so shocked by this dreadful remark that it hastily inserted a rider to say that it withheld all comment on the article.

Nevertheless, the historian will continue, instead of absorbing the first products of cross-breeding and permitting the status of racing ponies gradually to evolve into the remarkable animal we have today, the transient treaty-port residents drew up racing laws against the crossbreed, and segregated it into a separate class. However, it will be written, this segregation in itself was the most unfortunate act of a generally unfortunate series, for it at once established a contrast between the performance of the so-called pure China ponies and the crossbreed, in which contrast the poor little 'thoroughbred' suffered deeply.

This, the first step in the evolution of our present racing animals, may be said to have dated from 1924, when the segregated or B

Class ponies astonished the racing fraternity of the Far East by smashing three all-China records.

In such a manner, we believe, will the racing historian discourse on the evolution of race ponies two decades hence.

Six decades have passed since that was written, and it is difficult not to agree with every word of it. The entire basis of racing, from its beginnings, has been to test and demonstrate improvement of the breed.

He went on to say that the so-called 'small' owner may or may not have visions of annexing large sums of money through the prowess of his pure Mongol steed, but he usually figures on getting his money back.

This, of course, is the theory of amateur racing. In practice it is otherwise. The big owners — the Taipan class — make all the money there is to be made, and usually make it at the expense of the small owner. It cannot be otherwise with men who can afford to call their head mafoos and say 'Mafoo, here's ten thousand dollars, go Kalgan side more far catchee me four five fast pony — see?' Pure China pony or crossbreed, it makes no difference, the rich amateur has the advantage all the time. It's the Morriss, Arnhold, Toegs, J.M.D., Major Nathan, Howell, Morling and the many 'Ewo' taipan stables that provide the bulk of successful racing history.[19]

He then came to the Chinese:

The few hundred dollars difference in price between a Mongol pony and a crossbreed will mean nothing to rich Chinese owners, even though they should maintain racing on an amateur basis. If racing should become professionalized in China, the crossbred will without doubt supersede the China pony almost immediately.

Two years later the argument still raged. Each club having dealt with the matter in its own way, the result, as a correspondent pointed out, had been chaos. No two clubs had exactly the same heights and weights for crossbred ponies, while a B Class pony in Tientsin was a Z Class pony in Shanghai. It was now proposed to introduce the further complication of classified races — seven classes in all. Already, due to segregation, a China pony which could beat any crossbreed was not allowed to try. Classified races simply meant marginal public interest in races of low classification. Small owners won small victories.

19. Henry Morriss and his sons Harry and Hayley, Charlie and Harry Arnhold, who were brothers, Raymong Toeg and his son Edmund, all of Shanghai; and J.M. Dickinson, Major Nathan, Willie Howell of Liddell Bros., and C.R. Morling, all of Tientsin.

The simple solution — a subscription system based solely on merit, disregarding whether a pony was crossbred or pure, and with the usual weights for inches — could not be introduced against the weight of conservative opinion. Ada Law, Shanghai's first lady owner-trainer — 'walking like a man, big voice bellowing forth', as a friend once described her — in a sense personified the sentiment.

'I raced real ponies,' she said defiantly. 'I never had anything to do with those crossbreeds and Walers they raced down there in Hongkong.'

That was spoken 55 years later. Clearly feelings had not changed.

In the Tsingtao club the non-Chinese Stewards were divided on the issue. Three of them resigned and were not replaced. This conveniently gave a Board of six Chinese and three others. It meant victory for crossbreeds. Emotions rose to such a pitch that the Shanghai Race Club boycotted the Tsingtao races, while Britons in Tsingtao made as much trouble as they could, trying to rally sympathy for their cause.

The crisis came in February 1926, when a group of three Chinese bought from Shanghai a pony called *Tarsus*, certificated at 13 hands 2 inches. When measured on arrival in Tsingtao, he was found to be 13 hands 3 inches. There was an outburst. One Briton, whose name is best forgotten, publicly dubbed the Chinese racing men as 'profiteers'. Considering that one of the three buyers was Y.S. Chang, top jockey of Tsingtao, well-known at the Kiangwan races, and indisputably one of the foremost sportsmen of the time, the word was ill-chosen.

It created a sensation locally. The *Tsingtao Times* came out with a leading article beseeching the officials of the Recreation Club to bring themselves to order, since they were damaging the reputation of club and port. (The simple truth, nowhere mentioned, was that *Tarsus*, certificated more than a year before in Shanghai, had grown.)

In April, after four months of British rudeness and bad manners without parallel in a country in which they were guests, the *North-China Herald* reported that 'the differences with the Chinese' had been resolved, and that races were held with one of the greatest crowds ever gathered. New railings had been put in, the former ones having been lost due to the depredations of Chinese soldiers. Chinese, Japanese (three outstanding riders), Russians and Dutchmen raced. Vic van der Needa, a top Shanghai jockey, did the hat-trick. Y.S.

Chang was the hero of the day, with four wins. It was noted that people put their money on his name, not on the pony. British jockeys were conspicuously few, and did not do well.

Chinese expressed their views on the matter when the Kiangwan club announced the first-ever National Championship race for all ponies of either sex and any class, open to members of all recognized clubs in China, and made it the most valuable race ever run in that country, $10,000 to the winner, $2,000 for second place, $1,000 for third.

It was run on 12 June 1926, and unfortunately it was a very wet day. Ed Sheng won it with *Reinforcement*, J. Liou up; *Warrenfield*, transferred from the Harry Morriss stable to that of Sir Victor Sassoon, was second, Raymond Toeg's *Rosebery* third. The race, 1¼ miles, was run in 2 minutes and a fraction under 36 seconds, described as amazing considering how heavy the course was. There was a field of 13. *Warrenfield*, at 13 hands 1 inch the smallest entrant, showed a distinct touch of Arab. Both the other winners were 13 hands 2 inches. Several others in the race were 13 hands 3 inches. From this it can be seen that all were of mixed breed of one kind or another.

There were of course two championships by now, one for Y Class (China) ponies, the other for Z Class ponies. In general Z Class speeds in these races — they were run consecutively — showed that crossbreeds were slightly faster.

The Oldest Broker. Raymond Toeg — 'Sir John' — of Shanghai, doyen of the races, as seen in caricature by his son, Edmund Toeg.

Bengal

NOT always, however.

In the summer of 1923 Duke Larson made a very long journey indeed, to the far west of Outer Mongolia, well beyond Urga. In a breeding ground in that remote region he found and acquired a nice-looking grey of 13 hands 1 inch, of whom there could be no doubt, provided he made the vast journey across the two Mongolias and down into China safely.

This was *Bengal*, the wonder-pony of a century of racing, greater than *Hero*, greater than *Black Satin*, and of whose career there is a particularly full record because he was so obviously sensational.

Appreciating that when people in Tientsin saw his speed there would be no lack of 'experts' to come forward to declare he was crossbred, thus debarring him from racing, Duke Larson prudently took him to Peking instead. Peking did not have the fanciful restrictions and classifications of the Treaty Ports. In Peking a pony was a pony, the faster the better. In Peking one was dealing with people very different from those in the ports. The Diplomatic Corps and the Maritime Customs chiefs were not beholden to groups of merchants, however wealthy, such as those of the Shanghai Race Club. On various occasions the Tientsin Race Club tried to assert the race circuit's authority by debarring Peking owners from entering the Tientsin races, saying that their club was not 'recognized', at the same time not 'recognizing' any griffins first entered at Pao Ma Chang. Peking never retaliated. Pao Ma Chang was ever open to Tientsin owners and riders. However, their Club having been politely told it was being rather silly, after a season or so, back things went to acceptance of a difference between clubs, as of a difference between people.

The crossbreed was at the root of this, one need hardly explain. The amount of trouble caused by the British treaty-port reaction to the crossbreed is almost unbelievable. Harry Morriss considered it fatuous. The foreign aristocrats of Peking found it incomprehensible. They had the advantage, moreover, of phrases such as 'rather silly', which on the lips of the lady of a diplomatic residence are apt to issue with the effect of a cannon.

At the moment when *Bengal* was brought into China, peace prevailed between the clubs. There is no doubt, though, that had Duke Larson brought the pony for inspection at Tientsin first, *Bengal* would never have been heard of.

As it was, Larson brought him down to Peking either before or just after the winter, and sold him to David Fraser, who was Reuter's Peking correspondent and a notably successful owner at the Peking and Tientsin races. *Bengal* was clipped for the first time. His long tail looped up with bright braid, his mane unshorn, as had been the custom for more than seventy years, he would be entered as a griffin for the Peking Spring Meeting of 1924.

The Tientsin meetings were held in advance of those of Peking. As usual, Tientsin owners brought up their winners to race at Pao Ma Chang. Among the owners was Roy Davis, who by chance that year did not have a griffin to enter for the Maiden Stakes. Very friendly with David Fraser and his wife, he was invited to ride *Bengal*.

Thus began the most remarkable association between man and mount in the history of the China races. Roy Davis rode *Bengal* throughout the pony's racing career. Not even M.C. Nickels on *Black Satin* had quite such a tale to tell.

That spring in Peking *Bengal* was entered for three races, the Maidens, the Derby, and the Nanyuan Club Cup, and won them all. In the autumn, at the Nanyuan Club near Peking, he was entered for the St. Leger, and won at the same speed as David Sassoon's *Eureka*, a time only once excelled, by Eric Moller on *Vancouver* in 1903. He won the Champions as well.

He went on to win the same two races — the St. Leger and the Champions — at Pao Ma Chang and at the Tientsin Interclub Meeting. On the latter occasion he won the Champions in 2 minutes and a fraction over 33 seconds, an all-China record and a stunning one, knocking nearly four seconds off the existing record, that of *Loyalty* in 1899. In the autumn of 1925, in the same race, he repeated this time, and in the spring of 1926, again at the Tientsin Interclub Meeting, reduced his time by one-fifth of a second, to 2 minutes 33 and two-fifths seconds. This was the fastest Champions ever run by a pony in China.

At the Tientsin races of November 1925 he won the Trial Plate, one mile, in 2 minutes and a fraction over one second, clipping three seconds off the all-China record. In six seasons, from Spring 1924 to Autumn 1926, at the various racecourses of Peking and Tientsin he won 13 Champions, established 10 records, 4 of them all-China records, and out of 42 starts had 41 wins, all under the same jockey. This, an unprecedented series of wins with the same rider, is almost certainly a world record. China, of course, was in some ways so remote from

David Fraser, Reuter's correspondent, on Bengal, greatest of all the China ponies, Peking 1923.

the rest of the world that matters of this kind passed unobserved.

On the first occasion when *Bengal* won the Tientsin Interclub Champions, in November 1924, he did so by six lengths, and this in his career was not unusual. He was totally outstanding.

The gossip surrounding *Bengal* down in Shanghai and other places was phenomenal. Everyone was convinced that he was a crossbreed. Mysterious stories were circulated on good authority, or worse still, by those 'who knew'. He came from Chinese Turkestan (he wouldn't have won a single race if he had), and there, as was known . . . Since nothing was known, this was convenient.

In fact, as can be seen in a surviving photograph — *Bengal* walking with David Fraser in the saddle — the pony was simply a very beautiful specimen of a Mongolian horse. In addition, nearly all the best ponies he raced against were crossbred, whether the purists liked it or not, and *Bengal* was faster than any of them.

Mid-career, in 1925, *Bengal* was sold to one of the most colourful characters of the warlord period, One-Arm Sutton. It has to be admitted that, from Duke Larson onwards, *Bengal* was a member of an all-star cast.

Major Frank Sutton had signed himself out of the British Army and had joined Marshal Chang Tso-lin, who made him a Brigadier-General, with headquarters in Mukden and a residence in Tientsin, where he raced. He had a ghastly pony called *Baroon*, who savaged any animal who threatened to pass him.

Sutton was to be found in various parts of China, usually connected with the extraordinary. On one occasion he won £30,000 in a Shanghai sweepstake. On another occasion, in Chungking in 1921, he held the Mint at odds of 10 to 1, and slew General Ma Jui in single combat.

In short, a man to be reckoned with. He was also an extremely able soldier, capable of raising and training armies.

The announcement that he had bought *Bengal* was accompanied by an adumbration that General Sutton would shortly issue a challenge to Harry Morriss for a $50,000 match race between *Bengal* and *Warrenfield*. Excitement in Shanghai knew no bounds. This would be the race of a century. These two were unquestionably the best in China.

Strange, though. *Bengal* did not come down for the Shanghai Autumn Meeting of 1925. There had been grave doubts whether, his owner being a resident of Mukden and a member of an unrecognized club, *Bengal* would be allowed to enter in Shanghai. These doubts were dispelled by the excitement. It was explained that General Sutton might have had doubts about bringing *Bengal* down by train — trains which, as everyone knew, were not working most of the time because of warlords.

Early next year, when Kiangwan announced the first National Championship race, the name *Bengal* headed the list of entrants, though doubts were expressed whether the pony would come down. General Sutton had issued a challenge the previous year, however, and since *Warrenfield* was entered, surely this time *Bengal* would be there.

He was not. An announcement was made that due to the uncertainty of rail transport General Sutton had decided against it.

Now, a moment's pause.

Whoever heard of a horse being transported from Tientsin to Shanghai by train? On that route ponies travelled by steamer.

Yet somehow the Shanghai racing world accepted this dubious apology by One-Arm Sutton without seeing how odd it was.

Shift sights to Mukden and Tientsin. There it is to be found that no one knew about General Sutton's challenge — not even General Sutton — still less about the excitement it was causing in Shanghai. One is obliged, furthermore, reluctantly to assume that this was a myth introduced with malice. It was cleverly done, maintained to the end; and it achieved its purpose. When Frank Sutton failed to sustain his 'challenge' by not sending *Bengal*, it was in every Shanghai newspaper, and Sutton lost face. This, clearly, was someone's intention. It has to be remembered that many Britons regarded One-Arm Sutton as a renegade, which he was not. He was simply an unusual character and a tough nut, and he had luck. In consequence, he was envied.

That is the story of the famous *Bengal–Warrenfield* challenge, which damaged One-Arm Sutton's reputation for a considerable time. There was no such challenge. It is doubtful if Sutton knew much about *Warrenfield* anyway, faraway down there in the South in Shanghai. With *Bengal* and that ghastly *Baroon*, why should he?

Yet on it remorselessly went. On 6 November 1926 the *North-China Herald* carried a heading: 'TIENTSIN'S WONDER PONY'. The article began:

So much has been heard during the last two years of *Bengal*, the invincible pony of North China, that racing men in Shanghai would dearly love to see this amazing animal on one of our local courses, matched against half a dozen of our best. He was to have come down for the National Championship at Kiangwan last June, but owing to the uncertainty of transportation General Sutton, his owner, decided not to send him.

Thus this sewer mind of envy, with access to China's leading newspaper, pursued his inexorable projection of a defamation and a lie.

At the Tientsin Spring Meeting of 1925, when *Bengal* was appearing for the second time, there was the largest crowd ever seen at the Tientsin racecourse. This was the meeting at which J.M. Dickinson introduced the two fine crossbreeds which the Race Club, turning a blind eye, had deemed acceptable, with the idea that really the old boy should have a chance of winning the Champions. Their names were *Lyric* and *Rambler*.

Gamely, knowing *Bengal* was entered for the Stayer's Cup, $1\frac{1}{2}$ miles, Dickinson entered both of his for the same race, and *Bengal* beat them hollow. They qualified, however, for the Champions, whereupon *Bengal* beat them both again. The sad fact is that the Tientsin Race Club's two tacit and graceful exceptions to their own rules happened to coincide with a marvel.

At the Autumn Meeting of 1926, however, Dickinson had another griffin, *Gobi Eve*, unquestionably another blind-eye crossbreed, and this time pretty well a certainty for the Champions. However . . .

In the race for the Tientsin Champions last week, *Bengal* ran a remarkable race, and in the first mile smashed two pony records for all China, finishing the race in a common canter, and winning by a distance from a very good-class field.

A distance.

Here it is from the correspondent of the *Peking and Tientsin Times*.

Bengal made no mistake about the Champions. He beat *Gobi Eve* in the rush for the rails at the start, allowing the griffin to accompany him a little way past the mile post, and then opened the throttle, so to speak. He left the rest of the field standing, did the second quarter in 26.3, completed the three-quarters in 1.27, and the mile in 2.00.2. At that point he was the better part of a furlong from the leader of the bulk of the field, and obviously could never be caught. He came down the straight in the teeth of the gale at a comfortable pace, doing the entire distance in 2.35.4, and had plenty of reserve left. He looked, indeed, as if he were quite capable of doing another half-mile. Had it been a still day, or had the wind been in another direction, the last quarter could have been rattled off in 30 seconds or so, and the China record could have gone.

Bengal already held the all-China record. What the correspondent means is that the pony might have broken his own record a *second* time.

A more extraordinary race has not been seen for a long time. *Bengal* simply streaked away from the field after turning out of the back straight, and as he widened the margin at every stride to the half-mile post, spectators on the Stand began to jump and cheer. Mr Davis on this occasion completely altered his usual strategy when riding *Bengal*. Instead of permitting another to make the running, and trusting to the superior speed of his mount to get into the lead on the turn into the home straight, he decided to get away first and stay there. The wisdom of the decision cannot be questioned, for there was such a gale blowing up the straight that anything might have happened if the race was left to be fought out in the last quarter-mile.

This was not the whole story, however. The rest of the race — the race for second and third place — was tremendously exciting. They were in effect watching two races simultaneously, requiring two pairs of eyes, one pair fixed on *Bengal*, the other on the rest, which included the Dickinson beauties and the whole top echelon of the Tientsin races.

At the end of that season, by which time *Bengal* had won 41 races out of 42 starts, Frank Sutton unaccountably sold him to a Hongkong owner.

Roy Davis saw him safely boxed for the steamer journey from Tientsin to Hongkong. There is not much room for sentiment in racing, yet saying goodbye to one's animal partner in a world record achievement is upsetting enough.

'I never had a single letter from the Hongkong owner,' Roy Davis reflected later, 'which seemed quite strange.'

Some months afterwards he heard indirectly that *Bengal* had reached Hongkong with hoof trouble.

'I don't know whether he even started in Hongkong,' he wrote many years later. 'Poor, poor *Bengal*!'

He would have felt differently if he had known the truth.

Bengal's actual buyer, concealed behind the name of some unknown, harmless Hongkong purchaser, was Sir Victor Sassoon. The price was already undoubtedly high — one cannot envision One-Arm Sutton selling if it had not been. It would have been double or triple if he had known who the real buyer was. Nor would Sir Victor Sassoon have wished to see his name in any way connected with that of One-Arm Sutton.

Thus the silence.

Bengal was purchased for the Sassoon stable in Hongkong. At Happy Valley in February 1928 he won the Great Southern Stakes, Jimmie Pote-Hunt riding, beating *Baker's Bay*, of the almost unbeatable Lambert Dunbar stable, Buffy Maitland up. In the Champions, however, *Elliot Bay*, pride of the Dunbar stable, was the winner, Buffy Maitland up again. *Bengal* came third.

Perhaps it was hoof trouble, as in the obscure rumour reaching Tientsin. In any case, *Bengal*, greatest of all the China ponies, who showed no signs of a cross with any other breed, and who under his own jockey was faster than any crossbreed, was never heard of again.

What happened to race ponies when they were past their prime was a question that beset many owners. There was no way of putting a pony out to pasture. Many owners — and all Chinese owners — having the sense that one should not take life, consequently sold their cast-offs to become pack animals or draw carts. The problem here was that the rise and fall in the fortunes of the pony depended on those of the owner of the cart.

Some owners could not face this. They could not bear the thought of coming unexpectedly upon their former prize winner drawing a cart in a Shanghai street and looking more dead than alive. Ada Law was among those of this persuasion. The moment any pony of hers showed signs of being past its prime, she had it put down.

Chinese instinctively revolt at this. Other Europeans found it tough reality. Keeping a contingent of discarded race ponies in China would be economically absurd. Anything better than drawing a cart, though.

Elise Andrews, another notable owner-trainer and horsewoman, who will appear in more detail in a moment, had an additional refinement in this matter. When for any reason a pony had to be put down, she would never, with her love of animals, allow this to be left to others. She would stay with the pony to the end, then feed it a carrot as the marksman took aim, so that the animal had no premonition of what was to happen, and was dead before he knew it — happy.

11. Away from the Flat Tally-ho!

The Thump of Steeplechases

EVER in the background of this narrative there has been the thump of steeplechases and the pounding of paper hunts. These have been kept in the background for various simplistic reasons. It was for the flat that the races started; it was from the flat that the race clubs developed; the flat was where the money was.

There was symbolism in the fact that the steeplechase track was inside the flat, not outside. Chinese of different provinces disagree on many matters, but on one thing they are united, or were in the days of racing. They do not bet on steeplechases.

When one thinks of the enormous number of things they do bet on, this is unexpected. No one tried to explain it. It was simply accepted as a fact. 'Too risky' is the usual Chinese explanation given. Another is 'just sport' — meaning just fun racing. With all the upsets and uncertainties, it was not serious racing which one could give one's mind to.

Chinese were not the only ones who had feelings about it. George Sofronoff, a Siberian Russian born and brought up surrounded by horses, who began his professional career with Eric Moller in Shanghai, and came to be the most sought-after trainer on the China coast, would have nothing to do with steeplechasing. He trained solely for the flat. Even for Eric Moller, with his string of sixty race ponies in Shanghai and another dozen in Hongkong, George Sofronoff would not train jumpers. He said it was 'a hard job for horses and dangerous for people.' This is a sentiment the vast majority of Chinese would agree with. Were a meeting held consisting entirely of jumping races, not more than a handful of Chinese would turn up.

A minor problem concerned with steeplechasing was viewer reaction. Whenever there was a serious tumble and Europeans gasped with horror, Chinese burst out laughing. Not exactly the best thing for improving race relations.

There were, of course, the ponies who simply loved jumping. In general, these were either very difficult animals, or natural show-offs. Most famous of the latter variety was *Old Bill*, who was a winner for nine years at the Shanghai and Kiangwan racecourses — from 1920 to 1928. Whenever *Old Bill* received an ovation he signified his appreciation by waltzing through the paddock.

Purists living and dead will be pleased to note that he was a 'pure' China pony, registered as Y Class — the truly pure,

Old Bill, champion of steeplechase champions in China, who won the Shanghai Grand National 12 times in succession, and on one occasion the Grand National and the Champions on the same day. These were unique achievements. Sketch by Juel Madsen.

as defined by those who truly knew. He was owned by a confederacy of Britons with the uninspiring name of Campox, and came into his own at the Shanghai Spring Meeting of 1921, when he won the Champions and the Grand National Steeplechase on the same day, the only time this was ever done. He won the Criterion Stakes three times in succession, then went on to his truly extraordinary series of Grand National wins. He won this race twice a year for six years, often winning the Kiangwan equivalent as well. His performance achieved a kind of perfection. He knew every inch of the course, never seemed to hurry, almost floated over each jump, and of course — not to be forgotten — loved it. The public were fascinated by him, as year after year he gave this perfect exhibition. One of his owners had a house adjacent to that of Lord Rosebery at Epsom. Rosebery was so intrigued by what he was told by his neighbour about *Old Bill* that an arrangement was made for the pony, on retirement, to be pensioned off in one of Lord Rosebery's paddocks.

At the Spring Meeting of 1928 *Old Bill* won the Kiangsu Cup, two miles, beating F.B. Marshall's *Larch Tree*, and entered as usual for the Grand National. He made a slow start, took the first two jumps dangerously, and was withdrawn. An audible sigh of sympathy arose from the entire Grand Stand. The beloved pony would never race again.

Steeplechasing can of course be therapeutic. That year, 1928, two of Ada Law's ponies came first and second in the Derby, the only time this ever happened. The winner, *Glen Dochert*, for two years won everything he entered, and became impossible. Every time Ada Law came near him he put his ears flat, and would get upset at the slightest thing. She realized that the animal had had enough. Yet he was still in ideal form. Acting on a hunch, she put him in for a steeplechase. After only the first trial run he simmered down, became completely his old self again, and won the Grand National.

Billie Liddell had a dreadful animal called *Going Slow*. No rider seemed to be able to manage him. He behaved so badly he got nowhere, and consequently had a terrible reputation. When Billie Liddell entered him for the Grand National, no one would ride him. She knew and could command the services of every jockey in town — except to ride *Going Slow*. On the morning of the race, in despair, she contacted Eric Moller's eldest son, Eric Blechynden Moller, and asked him if he would take it on. With befitting gallantry he said he would, never having heard of the horse. He arrived at the course to find himself surrounded by consternation. Had he taken leave of his senses? *That* horse? He would end with a broken neck.

Somewhat unnerved, he was relieved to note that Billie Liddell was very calm. Her parting words to him were, 'Sit still; don't move.'

This he did, just raising his eyes at the jumps and lowering them once over. He had a sensational win and, the pony's reputation being known, an equally sensational dividend. Perfectly trained, *Going Slow* was a pony who could not stand being interfered with. He wanted to do it all himself. E.B. let him.[20]

Elise Andrews — 'I never walked; I always rode' — had an infuriating pony called *Maltese Cat*. He had been given to her by Captain McLaren when he left Peking to drive to Europe by car. Elise Andrews, born and brought up in palatial grandeur in Petersburg, Anglo-Swedish but very Russian, her parents personal friends of the Czar and Czarina, her entire family murdered in the Bolshevik Revolution of 1917, could not get this pony to come to terms with her. He was naughty, to use her benevolent word.

Elise decided to ride him from Tientsin to Kalgan and back.

20. Eric B. Moller won the 1983 Epsom Derby with *Tenoso*, Lester Piggott riding, in the presence of the Queen.

She took a little food for him, just in case, and a dog — very sensible. As a Mongol pony, *Maltese Cat* could keep going largely on grass. Even Elise was astonished by the warmth of affection and the hospitality she received from Chinese along the whole of that long and by no means easy route. She herself of course — a European brunette in hacking jacket, hat, jodhpurs and boots, all on her own with a horse and a dog — was a phenomenon, though no one let her feel she was. This was very much of the North, the horse and the dog helping to make her seem part of the landscape.

The journey to and from Kalgan took 17 days.

'*Maltese Cat* and I were intimate friends by that time,' she said quietly.

In her own way, without annoying him, she had mastered him. He went on to become a notable winner. The win everybody remembered was when Ted McBain, one of the wealthiest owner-riders, brought up from Shanghai a pony called *Captain Castle*, with which he clearly intended to sweep the Tientsin floor.

The jubilation when *Maltese Cat* beat him was perfect.

The Pounding of Paper Hunts

THERE were cross-country races as well as paper hunts, and of course there was polo. 'I went cross-country,' said Ada Law with a hint of challenge, 'not in paper hunts.'

There were these subtle preferences. There was a distinct paper hunt social set. Many leading Race Club members belonged to it; others, including some of the most important, did not. Complicating their infuriating custom of giving themselves pseudonyms, a Race Club pseudonym could not be used in paper hunt circles, so anyone who was a member of both clubs had two pseudonyms. For people wishing to inter themselves prematurely, they could not have done it better. Jockeys, incidentally, bore their own names. It was only the owners who were coy about themselves. There were several notable exceptions, F.B. Marshall and Madame A.V. Labis being the ones who immediately come to mind. In Peking pseudonyms were seldom used. Most of the Tientsin owners in Peking raced under their initials, making them slightly easier to disinter.

Paper hunts as children's games must be nearly as old as paper itself. Paper hunts on horseback seem to date from the Crimea, later adopted in India, as a substitute for fox-hunting.

A paper hunt, to quote Baron von Delwig,

is an interrupted *parcours*, not less than ten kilometres, and not more than eighteen kilometres. The whole *parcours* is divided into not less than three and usually not more than five runs, with intervals of enforced trot between them. All the runs in Shanghai were marked with strips of coloured paper, each run having its own colour. The first run ceased when there was no more paper, and the first rider to reach the end of the run was to stop, dismount, look at his watch and carefully mark the time. Gradually other riders arrived; most of them dismounted and looked over the saddlery. Five minutes after his arrival at the end of the run, the first rider gave the words, 'Mount, please', upon which the field proceeded at a trot in any direction, looking for the next run. Galloping between the runs was strictly forbidden. The rider who found the second run was to shout 'Tally-ho!' which was to be distinctly heard by the riders near to him, and galloped away. The first rider at the end of the second run had to pull up to a trot, but did not have to stop and wait for the field. He went immediately ahead at a trot, looking for the next run. This was repeated until the field came to the last run.

The last half of the last run was marked by flags on each side of the jumps. This last run was ridden like a steeplechase at a full pace, and very tight finishes were fought out. It was a dangerous game, but fatal accidents were scarcely known. Presentation of the Cups, usually by a lady, took place immediately after the hunt, and a hunt tiffin followed. In Tientsin the hunt was ridden after lunch, which idea I personally did not relish too much. Pink coats were allowed to be worn only by riders who won a hunt. It was a great honour in China to win one. When a young man won his first hunt, a pink coat was usually presented to him by the manager of his firm. Himself as a rule would give a big party with lots of drinks. It was the duty of the winner to lay the next hunt.

Two Cups were given, a lightweight cup for the winner, a heavyweight cup for the first heavy to make it.

All members of the club were usually cautioned not to hack in the country in which the winner would be laying the next hunt, so that they would not find out in advance the secrets of the lay-out. He was assisted by the winner of the heavyweight cup and by the hunt mafoos. When the hunt was prepared, it was his duty to go over all the runs and take each jump. This was a wise precaution, in order to eliminate the danger of a new man laying a dangerous hunt with unjumpable ditches.

The Shanghai and Tientsin countrysides competed in the matter of dangerous ditches. Both were riddled with them. One travelled by ditch, it must be borne in mind. But on the flat, unless one knew the country extremely well, the ditches were totally unremarkable until one was upon one. Edmund Toeg, artist son of 'Sir John', in one of his best sketches caught it perfectly, with only slight exaggeration. And it will be noted in the sketch that there were people on the other side of the ditch. There were people everywhere, it being impossible to move in China without encountering people just when you think you are alone.

Of course, when foreign imperialism became the fashionable cry — after the Empire — political screeds appeared in numerous languages (written by people who did not ride) describing the miseries inflicted upon farmers by the destruction of their crops when a hunt passed through their fields. Admittedly it was somewhat astonishing, standing in one's field, minding one's own business, when an entire hunt of foreign devils on horseback leaped over ditches and thundered through. Farmers complained at the tops of their voices, creating almost as much disturbance as the hunt.

The politicians got it wrong, however. The farmers knew very well that all damage was noted, and that they would be recompensed to a tune of at least three times the value of anything damaged. It was simply a matter of making a show, as in Chinese opera, where the actors play their parts at the tops of their voices according to strict convention. All gunfire is imitation.

Hunts were held after the harvest, causing minimum inconvenience to farmers. The point the polemicists cautiously chose to ignore was that when a mud jump was required somewhere, it was the farmers who, on grateful receipt of a modest fee, produced it. They continued to holler, naturally — to keep the price up.

The winner of the precedent hunt was not allowed to compete in the next one, nor was the winner of the heavyweight cup. The classic hunts, such as the Christmas Hunt and the Inter-Club Hunt, were not subject to this rule, and were laid by the Master of the Hunt Club. In some clubs, as in Tientsin, the winner was not allowed to compete in the next two hunts, and even the winning pony was not allowed to compete in the next one. These rules were introduced to give better chances to the beginners.

The tragic and the comical are often mixed together.

Billie Coutts, top-flight owner-trainer in Shanghai, winner of 27 Paper Hunt Cups. As seen by Edmund Toeg.

One of two sporting brothers had been Master of the Tientsin Paper Hunt Club for many years. He was a very fine sportsman and was very fond of making speeches, especially after-dinner speeches, though he stammered quite a lot. He was transferred from Tientsin to Shanghai, and a couple of years later, on his way to Europe, decided to make a visit to Tientsin. Next day after his arrival, he was given an old white pony to ride on the Tientsin Racecourse. He rode a couple of times round the polo field near the steeplechase course, and suddenly was not seen any more. Half an hour later, someone found his white pony lying dead of heart failure, and himself unconscious with a fractured skull. Next day he was dead.

A few days later there was a big Christmas Day paper hunt. Over thirty riders were lined up before the first large jump on a bitterly cold December morning, ponies fidgeting from cold and nervousness. The Master of the Hunt made his usual speech, gave his last instructions, and then said:

'Ladies and gentlemen, I have to announce some very sad news. Three days ago, a former Master of our Hunt, beloved by all, and whom many of you will remember, met his untimely death on our racecourse. It was a death fitting for a sportsman. I propose a one-minute silence.'

'Thank you,' said the Master after the lapse of one minute, and the hunting caps were put back on the sportsmen's heads.

'And now,' said the Master, 'we will sing our traditional song,' and the whole field sang:

   'And the birds of the air fell a-sighin' and a-sobbin'
   When they heard of the death of poor old robin.'

'Ladies and gentlemen, you may go,' said the Master, who wheeled his horse, galloped straight towards the first obstacle, and fell headlong into the ditch. The field followed, and four more joined the Master in the ditch. There was a great mix-up of horses' and men's legs and arms.

Paper hunts in China were a kind of romance, with a glamour all their own, reinforced by the fact that ladies rode in them, many of them wearing pink coats, many of them with more than one silver cup to their credit. Billie Liddell won 27.

The ladies presented certain problems, however, if one wished to win a Cup. Maurice Lister, in the late 1920s and early 1930s, was the British American Tobacco representative in Peking. Daniele Varè, author of the *The Maker of Heavenly Trousers* and so many other delightful books — he was in the Italian Legation — had an exceedingly beautiful daughter who adored paper hunts.

'But it wasn't fair,' Maurice Lister complained on reflexion many years later. 'If she fell off, what did one do?'

And as Ann Bridge observed, they fell off in armfuls.

Mukden presented peculiar paper hunt problems. Sir Paul Butler, who was British Consul-General in Mukden between 1936 and 1938, stimulated the introduction of racing there, even in the abnormal conditions of the Japanese-created Empire of Manchoukuo, which the Outer Province of Manchuria had become.

Because of the harvest problem, paper hunts were essentially a winter event. In Manchuria in winter, however, the winds are so fierce that no hunt could possibly be laid with paper. Instead, whitewash was used, daubed on rocks, posts, or anything noticeable, and on the jumps, indicating the way.

At that time Austin Giles, nephew of the great sinologue whose Chinese transliteration system is used here, was with the Hongkong and Shanghai Bank in Mukden. One winter his wife won the paper hunt, and had to lay the next one.

She set off in the usual way, on horseback, wrapped in everything she could think of, wearing Russian boots as protection against the cold, accompanied by a hunt mafoo, similarly mounted, bearing a large bucket of whitewash.

'It was so cold I was nearly dying,' she said, 'and it all had to be laid before dark. We were about half-way when the mafoo said we must go home. I said, "We can't! We must finish it!" '

' "No can, missie," he answered.'

'I said, "How can say no can?" '

Half a mile, half a mile onward; or in pidgin English, half a li, half a li more far. By Edmund Toeg.

The mafoo, from one horse to another, proferred her the bucket of whitewash.

It had totally frozen.

12. Shift to the South

Previous page: If I won the Champions: Georges Sapajou.

In the Shanghai Grandstands

WHEN the new grandstand and club at Kiangwan opened in February 1923, it was at once compared with the then-celebrated grandstand in Buenos Aires. Certainly there was nothing comparable with it in England or France. The Stand held 5,000 people with ease, 7,000 without undue crush. There were full club facilities, and the effect was sumptuous, the rooms teak-panelled throughout, with deep-set old English fireplaces. The scheme was the brainchild of T.U. Yih, who supervised every detail of the design and construction, and was, as Brodie Clarke, chairman of the club, put it, '95% of the whole business'.

The club was opened by General Ho Fêng-ling, the Defence Commissioner, who was saluted on arrival by two Chinese guards of honour, and entered the grandstand flanked by the chairman and John Johnstone, head of Jardine Matheson, followed by Hsü Yuan, Commissioner for Foreign Affairs, flanked by Chu Pao-san, by this time an octogenarian, and T.U. Yih. After the ceremony of anthem, flag-raising and speeches, the presentation gift to the General was made jointly by Brodie Clarke and T.U. Yih. Kiangwan not being in the treaty-port area, the trend of the proceedings was Chinese.

On the third day at this Kiangwan meeting Henry (Harry) Morriss had the most spectacular triumph of his career in the China races. He entered 6 ponies and had 7 wins. *Letchfield* won the Pari-Mutuel Stakes, *Danesfield* the Ladies' Purse, *Wyolesfield* the New Century Plate, *Grangefield* the Nil Desperandum Cup, *Petersfield* the Grand Stand Stakes, and *Patsfield* the Novices' Cup. The Champions, as can be imagined, was a charging mass of stable companions. *Letchfield* won it. This, of course, was the outcome of Henry Morriss' various visits to San Beiss in Outer Mongolia.

He went on to his supreme achievement in racing. On 29 April 1925 his *Manna*, with Steve Donoghue riding, won the Two Thousand Guineas at Newmarket. The excitement in Shanghai was terrific. Somehow they all felt they were in it. When it was learned that *Manna* was entered for the Epsom Derby, Henry Morriss in England was deluged with cables from Shanghai — people wanting him to put money on *Manna* for them.

On 25 May 1925, again with Steve Donoghue, *Manna* won the Derby. Edgar Wallace presided at the Press Club's Derby luncheon. That evening Henry Morriss gave dinner for forty at Claridge's.

Sassoon participation in the races was muted during the early 1920s. In 1926 the Sassoon family returned to the Shanghai races in force — David Sassoon and his nephew Sir Victor Sassoon, who had recently succeeded to the baronetcy created by King Edward VII in 1909. Aged 45, Victor Sassoon was a Member of the Legislative Assembly of India, and a few years later, in 1929, was appointed a Member of the Royal Commission for the Investigation of Labour Conditions in India, in which he played a significant part, having a life-long interest in labour affairs.

Entirely true to form, he and his uncle began by buying *Warrenfield*, the finest pony on the course and champion winner. *Warrenfield* in fact changed hands twice that year. Henry Morriss sold him to Speelman, head of the Russian-Asiatic Bank, and he sold him to Sir Victor Sassoon. The price was not disclosed, but a few years later David Sassoon sold Speelman his best pony, *Radiant Morn*, for $70,000.

More than thirty years had passed since David Sassoon was last encountered. Still with that narrow, seldom smiling face, still determined to win, yet something about him was different. It was almost a case of coming back in a different incarnation; he even had another name. Sir Victor, being his nephew, called him Nunckie; and this, being somehow right for him in his new incarnation, caught on to such an extent that in no time the whole of Shanghai society called him Nunckie. Older people, who remembered him from before, recalled him as 'the owner of the amazing *Hero*'. To younger people this meant nothing. When Sir John Keswick, who arrived to join Jardine Matheson in Shanghai in 1927, was asked what Nunckie's real name was, he had no idea. 'He was always Nunckie to me,' he said. It epitomizes the change which time had wrought.

Nunckie was the brains behind the Sassoon stable in Shanghai. Uncle and nephew raced as 'Morn' and 'Eve', David Sassoon being 'Morn'. As 'Mr Eve', Sir Victor Sassoon thus became the most distinguished of the hermaphrodite owners. It was said of him that he had a stable and a string in every place in the world where racing was worthy of the name. He was remembered on the China coast for having said that there were times when he wondered whether, of all his turf activities, he didn't most enjoy racing his China ponies.

David Sassoon — 'Nunckie' — leading in 'Peanut' Marshall on Radiant Morn, one of the great Sassoon ponies, Shanghai, November 1935.

In 1927, the year after the Sassoon resurgence, the top owners were Sir Victor Sassoon, Ada Law, and Raymond Toeg, in that order. Toeg — 'Sir John' — with a longer innings than almost anyone else, was the freely acknowledged *doyen* of the Shanghai town races. That winter he bought *Alligator*, the pride and despair of his life, who in May 1928 won the Shanghai Derby, Vic Haimovitch up.

All along, Raymond Toeg had striven to win the Shanghai Champions with a pony in his own sole ownership. In joint ownership he had won it three times. *Alligator* seemed to be the answer. Every expert eye in Shanghai said this was a pony unmatchable. With a temperament, however. In training runs he was unbeatable. All the experts who got up before dawn to go down to watch were agreed on this. Yet come the Champions, *Alligator*, having won everything he had entered, never made it to a win. His rider was Jimmie Pote-Hunt, son of an Admiralty pilot on the Yangtze, and himself the top jockey in Shanghai, known also as the gentlest and most patient of jockeys. If anyone could deal with *Alligator*, it was he. But the pony wouldn't co-operate.

This is one of the strangest instances of horse psychology in racing; because horse psychology it was. There is no other explanation for it. Some years afterwards, when he was getting on in life, Raymond Toeg said that if it were possible for a horse to break a human being's heart, it was *Alligator* who would have broken his.

High on the list of winning owners in 1927 was Lambert Dunbar, one of the very few American owners in the China races, and among the most successful of all owners, notably at Happy Valley. He and his wife, who had a string of her own, were particularly selective in their acquisitions. Their aim was a small stable, all winners; and they came very near it. Dunbar, who was a flour merchant, lived in Hongkong from 1920 to 1941. With his 'Bay' series he dominated the Happy Valley races in the 1930s, and with *Liberty Bay* had the next wonder-pony, who will be encountered in due course.

'Winsome & Hasty' — the Arnhold brothers, British of German descent, owners of another of the enormous China concerns which seemingly embraced everything — did well that year, though no longer at the top of the racing tree, as they had once been. Eric Moller, George Dallas, Jack Liddell, Fred Elias — all were in roughly the same winning category.

A study in legs, and what to do with them when being photographed, each having her own technique, Billie Liddell's being the firmest. Alone in not worrying is the only man in the picture, the future Chairman of Reuter's, Sir Christopher Chancellor, at this time Reuter's correspondent in Shanghai.

Then came 'We Two', which was the racing partnership of Billie Liddell and Vera McBain.

The principal McBain interest was mining, in which they were undisputed experts and the biggest people in the field. Neville McBain ran the Mentoukou mines in the approaches to the Western Hills. Any day his lines of camels could be seen bearing coal to Peking. Hongkong people remembered the McBains because they had a kaolin quarry in the hills just behind Kwun Tong, facing Hongkong harbour.

The father, George McBain, with nine children, built a house in Shanghai large enough for all of them, even married with children, to live under one roof. The situation created was finally solved by the house becoming — the only thing it was fit for — a hotel.

Ted McBain was the racing son, a major owner-rider. His brother Willie's wife Vera had formerly played walk-on parts in the West End of London, where they met. Vera McBain and Billie Coutts — not yet married to Jack Liddell — formed what was to be a lifelong friendship, exemplified by their racing name 'We Two'. By 1927 the name was accentuated by the fact that both husbands had competing stables.

They all lived palatially, with the difference that they were relatively comfortable. Raymond Toeg lived in compradoric splendour, which was considered normal. Others spurned the compradoric, moving instead into the phantasmagoric. The Sassoons had an oak-panelled, mock-Tudor dining hall, complete with musicians' gallery. The Ezra family lived in Grand Trianon style, with Louis XV furniture throughout, a ballroom for 150 dancers, a music room to seat an audience of 80 in comfort, and elegantly designed French windows giving out on to 25 acres of garden, approached from Avenue Joffre in the French Concession.

All these people raced and worked. How the racing men did so is a mystery. Lorraine, future wife of artist-scholar-connoisseur Edmund Toeg, caught it perhaps as well as it can ever be understood:

'We would dance till 5 in the morning, and at 5.30 there he was at the racecourse training his ponies. Somehow one managed to fit in running a business.'

Strange Changes in Canton and Peking

BRITAIN had, till this time, regarded Peking as the capital of China, which in effect meant recognition of any warlord transiently in control of the city. The situation having become derisory, the thrust of British diplomacy shifted southward. In 1929 Marshal Li Chai-sum, head of government in Canton, and Sir Cecil Clementi, Governor of Hongkong, exchanged official visits, and Britain recognized the Kuomintang as the National Government of China.

The effect in Canton was remarkable. Where foreigners were concerned, everything seemed to improve. It was not long before there was talk of holding races.

The Provincial Commissioner, General Chan Ming-shü, and the head of the Navy, Admiral Chan Chak, as well as at least three members of the Provincial Council, were all keen sportsmen and expert riders. Patronage was conferred immediately. A convenient venue was found at Shek Pai, along the Canton-Kowloon Railway, and for once it was not on ricefields.

The first meeting was held on Saturday, 4 April 1931, and was a spectacular success, unlike any previous Canton race-meeting there had ever been. An estimated 10,000 people attended, the scenes along the road from Tungshan to Shek Pai being without precedent in Canton. Two miles of cars in a constant stream held the road for a solid hour, from 10.30 to 11.30 in the morning, with a never-ending procession of pedestrians on both sides of the road. By 11 a.m. it was impossible to hire a car from any garage either in Tungshan or Canton. All had gone to the races.

His Excellency General Chan Ming-shü arrived on horseback and performed the opening ceremony, after which he trotted round the entire course to a thunderous ovation, demonstrating the esteem in which he and the Kuomintang were held. He had already donated a special Cup for the Derby winner. At the end of the meeting he presented the prizes, receiving another ovation as he departed.

One is apt to forget today what a message of hope the Kuomintang held for the people of China at that time. It is characteristic, too, that one should perceive it so clearly at the races.

Shifting the capital of China to Nanking, which was the corollary to international recognition of the Kuomintang, had a noticeable effect on Peking socially. The stable elements of government which had endured since the Empire — the Customs, the Posts, and what remained of the various ministries — moved south. Peking became a quieter place. It shrank as well. By the mid-1930s there were quite large areas of vegetable and farm land inside the city walls.

Nominally the Legations established themselves in Nanking. In fact, the diplomats spent most of the year in Peking, which was a better listening-post. Racing continued throughout the 1930s in conditions of charming rusticity. In the Pao Ma Chang area there were numerous small temples which Europeans rented and used as modest country houses. Among those with a farm was the Tientsin branch of the Dallas family. Dallas is the only surname to span the entire century of racing. In the Peking races Oswald Dallas, great-nephew of Alexander Grant Dallas, the Shanghai pioneer of 1844, became virtually jockey-in-ordinary to the British Minister — a succession of them, including Sir Miles Lampson, later Lord Killearn (Minister in China, 1926–8), and Sir Hughe Knatchbull-Huguessen (Ambassador in China, 1936–8). Sir Miles Lampson, incidentally, must have been one of the heaviest men ever to ride a China pony, which he did with gusto, though not in races.

Macao, to Where it Started

EARLY in 1924 a syndicate of Chinese with interests in Macao and Shanghai approached the Governor of Macao for the grant of a concession to organize pony-racing in the Portuguese settlement.

There being no precedent — when racing first started no one asked anyone's permission — the Governor settled for comfortable words and apathy.

The syndicate settled for the comfortable words. A few days later, in April, the International Race and Recreation Club of Macao Ltd. was formed, and proceeded to negotiate a contract with the Government. The contract had to be sent to Lisbon for approval. To everyone's amazement it was debated in the National Assembly, where it created a minor political uproar. Why, no one in China ever knew, not even the Portuguese.

Providentially, at this moment a new Governor, Rodrigo Rodrigues, arrived. Enthusiastic about the idea, in July he informed his superiors in Lisbon that the project would bring nothing but economic benefit to Macao, and must go ahead. With this encouragement the Club publicly announced its plans. T.U. Yih had by this time become a director. It looked set to go, and most people — and all the newspapers — took the Club's announcement seriously.

There was to be a grandstand with theatre, ballroom, billiards room, and social hall, with a space for 100 ponies underneath the Stand. Ships were to be purchased to make the journey from Hongkong to Macao in $2\frac{1}{2}$ hours (a physical impossibility) with boxes for 70 ponies. Races would be on Sundays, at night in summer, from 10 p.m. to 1 a.m.

Sunday racing was the great lure for racing people from Hongkong, where religious piety shunned such misdeeds. In this respect Macao, despite its seminaries, convents and churches, was not nearly so religious as Hongkong. Indeed the first race-meeting observed — in Macao in 1637 — was held on a Sunday in front of a church.

The site chosen faced the Pearl River. It was just beyond the old city wall, long since dismantled. Port works were in progress in the area to enlarge and develop the eastern side of the Macao peninsula. By this stage of the development there was a lake in the middle of the proposed course which the Government agreed to fill in. Various small plots and some village-style Chinese dwellings needed moving. It did not seem difficult.

When the Government made to take over the land, however, it was found that the compensation payable would be $1,000,000. Worse, it was found that by the terms of the contract the Government of Macao had to pay these costs, not the Race Club. And there was no money.

It now looked like no go. Then 'Pegasus', racing correspondent and senior tipster of the *South China Morning Post* in Hongkong, having seen a diagram of the projected Macao port works, observed that right up at the top end, facing the Pearl River, there was a space marked in small letters *Recreio* — for recreation.

The intention had been to have a football field there. When 'Pegasus' suggested that instead it be a racecourse, things suddenly sprang to life. In October the Governor-in-Council approved the change of venue. The Governor, Colonel Maia Magalhães, had the squatters moved off the land required for the grandstand. Admiral Hugo de Lacerda, in overall charge of the port works, shifted the greater part of his year's budget to reclaiming the racecourse site as a priority.

Racing returned to where it first started. The piece of reclaimed land was directly in front of the old Areia Preta racecourse, which was now occupied by a government-owned fireworks factory and many vegetable plots. If Harriet Low, seated in the bamboo grandstand, had looked slightly to the right, in what was then sea, she would have seen the new, massive, concrete Stand.

Dream of the Race Meeting: Georges Sapajou.

The organizers had moderated their ambitions. The theatre and other extravagances had been forgotten, and they had discovered the speed of ships. The end-result was the most attractive racecourse in South China, with that same glorious view of the Pearl River — and entirely correctly — the same name, Areia Preta. For Hongkong people of any colour these were the happiest racing occasions. They were completely informal, combining a meeting with an excursion, and for Portuguese and Chinese, all of them with cousins on the other side of the river, they provided the opportunity for a family get-together. For the British the great thing was the Ladies' Race — last in the programme, but which made the day. The ladies, moreover, were good riders. Unlike in Peking, here they did not fall off in armfuls.

It was a one-mile course. The first meeting was held on Saturday, 19 March 1927. Governor de Sousa Barbosa — governors changed with bewildering rapidity at this time — attended, with his wife and daughter. HMS *Petersfield* brought Lady Tyrwhitt over. A mass of people came from Hongkong. There were speeches. The first was made by the presiding genius on the Macao side, Lou Lim Ieoc, founder of the Po Seng Bank, the first Chinese bank in Macao to be run on Western lines. The Governor spoke next. Then — never put a good Jardine man down — came Ho Kom-tong. That evening Lou Lim Ieoc gave a party for more or less everybody in his stately colonial-style mansion.

The meeting was such a success, and the response from Hongkong so reassuring, that steps were taken immediately to enlarge the grandstand and improve the amenities. A special bus service was laid on to meet ships bringing racegoers, to transport them direct from the inner harbour wharves to the racecourse. The Club's director, K.H. Chun, collared the shipping company which ran the Pearl River and delta service, and persuaded them to divert the *Taishan*, the largest and fastest steamer, usually on the Hongkong to Canton run, to operate between Hongkong and Macao on race days.

The *Taishan*, on her special service, left Hongkong at 9 a.m. on Sunday — church bells ringing — and set off from Macao on the return journey at 5.30 p.m. Using the special bus service, day visitors could spend four and a half hours at Areia Preta. The service was vitally necessary too, because from the day of the first meeting the Boa Vista, the Riviera, all the hotels in Macao were fully booked on race weekends.

Actually it was the more sedate who took the *Taishan* both ways. Others preferred to risk their luck at fantan at the Central and take a night boat back. There were cabins, though these were not much used. Return crossings tended to consist of all-night card games. The ship sailed at 3 a.m., and the bar was open until about 5 a.m. At this hour the ship entered the deeply religious waters of Hongkong, and the bar shut. One disembarked at 7 a.m. to hear the Cathedral bell ringing for Monday matins.

With the advent of racing, Macao, normally a sleepy hollow, woke up. Portuguese and Macao Chinese owners burst upon the scene at Happy Valley. At the Christmas meeting of the Fanling Hunt Club that year there were so many Macao entrants that it was the biggest hunt there had ever been. The Macao races being on Sundays, there was no danger of a clash with Happy Valley. Week after week peaceful Areia Preta surged into activity, and nearly always there was the captivating spectacle of an important Chinese owner leading in the winner, his jockey being an English young lady.

Edna Farr being led in at the Fanling hurdle races after a win on Estrellita, owned by H.S. Yung, 1932. She rode Estrellita in Macao as well. (By courtesy: Mrs E.M. Baldwin, Sinnington, York.)

241

May came, the weather hotted up. Still the races went on. June came — hotter still. The races went on. July came — first cousin to a furnace. The races still went on.

This is the first occasion in South China when races were held in the month of July. That it was physically possible was due to Areia Preta's exceptional geographical position. Being situated on reclaimed land, sticking out into the sea, it was perfectly exposed to the breath of the summer monsoon, blowing steadily from the south with winds which, even on the hottest day, can be surprisingly cool.

The races stopped in August, amazing to relate. It was due to the rain, not the heat. They resumed in September, beginning the season with Saturday night open-air dancing at the racecourse, with an excellent Portuguese band.

Thus it went on, flush and flat-out, until the end of the 1929 season in July, when there were murmurs at the end of the last meeting. A reorganization of the company was being contemplated. The reorganization was such that there were no more races.

What had gone wrong was never explained. There was the obvious difficulty that the organizational axis of the company lay between Macao and Shanghai. More significant, however, is that after only six months of racing in Macao the guiding spirit of it, Lou Lim Ieoc, died at the early age of 50. As a banker and man of wide ideas, it was he who had kept the balance with the Shanghai confederates. For nearly two years there were no races.

The Government soon felt the shortfall in income. The hotels were not doing so well, neither were the shops. In a small place like Macao, the Hongkong racing visitors, without noticing it, had been bringing in a good deal of money. Complaints were shortly aired.

In February 1931 George Hutton Potts, who had moved his brokerage from Shanghai to Hongkong, went over to see the Governor of Macao, and came away with an extraordinary concession — a racing concession for a company not yet formed, which, when it was, would be formed in Hongkong, not Macao.

This was the Macao Jockey Club, which ran races at Areia Preta from late 1931 until the Japanese War. Ponies were by this time categorized into five classes, A to E, based on performance. Usually only D and E Class ponies raced at Macao. All the principal Hongkong and Shanghai jockeys, however, were to be seen racing there at one time or another.

New Territories

EQUESTRIAN activities in the New Territories started with the Fanling Hunt, around 1922. Hurdle races started in 1928, the Hunt Club becoming the Fanling Hunt and Race Club. The races were not actually held at Fanling, but at Kwanti some miles to the east, off the road — in those days a track — to Shataukok. There was a training track at Kwanti,[21] where in an English country club atmosphere there were a number of activities throughout the year, and where owners sent their ponies to graze in summer, those, that is, who felt they could not run to sea-bathing at Tsingtao.

Up to a point the hurdle races were a success in an ambience of this kind. But the Club had run up against the problem that Chinese are simply not interested in jumping, certainly not as far as gambling is concerned. Very few Chinese were to be seen. Finally, in 1931, the Club decided they must be practical and make more money. One flat race per meeting was introduced. Chinese promptly appeared, and the Club's financial position improved.

Edna Farr was among those who raced at Macao and Fanling. 'Fanling was a lovely little course,' she reminisced, 'all grass, and with the wonderful hills behind. I think Fanling was very dashing, because in those days in England ladies could only ride in point-to-points. Of course I used to go racing at Happy Valley, and it was wonderful high up in the boxes and stands even in 1932.'

In Macao she rode for H.S. Yung, one of the leading owners, and had several wins. The 'present' on such occasions was a slap-up Chinese dinner given by Yung and his wife for all the lady riders on their return to Hongkong.

The country in the northern part of the New Territories, sparsely populated and open, was ideal for good riding, presenting a varied terrain and many unexpected obstacles. The hunts sometimes went high into the foothills of Taimoshan, and could be challenging — granite with a shallow topsoil is not the easiest thing to take on horseback other than at a walking pace.

Here the China ponies came into their own. They had an almost uncanny facility for getting across difficult country. In the Fanling hunts they were taken for granted until 1931. In

21. W.L. (Bill) Stanton of the National City Bank of New York had a large bungalow at Kwanti, and by all-round agreement it became the clubhouse.

that year Japan invaded and seized Manchuria, and the arrangements for procuring China ponies were thrown into disorder. Hongkong, as usual, was hardest hit, being furthest away. Immediate recourse was had to Australia to obtain ponies.

'Les Girls', Macao, 1932. Second from the left is Mrs Leo Frost, wife of the champion of champions at Happy Valley, who rode Liberty Bay to 26 wins, never beaten. Note the junks in the background. The Macao racecourse projected right out into the sea. (By courtesy: Mrs E.M. Baldwin.)

Ponies, not horses. The truth is that Australian ponies had for some years been getting in by a side entrance at Happy Valley — on occasion in Shanghai as well. Provided they did not exceed 14 hands, the maximum for a Mongolian crossbreed; provided their papers were in order, meaning that a respectable dealer had vouched they were from Mongolia; provided . . . Well, they had somehow been getting in. From 1931 they took over at Happy Valley.

In the Fanling hunts it was another story. The China ponies instinctively understood the Chinese countryside. Approaching a semi-submerged tomb, grassy but with a nasty unseen stone obstacle somewhere in it, a China pony would apprehend it before his rider did, and either swerve or jump it without having to be told. Not so the Australian ponies, who in a Chinese countryside were more of a hazard than a help, and did not adapt easily to the peculiarities, pitfalls and obstacles. More than one rider said that for hunting in China they were hopeless. This is the more extraordinary when one reflects that the China pony is not a China pony. In Mongolia there are no obstacles remotely similar to those of a Chinese rural area. Yet a China pony adapted at once, somehow seeming to understand without being taught, while the Australian ponies did not.

Five New Dresses and the Hongkong Derby

THE Annual Meeting at Happy Valley, held in February, was the great social occasion of the Hongkong year — five days of racing, opening on Saturday, resuming from Monday to Thursday, with a gymkhana to end it off on Saturday. Everyone, of every hue and nationality, attended, even those not particularly interested in racing. The ladies, *de rigueur*, had to have new dresses — five, because they wore a different one each day. Not even Peking could beat this. There it was thought quite seemly for a young woman to be seen twice at the races in the same dress. The anxiety prevailing in Hongkong in dress-shop and boudoir was tremendous as the races approached, especially if one had unmarried daughters, who were virtually 'presented' at the races.

The great Shanghai jockeys who came down for this event — Jimmie Pote-Hunt, Johnny Heard, 'Peanut' Marshall, Buffy Maitland, Norman Dallas — were tremendous names in the racing world. In the evenings Hongkong racing buffs listened in wrapt amazement as they told stories (true ones) about fabulous Shanghai. They were heroes.

As mentioned earlier, Jimmie Pote-Hunt's father was an Admiralty pilot on the Yangtze, and he himself seems to have held down a job of some kind. Johnny Heard's family had one of the oldest firms on the China coast, Heard & Co., which eventually sold out to Jardine's, Johnny Heard becoming a Jardine departmental manager. 'Peanut' Marshall was a nephew of F.B. Marshall of the famous 'Tree' series, which prior to the development of contacts with Mongolia produced an astonishing succession of winners. 'Peanut' Marshall had very long ears. In Shanghai, when the ponies paraded and he felt he was on a sure winner, he would tuck his ears under his cap, as a secret signal to his lady friends to rush and place a last-minute bet.

Buffy Maitland was another nephew. His uncle, Frank Maitland, founder of the firm of that name — another of those firms which from nothing seemed to spread a long way in all directions — was a tremendous figure in Shanghai paper hunt circles. Tremendous in weight too. At 224 pounds he probably beat even Sir Miles Lampson. His nephew Hugh (Buffy) was a neat little chap with a perfect jockey figure. Of him it is firmly stated that he never did a day's work in his life. In fact, for a good rider, it had become steadily more difficult to be a real amateur.

Norman Dallas, third generation at the Shanghai races, was nominally employed in the silk department of Jardine Matheson. Technically the best jockey of his day, and the most elegantly dressed, his wins were calculated to perfection rarely seen. Fantastically applauded always for the finesse of his victories on the course, he was in fact a cold, unlikeable man with few if any friends. As one of his own cousins said of him, he had 'an almost livid temper under utter control. If he disliked the owner of the pony in front of him, he made a pony fly like the wind.'

Hongkong had only one jockey who could compete with these men. This was Leo Frost, who came to the Far East in 1920 to join Jardine Matheson. He first made his mark in the Tientsin races, where his main adversary was another great jockey, Edgar Leighton, with the reputation of being the finest rider in North China. In 1930 Frost was posted to the head office of Jardine's in Hongkong, and from then until 1937, when he was appointed manager of Jardine's Canton office, he reigned supreme at Happy Valley as champion jockey, indeed as champion of champions, in that his record of wins surpassed that of any other rider on this course.

Billy Hill, with the greatest number of wins of any rider in China, but who could not be regarded as an amateur, was racing at Happy Valley during Leo Frost's first two years there, winning the Champions in 1930 on *Diana Bay*. The 'Bay' stable was that of Lambert Dunbar, the American owner mentioned earlier. In 1932 Leo Frost became his jockey.

Mrs Dunbar had some notably successful animals in her string, the most famous being *Sitting Bull* who, usually with Buffy Maitland riding, won all the major races at Happy Valley. When it came to retiring the pony, she solved the problem in an unusual way. She sent him back to Hailar, where he came from. At least up there no danger existed of him ever having to draw a cart.

In the summer of 1935 Leo Frost trained jockeys, with a notable general rise in standards at Happy Valley. Donald Black, short and light, an accountant with the firm of Peat, Marwick and Mitchell, was the next champion, with H.C. Pih in third place, the first Chinese rider to reach the top three. High tribute was paid at the time to H.C. Pih's fine jockeyship.

The Hongkong Derby had now become one of the most coveted wins on the China coast — something one would never have expected to happen, say, ten years earlier. Lambert Dunbar won it with *Elliot Bay* in 1927, his wife winning it the next year with *Sitting Bull*. Ho Kom-tong won it in 1929 with *President Hall*. Lambert Dunbar won it again in 1930 with *Diana Bay*. Then at last, in 1931, T.E. (Tam) Pearce won it with *King's Service* — he had missed it in 1923 by a nose. This is extraordinary, because Tam Pearce — he headed one of the largest Hongkong firms, John D. Hutchison, and became Chairman of the Jockey Club — owned the 'Dynasty' stable, which was one of the strongest and best, winning everywhere it went. Yet somehow that Hongkong Derby had eluded him all those years. He was not the only one. A round dozen of owners went at it for years and never made it.

Most notable of the aspirants was Sir Victor Sassoon, who went at it every year from 1928 onwards, and finally won it with *Honeymoon Eve* in 1936. Next year — Coronation Year — Steve Donoghue won The Oaks for him on *Exhibitionist*.

H.C. Pih, Shanghai-born, who raced in Hongkong in the 1930s, and was among the top three jockeys. In Macao, 1936, being led in by his wife, who is wearing the last word in chic. (By courtesy: Government of Macao.)

Liberty Bay and Silkylight

THE most sensational animal from the Dunbar stable —
and between the two of them they had a series of
sensations, as their Derby winners show — was *Liberty Bay*,
who won the Hongkong Derby of 1932. He was a Mongolian
crossbreed streets ahead of any other at Happy Valley. That
November he won the Hongkong St. Leger by six lengths.
Liberty Bay marks the climax of Leo Frost's career as a
gentleman rider — 26 entries, 26 wins, never beaten. In 1933
Liberty Bay broke a record every time he faced the Starter.
His record for the mile and a half was unique, a fifth of a
second better than the Australian pony record.

Liberty Bay was one of the greatest of all ponies from the
plateaux, in the same rank as *Bengal*, and as *Hero* before him.
He won the Hongkong Champions three years in succession,
always ridden by Leo Frost. He raced solely with Leo Frost,
who nearly always rode him on the same principle: first off
the mark, in the lead all the way. His track record of 26
victories, never beaten, was sensational enough. Equally
astonishing were the margins of his wins. Six lengths was
ordinary. The racing correspondents were eventually reduced
to saying 'by many lengths', because nobody could say for
sure how many.

Liberty Bay won at Happy Valley with such ease that
occasionally Lambert Dunbar would deliberately not enter
him for certain races. The pony was in a class of its own, and
it seemed unfair to other owners and riders. In 1935 the
Stewards decided — and Dunbar courteously agreed — that
the pony's name must no longer be shown on the *pari mutuel*.
It never again was. In any subsequent race *Liberty Bay* ran in,
winning odds went to the second pony. In 1937 his owner
withdrew him for an entire year — he owned several other
winners. In the autumn of that year Leo Frost left for Canton
and retired from racing. Donald Black took over as principal
jockey for the 'Bay' stable. He was by this time the presiding
champion of the course. A few months later he went on home
leave. The scene was set for what has come down today as the
race of a century. A jockey had to be found for *Liberty Bay*.

Whether in Chinese or in English, anyone writing about
the China races, and who remembered it, will point to the
Hongkong Champions of 23 February 1938 as the most
dramatic race ever run on the China coast. *Liberty Bay* was

back after his year's holiday. That he had been removed from the *pari mutuel* did not mean that no one wagered on him. (Multiply by ten.) There was much excitement.

Eric Moller no longer rode in races. With three stalwart sons he did not have to. He sometimes threatened to, throwing his stable and his sons into dismay. The early 1930s had been perilous years. The Great Slump of 1929–31 did not hit the China coast at the time. It struck a year later and lasted longer, from 1932 to late 1936. Eric Moller left for America. George Sofronoff, working in his stable, the largest in Shanghai, feared that all the ponies would be sold, the stable closed down, and he and the rest would lose their jobs.

A loan was raised somewhere, and Moller was shortly buying ships at half their actual value. Well before the slump ended, the Moller Line was larger than it had ever been, as was the rest of the Moller empire. It was in this somewhat buoyant mood that in July 1937 he noticed a black griffin trotting round the Shanghai Racecourse 'in a very untrim and poor condition.' He was apparently destined for Hongkong. Albeit

Shanghai, 1935. The Race Club, with its imposing tower, was the most sumptuous of any such club in the world. The Grand Stand was reputedly the largest in the world, and probably was. The turf was described as 'smooth as a billiard table'. Beside the complex runs Bubbling Well Road. (By courtesy: Charles E. Wolnizer, Esq.)

an animal 'of quite unpretentious condition and shape', Moller had his eye on him.

In the latter half of August 1937, early in the morning, the Chinese Air Force launched a sortie on Japanese warships on the river. The bombs fell short, and in a few seconds the racecourse was a mass of falling shrapnel. Seven mafoos were flattened, five ponies hit. Eric Moller, who happened to be there, dived for protection under the concrete of the Mafoos' Stand.

On emerging, he found that this same black pony had been wounded in several places. He arranged for him to be sent to be cared for by the Moller stable vets, and bought the pony. This incident is typical of Eric Moller. Every day in Shanghai, on his way to the office early in the morning, he would stop at his racing stables off Bubbling Well Road, and accompanied by a member of the stable staff carrying a big basket of fodder, would go round and talk to each of his 60 racing ponies, personally giving each one a handful to eat.

They named the wounded pony *Silkylight*, and took it slowly building him up. He still had his unpretentious shape, but on his first trial gallop he was clocked — jointly by F.B. Marshall and Eric Moller — with a remarkable time for the mile and a quarter. At his next gallop he repeated this performance, whereupon it was decided to enter him for the Hongkong races of February 1938. In due course he was shipped down with Moller's top trainer in the express Italian mail steamer *Conte Verde*.

As Eric Moller recalled it: 'After a few days he was placed at exercise, and it wasn't very long before every third man on the rails at Happy Valley decided that he would be of very little use.'

Though he won the Maiden Stakes on the first day, few had much confidence in him for the Derby. The *Hongkong Telegraph*, best newspaper for the races, observed that pitted against an Australian subscription griffin he had acquitted himself magnificently in a trial. The punters were not impressed; so little impressed, indeed, that when he won the Derby the winning ticket yielded a staggering $141,380. 'A fortune awaits the lucky ticket holder,' the *Telegraph* exclaimed that evening.

Next morning the win was a banner front-page headline. Ah San-so was an amah employed by a Mr Ribeiro in Kowloon. Influenced by the fact that she had won $2,000 in a cash sweep, she had got her friends together, formed a syndicate of 250 amahs, and bought $300 worth of tickets divided into 280 shares, the largest having 10 shares. Each member must have made at least $500.

This was exciting enough. Next came the Champions. Having already won the Maidens and the Derby, *Silkylight*, if he won this, would gain what was known in Hongkong as the 'triple crown'. To return to Eric Moller:

In the Champions *Silkylight* met the most formidable race pony in China, the unbeatable *Liberty Bay*, which his owner Mr Dunbar raced in Hongkong for five years, with the magnificent record that *Liberty Bay* had never known defeat.

Thus it was perfectly understandable that the confidence of the public should still reign supreme that *Liberty Bay* would gallop away with the Champions in accordance with his usual custom, so much was the confidence of Hongkong folks centred in their grand pony.

The Hongkong Champions! Never will I forget it in all my life! Not only was it an intensely exciting race, but veritably it was most awe-inspiring in the majesty of its momentary spectacle.

At its very commencement, *Silkylight* leaped away from the gate with a lead of two lengths before any other pony got started. On former occasions it had been customary for *Liberty Bay* to start off at a great pace and never to be headed. [This was the Leo Frost technique with this particular pony. Today Buffy Maitland was riding him.]

On this occasion, in my opinion, the February Champions was won at the gate — because those two lengths which we gained from the very start were an invaluable asset at the finish, which indeed was a mighty and glorious one.

Finding this stranger two lengths ahead of him, *Liberty Bay* passed our pony like a whirlwind, and before the first three furlongs were done *Liberty Bay* led the whole field by about ten lengths — reaching the first mile post in 1 minute 54 seconds, which was record-breaking for the Hongkong mile distance.

It was quite noticeable that the racing public simply sat itself down to witness the usual run-in of the Champions, with *Liberty Bay* winning as he liked, and the rest of the field nowhere. At this moment *Liberty Bay* increased his lead, so that, when passing the Black Rock, all of those watching the race were positively satisfied and confident that the customary occurrence would be witnessed once more.

But after passing the Black Rock a slight change took place in the situation, because one could see that *King's Warden* [Tam Pearce's 'Dynasty' stable] and *Silkylight* were gradually commencing slightly to close the distance — but so slightly as to give no inkling of the amazing result of the actual finish which then swiftly took place.

Just before entering the straight I noticed that *Silkylight's* jockey — my son, Ralph B. Moller — asked the pony for a little, and to my unbounded astonishment I saw our pony answer like an arrow from a bow, for although *Liberty Bay* entered the last quarter about nine lengths ahead of our pony, I began to see that *Silkylight* was gradually and appreciably lessening the distance — and then, at that critical moment, I could see our jockey take out his whip and give his mount a definite demand for more speed, and it is impossible to realize the wondrous thrill of the answer this grand animal gave to the tremendous effort thus required of him.

No one on the Members' Stand seemed to realize for some moments what was actually happening, when all of a sudden we commenced to hear a rumble, increasing to a roar, which was coming from the faraway Public Stand where the people there could see better than we could that *Silkylight*, veritably and actually, was giving the hitherto unbeaten *Liberty Bay* a great race for the Champions; and as the ponies speeded along the last quarter, the shouts extended down to the Members' Stand, and it was plain to all that a great battle was being fought out for that finish of the Champions.

It seemed as if the whole multitude of spectators stood up in their places, shouting for all they were worth, and calling upon our *Silkylight* to give the veteran Champion a struggle for his crown of racing triumph. The finishing ride between that fine jockey Buffy Maitland on *Liberty Bay*, and my son Ralph on *Silkylight* was a truly terrific tussle during that last furlong, for both men rode out their mounts to their utmost capacity.

I was atop the Grand Stand watching the race through my glasses, and I noticed *Silkylight* come up and along with his head just about abaft the neck of *Liberty Bay* — and then our pony staggered, and I verily feared he had given his best and final effort, failing just short of victory.

But no! My boy, Ralph, gave him two cuts asking the great-hearted animal to come again, and the pony promptly responded nobly, and then, to the astonishment of all present, *Silkylight* streaked past the old Champion, *Liberty Bay*, winning his race comfortably by about a length and a half.

The race was run in 2 minutes 24 and two-fifths seconds, and this on a somewhat heavy course with shoes on.

It so happens that the foregoing is the only discoverable description of a China race given by a winning owner. By a happy fortuity it was one of the most important races ever run in China. More has probably been written about it than about any other China race. Years later — after the Second World War — accounts of it, mainly Chinese, given by those who remembered it and were there, accord with private English accounts putting Buffy Maitland's defeat down to over-confidence. It may have been; but from Eric Moller's description it does not sound like it.

Lambert Dunbar was said to have been deeply upset. He withdrew *Liberty Bay*, and never allowed him to race again. In fact, such was the glamour surrounding the pony, there was no alternative.

Silkylight had won the 'triple crown'. He went on to a notable future. In November he won the Hongkong St. Leger in a record 3 minutes 29 and three-fifths seconds, the fastest ever by a China pony since racing was inaugurated, three seconds faster than *Liberty Bay*'s record of 1932. Next month *Silkylight* won the Autumn Champions in record time, by many lengths, beating *Liberty Bay*'s 1933 record by over two seconds.

It does not sound as if Buffy Maitland was to blame. *Silkylight* was just a very fast pony.

13. Against Blackened Skies

Not to be Outdone by Dogs

SINCE no one believed the curtain could ever fall on brilliant and successful Shanghai, the fact that it was falling was barely noticed, particularly as far as the races were concerned.

Things had settled down after Chiang Kai-shek's massacre of the communists. At the Autumn Meeting of 1927 various races were for the first time officially designated Classics. These were the Criterion Stakes, the Shanghai Stakes (usually a very large race, with seldom less than 30 at the post, seldom less than 90 entries), the St. Leger, the Subscription Griffins' St. Leger, and the Shaforce Challenge Cup and Champions' Stakes.

Way up north in Newchwang that season they had the largest meeting ever, with a record Chinese attendance. In Hankow, already back to normal despite the devastated Chinese city, Madame Labis reigned supreme as usual, engaging British jockeys these days.[22]

Not for the first time, conditions around Tientsin were disturbed. The races of May 1928 had to be held with the entire racecourse guarded by foreign troops. Willie Howell, Tientsin manager of Liddell Bros., won the Champions that year with *Gobi Eve*, who later repeated the performance several times.[23] Strangely enough, in Shanghai at exactly the same moment Jack Liddell was doing the same with *Wheatcroft*, who won the Champions four times.

An intriguing figure at the Tientsin races was Dr R.J. Hoch, an American vet who bred and raced his own ponies, and who in due course achieved the unique distinction of successfully breeding a racing pony on Chinese soil. *Serene World* was conceived, born and bred in Tientsin, and had a respectable racing career. It is the only known instance of such a thing in China. Foals were born at other places — one was born in Hongkong, another in Shanghai — but they were useless as racing animals.

22. Her prize catch in this respect was Wilfred Bowling of ICI, who had recently been transferred to Hankow from Newchwang, where he was known as the Steve Donoghue of Manchuria.

23. *Gobi Eve* had previously belonged to J.M. Dickinson, who had been bankrupted when the Chinese Government reneged on an agreement with him to provide luxury railway coaches, sleeping cars, and restaurant cars. The coaches were ready for delivery when the Government disowned the agreement. In the ordinary way the British Consul-General would have come to the rescue, but on this occasion could not, because the coaches were made in Germany.

Second to Willie Howell's *Gobi Eve* at the Tientsin races was *Romanie*, owned by Margot Martell and her husband, who was the French Minister in Peking. *Romanie* was trained by Elise Andrews. She and Margot Martell were close friends, each of similar social vintage, the one from Petersburg, the other from Paris.

There were some notably successful Japanese owners in Tientsin at this time, as also at Newchwang. Ever since international-style racing was inaugurated in Japan, in 1906, where owners were concerned it had been the sport of the aristocracy and landed gentry. Japanese owners and riders in China were far removed from the fanatics who were to wreak such havoc on Asia and, in the end, on themselves.

The Chinese Jockey Club at Yangtzepoo held enormous races, with very big fields, all the major jockeys and owners participating, even Sir Victor Sassoon, which shows that the stakes were respectable. An odd feature of Yangtzepoo was

Aerial photograph of Shanghai, 1937. In the foreground, the Grand Stand and Club. In the distance, the towers of the great buildings along the Bund, facing the Whangpoo river. The position of the third racecourse, of 1860–1, can be detected just beyond the existing course, where there is a crescent of buildings. These lined the third course, showing exactly where it was, after all other evidence of it had vanished.

that the Off-Day, which had died everywhere else, was treated with enthusiasm — a card of races for non-winners, with funny handicaps for ponies whose owners did not get the best of it.

Since 1926, under orders from Marshal Sun Chuan-fang, the two Shanghai race clubs outside the foreign-controlled area had been paying municipal taxes to the tune of 15 per thousand. With 20 meetings a year at each club, the sale of tickets ran to more than $40,000,000. The ascendancy of the Kuomintang, however, brought in the New Life Movement, which was profoundly moral. In May 1929 it was proposed that racing be suppressed in Greater Shanghai — the part outside the International Settlement and French Concession. This meant that Kiangwan and Yangtzepoo would have to go. The Chinese racing men wisely issued a press statement saying that this was impossible at present because the Greater Shanghai municipality was making $600,000 a year from the two clubs for municipal improvements. Heaven knows where the money actually went — profound morality was not the Kuomintang's strong point — but put that way it was an unassailable argument. The clubs survived.

A more serious threat came from the Luna Park canidrome, operated by a bunch of well-heeled Chinese crooks trying to break the Chinese Jockey Club, their business rivals. Greyhound races, with much publicity, coincided precisely with meetings at Yangtzepoo. Luna Park was much nearer and easier to get to; and greyhound racing involved a simpler form of gambling.

Yangtzepoo had a bad knock. Required improvements to the course had to be put off for lack of funds, almost incredible when one considers the amount of money passing through that club. An outcry started in the Chinese press. 'No wonder,' observed the *Herald*. 'The Chinese, with their ardent patronage of pony racing, are certainly not going to be overwhelmed by dog races.' Outcry developed into agitation, all in the Chinese newspapers. Still the Luna Park crooks carried on.

Unfortunately for themselves, they had not reckoned with the financial and political power of their adversaries. When polite methods through the press had clearly failed, pressure was brought to bear. The Luna Park canidrome was closed down by the Shanghai Municipal Council in 1933. Its *pari mutuel* at the time was taking $10,000,000 a year, the inventor of its machinery $100,000 a year.

Another canidrome was opened later in the French Concession. The owners were wise enough not to compete with horse-racing. As a result, they survived. To ensure they persevered in wisdom, Tu Yueh-sen, head of the Green Circle, became Chairman of the Chinese Jockey Club, a warning to be ignored at peril.

The Hankow Race Club decorated for the Coronation of King George VI, 1937. Note the charming German architectural features. The German library at the Hankow Club was the finest of its kind in Asia.

Once Hankow ceased to be a Treaty Port, the British all but disappeared from the racing scene there. In 1929 only two were left. The owners and riders of the Chinese Jockey Club at Yangtzepoo streamed up to Hankow on such a scale that there were no cabins left on the river steamers. Madame Labis became particularly selective about the races in which she entered her ponies. In fact, she was in that difficult position of changing from queen of the course into being its *grande dame*.

In August 1931, in conditions of heavy rain and flooding, the railway embankment which served as a dam to much of Hankow broke at various points, and a terrible inundation followed. Thousands of people were left homeless. The Chinese Race Club was badly under water. The Hankow Race Club had water up to the balcony of the grandstand. Five hundred racing ponies, which gives an idea of the size of the Hankow races, had to be evacuated to Shanghai, 600 miles down river, where they were billeted in private stables in the Kiangwan area, there being nowhere for them in any of the clubs.

Manchoukuo

THAT year, 1931, Japan invaded and occupied Manchuria. Though few realized it at the time, this event marked the beginning of the Second World War.

It was a different Manchuria from that encountered hitherto. Over a period of three years, of which the peak was 1928, untold millions of Chinese, in one of the greatest mass migrations in history, had poured northward along the railway line, some in trains, others walking beside the track. Manchuria had for the first time become overwhelmingly Chinese, with no government of any kind and with a free-booting, pioneer atmosphere.

Within a year the Newchwang races, which only four years before had had record attendances, collapsed. Manchoukuo, as it was now called, was a dangerous place. The Japanese were thin on the ground. Bandits and kidnappers took over on a large scale. Where Europeans were concerned, cars had to be put away because there was no petrol. Britons were warned by their Consul-General, Sir Paul Butler, not to ride out when the kaoliang was high.[24] The reason the Newchwang races came to an end was because of the danger of being kidnapped when going out to the racecourse. The Mukden Hunt, described earlier, was made up entirely of offshoots from the Newchwang racing stables. It was too dangerous to bring griffins down from Harbin, and would have been extremely expensive.

British-American Tobacco left, Shell left, British Petroleum left. To make matters more complicated, the Japanese detested Manchuria and greatly resented being posted there.

Japanese official policy favoured a continuation of complete normality — without petrol. British policy was conformative. It was for this reason that Sir Paul Butler got the Mukden Hunt going. It was fairly safe near large places like Mukden. It reassured the Japanese that they were not friendless, and in any case, when the crunch came and all Britons had to leave, as an old French missionary observed, 'The British are so used to being massacred.'

Harbin, with its settled Russian and 'White' Russian community, with its importance in the breeding of horses and their transport down into China, was the obvious place to

24. Sorghum. It grows to heights greater than that of the head of a man on a horse, and makes ideal surroundings for kidnapping and stratagem.

organize (sporting) normality, despite the cold. In the autumn of 1933 a new Harbin Race Club was announced, under the auspices of the Military and Political Bureau of Changchun. General Ma Yu-fêng was to be President of the organization, with Major Kondo as Vice-President. Both were appointed by the Manchoukuo Government. Forty-five well-known and influential citizens of Harbin — 15 Japanese, 15 Manchoukuo citizens, 15 Europeans — were to be invited to become members of the organization and be responsible for its activities. A new racecourse was being laid down between old and new Harbin, and would be ready in a month. There would be a country club as well. Owners of horses would probably receive subsidies from the Government, while the value of prizes would be increased by 250 per cent.

It has a ring of disaster about it. One sees the Ezras and the Sassoons contemplating it in the Shanghai morning newspapers.

It apparently happened, however; and under 'advice' from Mukden, Britons — the few who were there — enrolled. From the British Government's point of view, it was a case of anything to keep the political temperature down.

The Military and Political Bureau of Changchun, however, does give pause for thought. There had always been military bands at races in China, when you could get one. There had been masses of sailors too, lining the course, mainly for fun.

Harbin is the only instance of political races.

Elasticity and the Fourteen-hander

AT Tientsin, as also in Peking and Newchwang, no distinctions were made any longer about crossbreeds. So long as a pony was 14 hands or under, it could race. Crossbreeds simply carried more weight.

The 14 hands business was slightly farcical. Ponies came down from the plateaux aged usually four or five, and a China pony grows until it is seven. Thus if one managed to get a 14-hander in, two years later it was quite likely to be 14 hands 1 inch, or even 14 hands 2 inches. This did not matter. In the tablets of Holy Writ it was recorded at the height it entered as a griffin.

Terrible things went on when one had a touch-and-go 14-hander, worse still when it was definitely over 14 hands. Baron von Delwig was the expert when this difficulty arose. He kept it dark, naturally, but what he did was starve the pony for several days, making sure it did not sleep or lie down. The pony consequently sank with exhaustion, turning into a wretched creature which was patronizingly allowed past, the experts realizing it could never pose a challenge to their own ponies. Having been registered at 13 hands whatever, it was taken home for a huge meal, told never to worry again, and rose once more to its proper height.

The interesting point, however, remembering that height and speed do not increase proportionately, is that the real winners, crossbred or not, tended to be 13 hands 2 inches or 13 hands 3 inches. This being their registered height as griffins, it means that they were slightly taller after a couple of years. The point is that the 14-hander was not necessarily a winner.

Another point is that a more or less pure China pony, one which showed all the classic characteristics physically, could still beat a crossbreed hollow. Baron von Delwig had several such. *Orestes*, who won the Tientsin St. Leger in 1930, thought nothing of crossbreeds.

Edgar Leighton and Andreas von Delwig, in their racing colours, Tientsin, 1928. 'We were at our best when Leighton rode and I trained.'

His rider on that occasion was Eric Watts, of the Kailan Mining Administration, and this raises yet another point. To a remarkable degree, racing in China ran in families. Eric

Watts' father, Arthur Watts, was another top rider; and Arthur Watts' brother was James Watts, who made the famous night ride to secure the relief of Tientsin in 1900. The family names flow smoothly through the scene: Dallas, Maitland, Forbes, Burkill, Liddell, Marshall, Soares, Arnhold, Ostroumoff, Moller, father and son or uncle and nephew as the case may be, while as for the Jardine family, one is left astonished. First there were the Jardines themselves, then all the descendants of Jean Jardine bearing other surnames but forming a family succession — Johnstone, Keswick, Bell-Irving, Paterson, Gresson, Landale — a racing legend which only the Dallas family could rival.

Baron von Delwig and Edgar Leighton were singularly suited to a racing partnership. Both worked in Wilson & Co., one of the oldest and most important English firms in Tientsin. The Baron was their wool expert; Leighton handled their book-keeping and insurance. *Apollo*, entered in Leighton's name, was one of their best winners, *Eros* one of the fastest. Among the popular jockeys of the time were the Samarcq brothers, Robert and Marcel, the latter in the French Police. On one occasion when Robert Samarcq rode *Eros* the pony went at such a pace that at the end of the race the jockey was sick. As Andrew von Delwig said of *Eros*, 'The more you rode him the faster he went.'

Diana, a crossbreed, was another of which he was proud — 51 races, never unplaced. In the spring of 1931, with Edgar Leighton riding, she was beaten by *Clontarf*, the owner-rider being the Jardine manager. '*Clontarf*, a crossbreed, was ridden incredibly badly, but won and broke the record for the mile — 1 minute 58 and four-fifths seconds.' Next season the partners introduced *Orontes*, who beat *Clontarf*. 'That was my greatest pride as a trainer,' Andrew von Delwig commented, adding, 'We were at our best when Leighton rode and I trained.'

An almost identical comment was made by Leo Frost, who knew them both in his Tientsin days. The Baron greatly admired Leo Frost's style of riding. He said, 'Such was his elasticity of muscular movement he could ride a finish without disturbing the horse.' It was Andrew von Delwig, too, who pointed out that rowers make particularly good jockeys, in that the elasticity of movement required in rowing is similar to that needed in a good rider.

In an earlier chapter his sense of macabre comedy was observed. Another example of this concerns the Tientsin

Starter, Dr Tinsey Moore, who drank two bottles of whisky a day. On one occasion they were all lined up at the tape, ready to go; but nothing happened. The ponies were restive. Why wouldn't the Starter let them off?

Peering over to find out what was going on, they saw that the Starter was in exactly his proper position, but he had dropped dead.

'On the bridge,' murmured the Baron.

In Happy-land

HANKOW recovered from the inundation of August 1931, and by November the racecourses were in running order. In 1933 they came up with a wonder-pony, *Boston Drill*, owned by Mrs W.S. Duprée. Her husband, who was English, worked in the Hongkong and Shanghai Bank in Hankow, and was keenly sought after as a jockey. He had his greatest successes on his wife's pony. *Boston Drill* stood only 12 hands 3 inches; he won the Hankow Champions two years running — four times. When Mrs Duprée led him in in November 1933 it was

Eric B. Moller, shipping magnate and industrialist, and Eric Cumine, architect, in the thick of it, Shanghai, 1938.

noted that *Boston Drill*, with Duprée riding, had in the past three weeks won the Champions at all three Hankow racecourses. Duprée's victory at the Chinese Race Club was in fact his eighteenth in succession.

It was always held that racing standards in Hankow were high. *Boston Drill* is the proof of it. After his exploits in 1933 Billie Liddell bought him and took him to Shanghai, where in the autumn of 1934 he won the Criterions and the Chinese Cup, and was winning confidently a year later, his rider Buffy Maitland.

The following year in Hankow they revived the Sunday morning race for novice jockeys, at which points were awarded for winners and those placed. The ponies were supplied by owners, and drawn by lot before the race. This was another matter on which in a sense Hankow was in advance of Shanghai, which should have been doing the same thing, but was not. Despite an acute shortage of jockeys there, the principal owners were giving no encouragement to novices. Eric Cumine, the distinguished architect, joined the Shanghai races as a novice at just this time — 1932 — and testified to the difficulty of getting a good ride. He seemed to find himself invariably at the tail end of any field.

Shanghai Spring Meeting, 1937. The Members' Stand decorated for the Coronation of King George VI.

A person of unlimited resourcefulness, he put the experience to good use. Being at the rear, he observed, was a perfect way of studying the technique of the leading jockeys and the abilities of winning ponies. The Cumine family owned the *Shanghai Mercury*, among other things. Eric Cumine went into print, becoming Shanghai's ace tipster. As he himself explained, 'Being always at the back of the field was like being in the referee boat in a boat race. I saw everything. I knew who tried, who did not, who tried but got cornered, boxed etc. It was in itself a great experience, and taught me how to "read" races.'

One day the Mollers asked if he would like to ride for them. 'They had so many horses they had to have three jockeys for each race, Francis Noodt, Chris Moller, and myself.'

His first ride with the Mollers was on *Joylight*.

I found this horse so tall I had to be lifted on to the saddle. China ponies, we got astride them like bicycles. Then I was told, 'No chance.' I cantered with the field, and could have won. I came third. I told the stable, 'I could easily win with a pony like this against all the donkeys I always ride.' Next time out it was an odds-on favourite.

I won ten races out of twelve rides that meeting. What the hell. Everything I rode cantered into the straight. Everybody riding his heart out, and I was holding. A dream situation.

It was a dream world for those who made it. Aged 27, he had a race box where he entertained about forty guests every race day, 'and we had about twenty-five days of racing a year, and then after 1937 we had sixty days.'

The year he joined the races, in 1932, 'We Two' — Billie Liddell and Vera McBain — at last won the Shanghai Champions, with *Mister Cinders*. In November 1933 the new grandstand was opened to the public, and in March 1934 the new Race Club opened. The grandstand was thought at the time to be the largest in the world, and probably was, while the Race Club, with its marble staircases, teak-panelled rooms, oak parquet floors, and its coffee room which was 100 feet by 47 feet with a huge fireplace, must certainly have ranked as the most sumptuous club of its kind yet built in any country. The *Herald* paid tribute to Ah Hong & Co., the builders:

Surely no Chinese construction firm has ever equalled them. They built the huge public stand in six months — between race meetings — with relays of men working continuously under a gigantic matshed. They completed the task to contract, and the only lament of No. 1 was that the scaffolding and matting had to be dismantled and would take several days, plus money. That very evening there arose a mighty wind which laid the whole contraption flat, and he was a very joyous builder who the next morning harnessed a few dozen coolies to the wreckage, and simply towed it away in a few minutes.

The Race Club was similarly built in six months, a feat which almost certainly none but Chinese could have achieved, and probably none but Ah Hong.

It does not sound as if the curtain was falling.

Illuminations and Splendid Racing

BEYOND the perimeter of the International Settlement and the French Concession, however, in Greater Shanghai, the situation was less secure. In January and February 1932 there was outright war between Chinese and Japanese forces and total disruption of the city, with thousands of refugees streaming into the Settlement. Despite this, the Racing Season began on time.

Law and order in Greater Shanghai broke down to such an extent that in 1936 the decision was reluctantly taken to close down the Kiangwan course with its 'beautiful, palatial grandstand, once the pride of Shanghailanders.' The last meeting was held there on 13 and 14 June 1936. Thereafter the International Recreation Club held its race-meetings at the town course, by arrangement with the Shanghai Race Club.

At the same time there was an ominous build-up of Japanese military forces in Hongkew, the industrial riverside area of the International Settlement north of Soochow Creek, which contained wharves, warehouses, docks, shipyards and manufacturing industries. If it was the Japanese intention to invade Greater Shanghai, obviously their first aim would be to seize the railway station. This would place the Yangtzepoo racecourse in the front line of fire. As a precaution, the Chinese Jockey Club decided to move further out still, to Ying Hsiang Ziang, where conditions might be safer.

Races were held there in December 1936. Everyone in the racing community rallied round. It was 'Nunckie' Sassoon's day. The major event was the China Gold Vase, a Classic. He won it with *Volcanic Morn*, 'Peanut' Marshall riding. *Naming Morn* was second, with Jimmie Pote-Hunt up; and *Nevada Morn* was very nearly third — he was beaten to third place by a nose.

Part of the crowd at the Shanghai Races, 1938.

In the early months of 1937 the situation deteriorated still further. There were now at least 9,000 Japanese troops in Hongkew. In April a meeting of the Chinese Jockey Club was called to decide whether attempts should be made to resume racing at Ying Hsiang Ziang, or whether the organization and its activities should be discontinued. So few members turned up that no decision could be made. By the time another meeting could be called, it was already too late. Japan had launched an all-out invasion of China.

On 13 August foreign troops and the Shanghai Volunteers were called out. Next day it was announced that a British battalion was on its way from Hongkong, the flagship making all speed from Tsingtao. That same day it began, exactly as feared, in the Yangtzepoo area. While Yangtzepoo burned, a polo match was taking place in the grounds within the Shanghai racecourse.

Chiang Kai-shek's German-trained troops replied with spirit. The worst casualty, however, was the International Settlement, which was bombed by Chinese planes trying to hit Japanese cruisers on the river, their bombs falling short, killing and wounding thousands of civilians. It was at that moment that Eric Moller bought the wounded *Silkylight*.

Stalemate continued until, in September, the Japanese were reinforced by 30,000 troops sent from Japan, and moved into the offensive. The same month Nanking was bombed. The Rape of Nanking took place, one of the unspeakable horrors of modern warfare. In Shanghai, around the entire perimeter, the sky was black with dense rolling smoke, streaks of flame leaping amidst it, a horrible but spectacular sight, the blackness rising so high that in the Settlement, which was undisturbed, it seemed as if everything was in semi-darkness.

That same autumn the Japanese occupied Peking. It was orderly and thorough, and even included a victory parade in front of the Forbidden City. The Legation Quarter was left strictly undisturbed. Racing continued as usual at Pao Ma Chang. The Tientsin races continued too, though always under military guard.

In Shanghai orders were given that no races were to be held without permission of the British Consul-General and the Municipal Council. In late November racing was resumed, everything normal. In June 1938, with Greater Shanghai firmly in Japanese hands, the Race Club were even negotiating to buy the Kiangwan race property — not for an aerodrome, as was loudly rumoured in the press, but for racing.

In October that year Canton was occupied by the Japanese, and Hongkong and Macao in consequence found themselves dealing with a China peculiarly different from that which they were accustomed to. They were becoming aware, also, how much they depended on supplies coming in by sea. It was the first hint of Hongkong's vulnerability.

The strange fact about Shanghai at this time — when with war blazing all around it, and the races at their apogee, it does seem to have parted company with reality — is that when the Japanese invasion took place, Shanghai, by the canons of a unique city, was just getting back to normal, after the Great Slump of 1932–6. Conditions during the Slump had been abnormal, financial anxiety everywhere, money tight, the word 'broke' travelling on the wind. When, towards the middle of

1936, financial conditions improved, this was far more important than anything to do with wars or invasions. They had lived with that all their lives. So had their parents. So in some cases had their grandparents. Wars and invasions meant nothing to them. It was slumps that mattered. These they were unaccustomed to.

Some, a few, did realize the danger of Japanese ambitions in China. As so often, scrutiny of the China races gives the politically barometric hints.

The Sassoons resumed racing in Shanghai in 1927, when they promptly appeared heading the list of winning owners. This, the second Sassoon onslaught on Shanghai racing, was not so devastating as the first — there was stronger opposition — though it bore some of the same results. With the 'Morn' stable to contend with as well as 'Mr Eve', fields grew smaller, until for the Criterions of Autumn 1936 — business booming again — only four came to the post.

It is worth noting, too, that 'Peanut' Marshall, the Sassoons' preferred jockey for their lead pony, after winning the Spring Champions of 1935 on *Opera Eve*, won the Autumn Champions that year on *Radiant Morn*, and never again rode an 'Eve' pony. There were no more under such name in Shanghai. Sir Victor Sassoon had seen the political writing on the wall in China. 'Eve' ponies continued to race in Hongkong, which was considered safe from the Japanese. It was held by the learned few that though Japan might be tempted to interfere with the Treaty Ports, she would never risk touching Hongkong.

Sir Victor Sassoon withdrew from China in 1937, four months before the Japanese invasion. By the autumn of 1938 all sign of the 'Morn' and 'Eve' stables had vanished from the race-cards.

No one else seemed to care much. The Shanghai illuminations for the Coronation of King George VI were magnificent, an outstanding feature being the floodlighting of the Race Club clock tower, which was described as 'startlingly beautiful.' In August, when bombs began to fall and an evacuation of British and American women and children was announced, it was considered somewhat exaggerated. Billie Liddell bought the winner of the St. Leger, who had beaten two 'Morn' ponies, changed his name to *Cordon Rouge*, and won the Criterions and numerous other races with him. With *French Leave* and *Early School* both doing well, and with *Boston Drill* too, she had four current winners.

Tientsin Racecourse, 1938, 1½ miles and — note the dust — a dirt track, as all courses had to be in North China, because of the grass problem. People at the rail are few. Japan had already launched an all-out invasion of China, and strict precautions had to be enforced on entry to the racecourse. Though a dirt track, this was the almost perfect course, dead flat, with the canal inside the course to keep the surrounding soil dry.

First Signs of Disaster

EARLY in 1939 Japanese attitudes hardened. The tone was set by Colonel Takashima of the Army General Staff, who declared that Japan had embarked on a 100-year war for the creation of a new world in keeping with the precepts of the Japanese Imperial Way. In Peking conditions were normal. In the country, resistance was developing with the formation of patriotic guerrilla bands who were able fighters. In Tientsin the Japanese were nervy, unaware that they were in fact besieged by the enormous country they sought to encompass, yet with a siege mentality nonetheless, deeply suspicious of Europeans, who were now called Third Nationals. Chinese hirelings of the Japanese infiltrated and spied everywhere.

For the Tientsin Spring Meeting of 1939 the Stewards announced that members only and their servants (mafoos) would be allowed in. The Russian Guards were instructed to refuse entry to all members of the public. Members were advised to wear their badges and to make sure their mafoos bore some clear form of identification. It was their aim, the Stewards stated, to keep the races alive in a difficult political situation. They hoped the members would support by their presence the efforts being made.

The meeting took place. Shortly afterwards the Japanese imposed a blockade on the entire area, and in summer the dykes, neglected, broke. There was a devastating flood. Eighteen months passed before there was any more racing.[25]

The Bank's Travail with the Races

BY July the situation had become clearer. In Tsingtao a Japanese-inspired Chinese mob attacked the British Consulate-General, the Chinese staff of which resigned *en masse*. In Shanghai a map appeared in all newspapers showing the specified areas outside the International Settlement in which Third Nationals might move about and reside by permission of the Japanese Commander. By September there was a grave rice shortage in Shanghai.

The races were magnificent. Billie Liddell won the Champions.

'Peanut' Marshall rode a magnificent race to win the 1939 Spring Champions on Mrs Jack Liddell's *Rain* in the presence of a huge crowd in one of the most thrilling races of the season, defeating Mr A.S. Henchman's griffin *Hindhead*. The large crowd that packed the stands to capacity cheered wildly while the two ponies fought out a close finish which started the moment they entered the straight.

Mention of A.S. Henchman, who was Shanghai manager of the Hongkong and Shanghai Banking Corporation, brings up the subject of the Bank and racing. From one end of China to the other it was a case of the Princely Hong and the Bank.

25. This was the period when Chiang Kai-shek, in one of the most questionable moments in his career, deliberately broke the dykes of the Yellow River as a means of stemming the Japanese advance, thereby rendering millions of Chinese homeless. It is just possible that the Tientsin dykes were broken on Kuomintang orders, but this has never been proved.

Other banks had to give their name. Only one was 'The Bank'. It also issued currency notes which were recognizable over a very large part of China. Occasionally, and in several places — notably Hankow, Foochow, Amoy, and Hongkong — the Bank maintained a small stable, racing under the Bank's Chinese name, Wayfoong. But whereas the Princely Hong has been encountered on almost every other page, nothing has been noticed of the Bank.

Max Haymes, a retired member of the Bank staff, who trained the Bank ponies at Happy Valley in the 1930s, may have provided part of the answer. It was extremely difficult for a Bank man to do anything in the way of outside activities. He had to be at the Bank by 8 a.m., and was lucky if he got away at 7 p.m. At each day's close of business, every note in circulation had to be counted by a European member of the staff. This included notes of $1 denomination which had been in rickshaw coolies' pockets at 90 degrees in the shade. It was a filthy business. Next morning, sometimes for more than two hours non-stop, the young bank clerk had to sign currency notes replacing the filth collected the previous evening.

Training ponies under these conditions of daily work was not easy. With the Princely Hong there was latitude. One could turn up late and depart early, if it was for the races. In the Bank this was out of the question. In stability amid chaos it was practically running China financially at various moments not obvious to the outsider. Like a clock, it could not stop for a second without throwing things into disorder.

Their best pony was *Wayworth*. As Ronald Wood of the Public Works Department — one of the very few Hongkong government servants to race — related,

Probably the best pony I rode — certainly the one I liked best — was *Wayworth*, the Wayfoong pony of 1940, a big, dark, bay Australian pony. He had, however, one bad fault. He was frightened of the starting gate. The first time I rode him, at the Annual Meeting, he just stood still and let the rest of the field get away.

Another rider had a go on him with the same result; and then Donald Black, the champion jockey, tried.

Again the same thing happened, and directly in front of the grandstand. Never in the races had a champion jockey suffered such a loss of face.

'What that bloody pony needs is a bullet,' said a seethingly angry rider to Max Haymes, the pony's trainer, as he got the wretched animal back to the stable.

The climax to the misdemeanours of *Wayworth* came in a 1¼-mile race when he whipped round as the gate went up, and started off in the wrong direction. Ronald Wood was riding him. *Wayworth*, needless to say, was on the rail. Within seconds it was clear that nothing could hold him and there was going to be a head-on disaster with the oncoming field. With marvellous speed of judgment, and great courage, a group of Chinese syces dashed out on the other side of the course and formed a line, forcing the pony to swerve to the outside. The syces then ducked under the rail, and a few seconds later the field passed.

It was potentially one of the most dangerous incidents ever witnessed at Happy Valley.

'It was a nasty few minutes,' said Ronald Wood.

A few meetings after that, I rode him again in a race with a very big field, and we were drawn in the second row, as there were too many ponies for the course. Although we were on the rails, I did not think much of our chances; but as it happened, the two ponies in front of us went off like rockets, *Wayworth* never saw the gate, and followed them. The result was that for the first time in his career we had a perfect position and won easily.

Where the Bank really scored was in its individuals, such as Duprée in Hankow, and above all A.S. Henchman — universally known as 'Hench' — in Shanghai. To appreciate the situation, it has to be remembered that the Shanghai branch of the Bank was three times the size of the head office in Hongkong, and something like ten times more important. Countless millions of people, as they passed its doors, touched the paws of the bronze lions for luck.

A.S. Henchman was one of the Bank's greatest managers, a financial wizard. On one occasion, in 1935, he saved China's currency from collapse. He enjoyed tremendous respect among Chinese, whose nickname for him meant Wise Old Fox, a great compliment. He and his wife were inveterate racegoers and had a stable, the ponies usually named after places in England where there were golf courses. Prior to his narrow miss of a win with *Hindhead* in the spring of 1939 he had for some years not been doing too well. He had had one trainer after another, none of them quite up to the mark.

The races of 1940 were spectacular. There is no other word for it. In the Siccawei Plate, for instance, *Hindhead*, beaten by a neck the year before by *White Parade* in the Champions, beat *White Parade* by half a length. It was similar throughout the card, a fine matching of well-trained animals from stables as good as any to be found elsewhere, including the world of professional racing.

At the Spring Meeting, as the first and second day proceeded, it seemed clear to the discerning that *Hindhead* was going to win the Champions. But he did not. The Clunies, another husband and wife team, captured it with *Cluniehouse*, *Hindhead* a neck behind.

Prior to this, Henchman had been persuaded to engage Elise Andrews, now a young widow, who was down in Shanghai from Tientsin, to be his trainer. The persuader was A.F. (Nobby) Clark, a former Bank employee who even after resigning remained Henchman's lead jockey.

Remembering all the earlier disappointments with trainers, Henchman asked wearily, 'How long will you keep her?'

Above and on the following page: The Shanghai Spring Race Meeting, 1939. (By courtesy: Illustrated London News Picture Library.)

The question was shrewder than he knew. In due course Nobby Clark and Elise Andrews got married.

Hindhead's series of narrow misses in the Champions had shown his quality. It had also set Elise Andrews thinking. On the last day before a pony was to race, even in the early morning of the day he raced, the mafoos in Shanghai had a near-irresistible urge to give him a gallop themselves. Elise had trained *Hindhead* to a condition in which, as she put it, he was *au point*. The day before the Champions of November 1940, to the fury of the mafoos, she got on him, and to make quite sure no one interfered with him, stayed in the stables all night. This was not only wise, but courageous. The Chinese mafoo, if crossed, is not the kindest of characters. To stay that night in the stables took some doing.

It produced dividends, however. Ridden by Charlie Encarnação, the top Portuguese jockey in Shanghai, *Hindhead* — and the Henchmans — had a splendid win, the pony pitted against the two best contenders, *Cluniehouse* and *Cluniehill*.

Final Victory in the Final Race

THIRD Nationals meanwhile had gone through a couple of unnerving incidents. An assassination attempt, clearly a Japanese put-up job, had been made on the life of Godfrey Phillips, Secretary of the Shanghai Municipal Council. This was early in 1940. A year later, on 23 January, at a meeting of ratepayers held at the racecourse, the unprecedented scene occurred of the head of the Japanese ratepayers walking up to William Johnstone Keswick, Chairman of the Municipal Council and head of Jardine's, and shooting him at pointblank range. Mercifully the outraged man held what was little more than a toy pistol. Keswick was wounded, but since it was an exceedingly cold day and he was in a heavy overcoat, the wound was not fatal. The meeting of ratepayers — a very large one — broke up in disorder. 'The uproar in the grandstand was greater than at any previous event, sporting or otherwise. Fisticuffs and missiles were exchanged until at last the police succeeded in clearing the course.'[26]

Ironically, one of the Japanese members of the Municipal Council had also caught the bullets, and both he and Keswick were taken to the same hospital. Morning dawned with William Keswick sitting up in bed, sending a message to the Japanese Councillor, expressing the hope that he was on the mend.

The Princely Hong was not misnamed.

The Shaforce Challenge Cup and Champions' Sweepstakes of 8 May 1941 was 'yet another chapter in the bitter struggle for supremacy between those sworn rivals, *Hindhead* and *Cluniehouse*, one of the most sensational races for the Champions witnessed in recent years, with the raging favourite, *Cluniehouse*, failing even to place.'

Before a crowd of over 20,000, 'with leaden skies put to shame by the early Summer fashions, broad-brimmed hats flaunting a suggestion of Ascot,' the ten beautifully conditioned, fidgety starters were 'off to a bunched start, *Phantom* streaking out into the lead, with *Silver Fox* lying second and *Cluniehouse* third on the rails.'

Halfway down the back stretch *Cluniehouse* came into the lead and stayed there, *Silver Fox* a close contender.

Into the home straight it was *Cluniehouse* and *Silver Fox*, stride-for-stride, length-by-length, with *Cluniehill*, *Hindhead*, *White Parade*, and *Magic Circle* close behind, breast-to-breast.

26. J.V. Davidson-Houston, *Yellow Creek*.

It seemed at that point that the raging favourite would win, but, sensationally, he flattened out when the big question was asked. Before the horrified gaze of thousands, *Cluniehouse* began to fade under the relentless drive of *Silver Fox*, who forged ahead into the lead. And then, while a tremendous roar went up from 20,000 throats, up came *Hindhead*, in the very shadow of the post, with a storming burst of speed that swept him on to snatch the victory.

Charlie Encarnação was congratulated on riding a perfectly judged race.
It was the last time the race was ever run.

A Few Months Later

AFTER eighteen months of blockade, floods, and political trouble with the Japanese, races were held again in Tientsin in October 1940, on three consecutive weekends. The Spring Meeting of 1941 had to be postponed twice because of heavy rain. By the time it was possible to hold it, it was mid-June, and the races were run in sweltering heat on a heavy course. Dr R.J. Hoch's *Super World*, bred by himself, won everything he entered with ease. The Tientsin Race Club had once again broken its rules to allow Michael Boycott, born and brought up in Tientsin, to race from the age of 16, from 1939. Boycott *pére* had come to North China as sales agent for Morris Oxford and Morris Cowley cars. His son moved as by nature into the world of the course, speaking effortlessly fluent Mandarin and with a perfect attunement to the cosmopolitan atmosphere of Tientsin and Peking. He rapidly became a popular jockey, seldom having less than three wins a day, and riding for all the best owners.

Baron von Delwig, in his pony-trap, would meet him at the Pao Ma Chang railway station, and drive him out towards that distant view of the Western Hills, to the course surrounded by willows and small mounds, with its stately tiered grandstand which Ann Bridge recalled as being decorated green and white, with potted oleanders and pink geraniums, around it the silver undersides of the willow leaves, above it the high cry of the kestrels, and from the swamp an occasional upsurge of snipe.

Andrew von Delwig had a field day that autumn in Peking
— three wins in succession. A group of friends, among them
Werner Jannings, brother of the film actor Emil Jannings,
urged him to try for a fourth win. Andrew's only available
pony was *Vulcan*, a fine winner in his day, but who was now
over 20 years old. Just for a joke he put him in, and the pony
won.

It called for a celebration. A sizeable group of them
adjourned to the Baron's country residence near the
racecourse, where in less than no time a lively party was in
progress. In the midst of it, however, Werner Jannings noticed
that their host was not taking any part at all.

'Andrew! Four wins in succession! You should be
celebrating!'

It had no effect. Several of them gathered about him.

'Andrew, what's the matter?' Werner Jannings asked.

The Baron replied slowly:

'I have a feeling I shall never ride another track pony.'

His intuition did not play him false.

The date was 6 December 1941.

Next day. Pearl Harbour.

A Few Days Later

IN the Treaty Ports the transition was straightforward. The
Japanese simply took over without fanfare. Flags changed
on buildings.

Hongkong was different. With an abnormally large garrison
of British, Canadians, and Indians, and with orders from the
War Cabinet to resist, it would have to be fought for. The
daylight spread westward from Pearl Harbour. As it dawned
in Hongkong, the Japanese invaded from the mainland of
China. In Asia it was 8 December.

Four days later they had complete control of the New
Territories and Kowloon. It remained to take Hongkong
Island, to which the defending force had withdrawn and
concentrated. After a Japanese attempt to negotiate a
surrender of the Island had been met with defiance, the Island
was shelled mercilessly for five days, prior to a night invasion.

The last Governor's Cup ever presented at the Fanling Hunt and Race Club in the New Territories, Hongkong, 1940. Presented by Sir Geoffry Northcote, it was won by Mrs Butcher's March Brown. (By courtesy: Mr and Mrs A.H.R. Butcher, Frith End, Bordon, Hampshire.)

On 15 December, late at night, in the midst of the shelling, before the invasion, bombs fell in Happy Valley. One of Hongkong's foremost and most popular jockeys, Benny Proulx, a Canadian, in ordinary life a broker, at this moment a Lieutenant RNVR, described the apocalyptic scene that followed:

Here among the bursting bombs a hundred or so race horses were running wild in the streets. The near-by Jockey Club's stables had been badly bombed and the horses had escaped. They thundered through the avenues, swirled around me, stopping, turning sideways, running back, as bombs and shells burst among them with spouts of dark débris and shrapnel. Blood on their silky coats, streaks of blood in their wide staring eyes, heads high in panic, they ran a futile race with death. A horse would suddenly slip and fall, another would balance himself, bewildered and helpless on three legs. Many lay dead in the littered streets.

One stood trembling, still bridled, and with the reins hanging limply from his mouth. I went up to him, but he seemed not to notice me. I started to unbridle him. Fifty feet away, a small shell burst with a high crack of noise and I instinctively ducked my head, but the horse stood motionless. Tossing the bridle away, I lingered for a moment stroking the sweaty neck. I left him finally, but as I turned the corner of the next block I glanced back. He still stood there, quite motionless, head down among the rest of the panicky herd — a creature frightened into insanity, but so beautiful that it seemed no bomb could touch him.

Doubtless within a few minutes he was dead. It was a bloodbath.

So it ended, and it is best to leave it so. There was racing of a kind in Hongkong afterwards — as in Manchoukuo, the Japanese insisted that ordinary life must go on — but it was rigged and dishonest. It ground to a halt in April 1945, four months before the war ended.

In Shanghai, which of all major cities occupied by the Japanese suffered least, racing went professional, horses and professional jockeys being brought down from Japan. It remained international, too. The champion jockey was a Vichy Frenchman from the Tientsin Race Club who went professional, there being no other means of earning a living.

How the Japs had us coming and going, by Eric Cumine. From his book of cartoons about internment in Shanghai by the Japanese, entitled Lunghua Cackles, published shortly after war ended.

14. Royal and Professional

Previous page: Racing at Happy Valley in the 1960s. It was still amateur racing, but the Stands, and their size, speak for themselves.

Getting Back

THREE years later they emerged from internment camps, or sent cables from thousands of miles away, all with the intention of getting back in quickly. The cables produced numerous losses of fortune. From afar it was not apparent how profoundly China had changed, how perilous was the state of her currency. With the aid of various ambiguous and entirely unnecessary international agencies, Shanghai surged back into life. Billie Liddell, Sir Victor Sassoon, Harry Morriss . . . they all came back. It was all going to be wonderful again.

At which point one leans back and takes a sad look at their lack of political sense. Perhaps they were too close to it, mentally if not geographically. They had had it so good for so long, and few things had interfered with the races — or with liaisons at the Beach City.

But from mid-1944 it had been clear to anyone with the least political perception that Mao Tse-tung and his communists, in their Yenan caves, were going to be the next government in China. Later it was widely said that corruption brought about the Kuomintang's downfall. This is not so. Corruption was peripheral. The Kuomintang died of exhaustion, and from around July 1944 it was quite clearly in the process of doing so.

Racing never resumed in Shanghai, partly because there were difficulties in obtaining horses and ponies, mainly because all were busy trying to get back in quickly, amid mounting obstacles, such as carrying a suitcase of currency notes to buy a loaf of bread, and which finally became insuperable, though even then quite a few would not recognize it. Billie Liddell was there when the communists marched in, so was Harry Morriss. Sassoon had evacuated. It was still all marvellous. Nothing, after all, could break the Chinese family system.

They knew absolutely nothing about the men and women from the Yenan caves.

Only when Billie Liddell found herself being ordered about did the penny drop. She left: in the opposite direction, of course — north. You could not get out to the south. In Tientsin, with less surveillance, she got aboard a ship bound for Hongkong. It was the last ship to leave before the port closed. Harry Morriss remained in Shanghai, and died there. The *North-China Daily News*, which he had re-opened, lasted until the morning when it announced that North Korea had invaded South Korea. This being contrary to sacred doctrine, the newspaper was closed down. And Harry Morriss stayed on . . .

There is the inescapable sense that many of the people in this narrative could never have flourished anywhere except on the China coast. Still, it was great fun while it lasted, and there has never been anything like it before or since.

There were no scandals, moreover. As Eric Cumine put it, 'No one noticed, and after a time it didn't matter.'

Up in Tientsin there was less unreality because the situation was much plainer. North China had been utterly wrecked by the warlords and the Japanese occupation. Most of the leading Tientsin foreign personalities went back, took a harrowed look round, came away, and never returned.

Oswald Dallas, owner of the largest of all stables in the North China races, was among them. He went up to Peking, to his country house at Pao Ma Chang, where he found everything in absolute order, his groom waiting for him, and his favourite ride, *Sultan*, a bay whose father was an Epsom Derby winner, loose in the yard. Dallas gave his special whistle to the horse, who turned, whinnied, and came to him at once. They had not seen each other for three years.

Sultan was bridled and saddled, and Oswald Dallas took him out on a two-hour ride, noting as he did the formidable deterioration in the countryside. Next morning he went again to the stable to find his groom with a face of utter misery. The horse had died in the night.

It was obvious, and the groom knew it too. *Sultan* had waited for three years, hoping to see his master again. He had now seen him.

Oswald Dallas was so moved that he never rode again.

The Royal Hong Kong Jockey Club

As the autumn of 1949 neared, everything depended on what the Red Army would do when it reached the Hongkong border. The communists were masters of all China. Only this extremely mountainous and essentially ridiculous oddment remained. There was Macao as well, of course, on the other side of the Pearl River; but as most of the leading communists — in fact, practically all leading men in China from about 1922 onward — had houses there, caution was desirable. There was no problem on that side. It was Hongkong that mattered. There only right-wing leading people had houses. There were only a few of them, it is true, but their presence made Hongkong vulnerable.

The Red Army stopped at the border in November 1949. Why, no one has ever known. More extraordinarily, it was they who sealed China off from Hongkong.

At this juncture Hongkong had two of the greatest men it ever had, Sir Alexander Grantham, the Governor, and Sir Arthur Morse, who was Chairman and Chief Manager of the Hongkong and Shanghai Banking Corporation, and in addition Chairman of the Board of Stewards of the Hong Kong Jockey Club. They were jointly faced with a peculiar situation. Thousands and thousands of the recent immigrants from China — who as Sir Alexander said, had 'voted with their feet' — were going to the races at Happy Valley. Within a year the turnover was $3,000,000 every Saturday.

A Betting Tax had been imposed since 1930, though standards of British morality insisted that minimal revenue be raised from it. The Jockey Club was charged at 2 per cent of its profits.

Racing returned to Happy Valley at the end of 1945 under British Army auspices. With the re-establishment of civil government the following year the Jockey Club resumed its activities, with Australian horses. From that moment began the phenomenal success of modern racing in Hongkong. By 1948 it had achieved such status, and was of such social consequence, that Sir Arthur Morse resolved that the Jockey Club must make application to become Royal, signifying recognition of the extraordinary position which racing held in the community.

Senior officers in the Secretariat squirmed uncomfortably in their seats, and wrote deprecating minutes in files. Sir Alexander Grantham, undeterred, inquired from London if an application would be considered. The Colonial Office behaved in exactly the same way as the Hongkong Secretariat. They were damning. The actual words used were 'not much chance' — diplomatic words. The fact is they did not even put the matter up to the Lord Chamberlain.

Meanwhile every year, in terms of people and finance, the races were becoming more enormous, and the 2 per cent tax more ridiculous. There was Hongkong with a government in desperate need of money for a mass of things which had never been needed before. Hongkong had always been a town of transients. With the fall of the Bamboo Curtain it had for the first time acquired a static residential population, more than a million of whom at that juncture were living in huts on hillsides. The need for hospitals, schools, clinics, all the amenities of a modern city, was of daunting proportion.

And there was all that money down there in Happy Valley.

To raise taxes was the answer; but the Governor and his Financial Secretary, Sir Geoffrey Follows, were resolutely opposed to this. To raise the Betting Tax — the core of the matter — could never be done. It would cause such uproar in the Colonial Office — uproar which would quickly and mysteriously reach Fleet Street — it was useless to think about the idea. Morals.

Grantham and Morse, though of very different character, had an attunement to each other. Morse, by taking frightful risks — Henchman-style — had put Hongkong on its feet commercially. Grantham held the reins — loosely, knowing the secret, which is that in Hongkong the less the Government does the better. Without being told, Sir Arthur Morse understood Sir Alexander's predicament over the Betting Tax. Early in 1952 he went up to Government House, and suggested that henceforth, *en principe*, the Jockey Club should make over one-third of its takings to civic and social undertakings, that the Government should advise on which projects it felt were worthy of support, but that of course the final decision on any such matter would rest with the Stewards.

There is nothing about this in writing. It happened verbally. But after Arthur Morse left Government House that day, a more joyous Governor could not be imagined. Morse had solved the problem: a million dollars for nothing every Saturday, and no need to refer to the Colonial Office.

Not that Sir Alexander Grantham ever referred to them very often. He was the first Governor of Hongkong to reverse the process. They referred to him.

Thus began the amazing system whereby a horse-racing club became one of the largest and most beneficent civic institutions in existence. The Jockey Club had always given a certain amount to what was called charity, rated at about $400,000 a year. This was not charity any more. It was promoted development. In the first year the figure ran to $5½ million.

So it went on, as this extraordinary racing fervour developed. As was said of the Peking races of 1865, no one

Happy Valley in the early 1960s, in the days when the public were admitted to the in-field.

in Europe or America would be able to imagine it. Nothing
had changed. The people of Europe and America would still
not be able to imagine it.

Donovan Benson, head of the Mercantile Bank of India,
and who chose to retire in Hongkong, took over as Chairman
of the Jockey Club when Sir Arthur Morse left. Benson, with
the full support of the Governor, Sir Robert Black,
inaugurated another go at the Royal problem. It had now
become absurd. The Jockey Club, the largest organization of
its kind in the world, in one of the last British territories left,
and per square mile the most affluent and successful of all
British colonies ever, simply had to be Royal.

In this attempt, in 1954, the truth came out. The trouble
was the Queen. Very early in her reign she had laid it down
that the Royal designation must be restricted to concerns
entirely devoted to charitable purposes, or, in the colonies, to
special organizations fostering social relations between
different races.

Well, the Hong Kong Jockey Club did all these things; but
as the Colonial Office did not have the courage to put it up
to the Lord Chamberlain, how was the Queen to know?

Sir Robert Black, who was determined this must go through,
asked Benson to give him a statement of the Jockey Club's
donations for 1960 — the correspondence had gone on for
six years. The statement ran to tens of millions of dollars for
one year.

Back from the Colonial Office came a letter of refusal, stating that in disregard of the Jockey Club's benefactions, it was not an institution 'devoted to charitable purposes' — the Queen's own words.

Sir Robert then used a trump card. Instead of going through the wearisome official channel, he contacted one of the beachcombers at the Colonial Office, W.I.J. Wallace. The beachcombers were ex-Governors and others who had personally ruled hundreds of thousands of people in many parts of the world, had become bored living on a pension, and having taken to a desk at the Colonial Office, working for practically nothing, were the only people who ever got anything done in that Ministry, or so it seemed.

Wallace was ex-Burma Civil Service. He knew Asia like the back of his hand. He had a contact somewhere — it was certainly not in the Lord Chamberlain's office — and he used it. A reply came back, 'Chances fairly good.' Donovan Benson wrote at once. At last the subject came to the attention of the Queen. Within a month it was the Royal Hong Kong Jockey Club.

Going Professional

ON 19 December 1968 the Jockey Club vet discovered that a horse called *Black Fury* had definitely been doped, and had raced. In a moment of aberration — nothing like this had ever happened before — instead of consulting the Stewards he reported the case to the Police.

A chain of events was set in motion.

Inside the Royal Hong Kong Police Force the gravity of the case was realized immediately. Tens of millions of dollars were involved. Under the command of an exceedingly experienced senior officer, an investigation started. No one except the Stewards — from the moment when they learned of the vet's grave but understandable mistake — knew that a police investigation was going on.

A year passed, and absolutely nothing came to light. It was too closely sealed. Yet, to the discerning, something sinister was going on. It was not just that one horse. The Police were as sure of it as were the Stewards, but were unable to pin it down.

At a meeting on 25 May 1970 one of the Stewards, Peter Williams, who was later to be Chairman of the Board of Stewards, and who in ordinary life was head of Dodwell & Co., one of Hongkong's major trading companies, and a Legislative Councillor, suggested that there be a study and report on the feasibility of introducing professional riding, with the Club establishing its own riding school for young apprentices, based on the lines of the Japan Racing Association.

The word 'shamateur' was first used in the 1930s in Shanghai. It applied to only a few, and since a number of them were men with a good financial background it did not matter much. In post-war Hongkong there were many more shamateur jockeys, and most of them, despite having offices and holding down so-called jobs, were in fact professionals, earning their living entirely from racing. Peter Williams' suggestion that the Jockey Club take the next logical step and go professional was a tacit acceptance of something which could not be discussed, but which everyone was aware of. The doping case had brought it to the fore. This was not Shanghai or Tientsin — still less Peking or charming Chefoo with those trees. Post-war Hongkong, magnified more than four or five times in population, and industrially and commercially a powerful city, was a tough number.

By January 1971 it was clear that the Royal Hong Kong Jockey Club had decided to go professional. It was also clear that a new and larger racecourse was required in the New Territories, and a site had been requested, to be on reclaimed land at the inlet end of the Sha Tin valley.

Suddenly the Police struck. On 9 February 1971 one of the leading and most popular jockeys, a Hongkong Portuguese, was arrested in his office in Ice House Street. He appeared in court next morning on a doping charge.

He was not the only one. There were several others, most of them Chinese. It turned out to be among the most extraordinary and complicated cases ever heard in a Hongkong court. It lasted more than nine months.

The Crown held that 53 horses had been doped, some of them several times, in 88 races over a period of two years. It was probably far more than this.

Stimulants and depressants had been used. Depressants had been found to be more effective. A drug in the feed the day before a race, the depressant kept on for the next two or three races, then with very few bets having been laid on the horse, a win.

There were two doping groups. Such was the secrecy in which they operated, for several years neither of them knew of each other's activities, though bumping into each other daily in the stables. In March 1970 they found out about each other, after which it became slightly more obvious. It was this which led to the tip-off to the Police to go into action.

The case was extraordinary because as it went on, so did the doping. Fresh pieces of evidence, totally disorganizing the existent pattern of evidence, kept on coming to light. Miles Jackson-Lipkin,[27] defending Counsel for the chief accused, revealed halfway through the trial that there was a third gang of dopers, about whom neither of the others knew. As need hardly be stated, this created a public sensation.

The following Monday, more evidence was introduced of doping at the previous Saturday's races. It was a judicial hearing and a criminal investigation running parallel — an extremely rare and highly interesting legal occurrence.

But the iniquity of what had been happening settled once and for all the suggestion put forward by Peter Williams that the races go professional. The Jockey Club's first wording of it was that amateurs be continued to allow to race, that there be special races for them, if required, and that there be stricter control of riders — they actually used the word 'shamateur' — and greater authority for trainers. Weatherby's was to be asked to re-draft the rules.

Michael Boycott was among those who had gone back to Tientsin, taken a heartbroken look and come away. As a gentleman rider at Happy Valley he already numbered among his successes a unique one — the Coronation Cup of 1953, which he won on Willie Stewart's *Ben Lomond*. At the present juncture Boycott was Secretary to the Jockey Club. He was now ordered to be responsible for all stables administration, including security, and 'to undertake to raise training standards to those comparable with training establishments elsewhere.' For one who had always regarded himself as an amateur rider, this must surely be one of the finest compliments ever paid. The truth is that the good riders in the China races knew — and had to know — more of horses and horsemanship than riders elsewhere.

In August 1971, halfway through the doping trial, with no sign of it coming to an end, the Royal Hong Kong Jockey Club, by unanimous vote — it included masses of Chinese —

27. Today Mr Justice Miles Jackson-Lipkin, Judge of the Supreme Court.

went totally professional. Sir John Saunders, head of the Hongkong and Shanghai Bank, was in the chair. It was announced that three top trainers were to be engaged, top jockeys sponsored and local boys indentured as apprentices to trainers with a view to producing professional jockeys. It was also hoped that top-flight jockeys of the calibre of Lester Piggott and George Moore might be expected to make guest appearances.

As indeed they did.

Meanwhile the trial went on. In the final defence address for his jockey client, Miles Jackson-Lipkin, a barrister superbly suave, gentle and disarming, for the one and only time in his life broke into abrasive words. He described the Crown witnesses as a succession of 'pimps, absconding debtors, perjurors, and unfilial sons.'

He lost the case. Four of the accused were sentenced to two years in prison. But it gives an idea of how shocking this case was — and that there was much more to it than ever came into court.

A Civic Institution

IT is surprising, one must admit, to find a Jockey Club becoming a major civic institution. Basically it is due to Chinese interest in racing. Money pours into the races on a fantastic scale, not comparable with any other place on earth. After prudent housekeeping, a great deal of it pours out, always with that discreet tie-in with the Government which, under the cautious but firm influence of Sir Robert Black (Governor, 1958–64), at last grudgingly conceded that it might derive revenue from gambling, provided that such was done indirectly — which it was.

Among the most valuable contributions made are the Jockey Club Clinics, of which there are 13 throughout the Hongkong territory, all of them built, equipped and maintained by the Club. Operating to the highest standards, and providing day-and-night emergency services, they are an invaluable part of the hospital system, particularly in areas outside the central urban region. There is also a floating clinic which provides a regular service to outlying islands.

The Jockey Club virtually built the Tsan Yuk Maternity Hospital, vitally needed at a time (1953) when the general hospitals were in danger of being swamped by maternity cases.[28] The hospital, built on the curve of a very steep slope, is one of the architectural masterpieces of Eric Cumine, who moved to Hongkong after 1949 and, irrepressible as ever, raced at Happy Valley as an owner, and in due course became a Steward.

Quite a crowd of Shanghai people were to be seen at Happy Valley in the years following the communist take-over of China: Buffy Maitland, Jimmie Pote-Hunt, Charlie Encarnação, Billie Liddell and Vera McBain, Elise Andrews, now Clark, and numerous others, including several prominent Chinese racing men. None of them liked Hongkong. It has sadly to be admitted, though, of most of them, that if they had tried to live anywhere else they would have come to grief. An unwise few made this mistake, and did.

Another aspect of the Jockey Club's munificence concerned, appropriately, public recreation. The first major demonstration of this was the creation of Victoria Park, which was reclaimed from what was formerly Causeway Bay, and became an invaluable urban lung, accessible to two of the most densely populated districts of the city of Victoria.

The next, on a much larger scale, was Ocean Park. For some years the Government had wanted Hongkong to have an oceanarium, but understandably did not want the burden of running it. It meant offering a piece of land, and publicly inviting any interested organization to put it to use for this specific purpose. A suitably dramatic site in open countryside on Hongkong Island was carefully selected, and in 1965 the Hongkong Tourist Association took the lead in commissioning a feasibility study from a former president of Marineland, Florida. A form of public offer then had to be devised. The preparatory work took a considerable time.

When the announcement and offer were at last made, it was August 1967, a time of grave civil disturbance, when an attempt was made to cause China's Cultural Revolution to overflow into Hongkong. The determination of the vast mass of the population that this must not happen, coupled with brilliant police work, saved the situation. But it did mean that the oceanarium announcement disappeared in the general

28. A government public relations campaign to persuade mothers to have their babies in hospital had met with an unexpectedly good response, temporarily upsetting hospital arrangements.

confusion, and was completely forgotten. There were no bidders.

Sir John (Jake) Saunders had for some time been thinking that the Jockey Club ought to undertake some large and challenging project for the public benefit, but was uncertain what to recommend. In December 1969 the Governor, Sir David Trench (1964–71), in his usual letter putting forward suggestions for Jockey Club donations, decided to resurrect the forgotten oceanarium idea.

'I mention this with some diffidence,' the Governor wrote, 'as it could cost up to $8 million, and would have to be organized as a non-official community project.'

It was exactly what Jake Saunders had been looking for. Two weeks later he brought it up at a Club committee meeting. A sub-committee of three — Sir Kenneth Fung Ping-fan, Dhun Ruttonjee and Peter Williams — was formed to investigate and report. This was in January 1970. In October the Stewards earmarked $12,000,000 for Ocean Park. A year later a separate company was formed to handle the oceanarium. In fact, much of the outline and a good deal of the detail was settled during 1970 in private discussions between Saunders and the Governor.

Designed over part of Brick Hill on Hongkong Island, approached by cable car, Ocean Park, apart from its performing seals and intelligent killer whales, has the most sensational aquarium in Asia, in which — all the fish swimming free — one walks gradually down and around, seeing everything on three levels: at the top the fish who need sunlight and warmth, at the second level the temperate fish, and at the bottom the fish who live watchfully but determinedly on the floor of the ocean. This amazing place, all derived from racing profits, has given pleasure to millions and is vital in one of the most densely populated areas on the surface of the globe.

There are many other parks, polyclinics, schools, hospitals and public swimming pools, all supported and most of them maintained by the Royal Hong Kong Jockey Club. The bill for their upkeep runs into hundreds of millions of dollars a year.

It is in recognition of this that the Crown rent charged for the Happy Valley racecourse, the most valuable piece of open land on earth, is one dollar per annum.

The Races Today

NIGHT racing — on Wednesday evenings at Happy Valley — started in October 1973, and was an instantaneous success. Against the background of thousands of lights in the homes around the Valley, night racing there, quite apart from anything else, is a scene of spectacular beauty. When the Queen and the Duke of Edinburgh came, in 1975 — it was the first visit to Hongkong by a British reigning monarch — they attended a night race-meeting. There the Queen presented the Queen Elizabeth II Cup at what was Happy Valley's most glamorous moment.

In retrospect there could hardly have been a more appropriate winner of the inaugural running of this race. It went to Mr and Mrs H.T. Barma's 3-year-old gelding *Nazakat*, who gallantly held off a strong challenge by the Chinese Recreation Club's *Celestial Call*. *Nazakat*, always in trainer Cheung Hok-man's stable, raced for 9 seasons and won 13 of his 74 races. His greatest triumphs were at the start of his career in front of the Queen at Happy Valley, and in his very last race, at Sha Tin, where on 5 March 1983, ridden by Lester Piggott, so often a rider for the Queen herself, *Nazakat* rallied superbly in the final strides to edge out an animal 7 years his junior. The old horse's retirement, previously determined on, had truly been well-earned through his last victory.

For reasons already noted, racehorses cannot be bred on Chinese soil. Every racehorse has to be imported. Even their feed has to be imported, another expensive complication, due to the calcium deficiency in all organic matter in China. Because space for stabling and training is limited, the horse population cannot exceed around 800 at the start of any given season.

The number of horses decrees the amount of racing which can sensibly be held when the weather is not too hot and humid; hence some 450 races take place each season — September to June — during 60 to 65 race fixtures. These are held on most Saturdays, on some Sundays at Sha Tin, and on two out of three Wednesday evenings at both racecourses. A recent innovation has been racing on grass at night at Happy Valley — normally the racing surface under floodlights is sand — where this breathtaking new spectacle was introduced in December 1980.

Royal Visit, May 1975. The Queen and Prince Philip with Stewards of the Royal Hong Kong Jockey Club and the winning owners of the Queen Elizabeth II Cup. Her Majesty, having just presented the Cup, receives a bouquet from A.K. Chean, who rode Nazakat to a win at a night race-meeting at Happy Valley. From left to right: Peter Gordon Williams (Chairman); David Newbigging; HM The Queen; Lamson Kwok; A.K. Chean; HRH Prince Philip, Duke of Edinburgh; Sir Douglas Clague; Mr and Mrs H.T. Barma (the winning owners); John Pearce; and Sir Kenneth Fung Ping-fan. Concealed by the Queen is Eric Cumine; concealed by Prince Philip is the the present Chairman, Michael Sandberg.

Dusk on a Wednesday at Happy Valley. Lights up. All set for the first race.

It is no easy matter both to have comparatively few horses in training and to organize competitive racing. More than 90 per cent of the races are therefore handicaps, the Handicapper adjusting the weights to be carried in order to equalize the horses' chances of winning. When professional racing started, the Stewards decided to choose a rather heavier weight scale than normal. The aim here was to encourage experienced overseas jockeys, who might well be having riding weight problems at home, to come to ride in Hongkong and help develop the talents of the locally trained apprentices.

The scheme — the weight scale extends from 140 pounds down to 116 pounds — worked well, and a Hongkong-born and locally trained jockey, Tony Cruz, has already been champion jockey twice, and has ridden with success in England and Australia as well. Cruz has been the most successful so far of the team of 15 or so Hongkong jockeys, who are already backed up by a similar number of apprentice riders trained in the Club's own apprentice school. This, intriguingly enough, is situated in the same rural area to which the racehorses retire when their racing days are over.

The public excitement in Hongkong on the various occasions when Tony Cruz and Gary Moore, with his international reputation, have competed for the position of Jockey of the Year has had to be seen to be believed. The money wagered on them must have been stupendous.

Many renowned overseas jockeys have contested regularly in Hongkong, two in particular. Gary Moore, the young Australian who won the 1981 Prix de l'Arc de Triomphe at Longchamps on *Gold River*, and has himself been six times champion in Hongkong, and Philippe Paquet, the former French champion, have ridden throughout the Hongkong racing season. Others, such as Lester Piggott, Yves St. Martin, Willie Carson, Joe Mercer, and Freddie Head, have chosen to come for shorter visits. All have added to the local spectacle and have contributed greatly to the development of local jockeys' skills.

The trainers' list is equally international. Half the 22 or so, at the last count, were Chinese, the rest being divided equally between Australian and British. One name stands out in the record. This is George Moore — father of Gary Moore. As a jockey one of the greatest riders ever, George Moore has been champion trainer of Hongkong every year except one since his first full training season in 1973–4. His sole defeat — 1978–9 — came at the hands of Allan Chan.

Since 1971–2 only thoroughbreds have been allowed to race, and these are of a high standard. Youngsters imported have included the progeny of such internationally renowned sires as *Great Nephew, Lyphard* and *Sir Tristram*. Previously raced imports have had place-getters in Pattern Races amongst their number, including a second in the Wellington Guineas beaten only by a neck.

No matter a horse's potential on breeding, however, nor what it may have achieved on other racecourses in the past, what counts in Hongkong is its performance in Hongkong. On that score two horses have stood out since professional racing started. These are the *Piccadilly Lane* (Irish) gelding *Super Win*, which won 18 races between 1974–7, and the *Town Crier* (English) grey gelding *Silver Lining* (raced in Australia as *Vintage Moon*) which, racing between 1978 and 1982, became the first — and so far the only — horse to win over a million Hongkong dollars.

While over 90 per cent of the races are handicaps, the most valuable races — as in all leading racing countries — are weight-for-age or terms events. These include a semi-Classic series of races for first- and second-season horses, and championship races at the end of each season — the Chairman's Prize for sprinters, and the Champions' and Chater Cup for middle-distance horses.

The Hongkong Derby continues to be the most valuable race in the season's programme. In 1983 it was worth HK$366,300. Because of the circumstances particular to racing in Hongkong, the Derby is a terms race for 4-year-olds only, run in late January each year over a distance of 1,800 metres, with weight for sex being the only allowance permissible.

The extra racecourse at Sha Tin, in the New Territories, opened in October 1978.[29] It is the largest course ever made in China, surrounding 250 acres of reclaimed land. The main

29. Sha Tin — it means Sandy Fields — once produced what was probably the finest rice in the world, a long, thin grain of exceptional fragrance. In former times the entire crop was purchased annually for the Imperial Court in Peking. After the Revolution it became possible for the first time for Hongkong people to purchase the rice, by going out to the valley and buying direct from farmers. The rice was never served in restaurants; it all went into private houses, and even there it was served only on very special occasions. The valley is now completely urban, and Sha Tin rice exists no more. Attempts were made to plant it in other parts of the New Territories, but it nowhere achieved the quality it had when grown in its home valley.

Sha Tin Racecourse, New Territories. The Stand holds 38,000 people, and is being extended. The course is the largest ever laid down on Chinese soil. In the foreground, in the middle of the course, the Penfold Garden, open to the public, for whom it has proved an enormously popular amenity. It is named for Major-General Sir Bernard Penfold, formerly general manager of the Jockey Club.

track is grass. It is 1,900 metres around and 100 feet wide throughout. The gentle bends are banked, and the back straight was built 8 feet higher than the home straight to provide better viewing for the spectators. The run-in from the home bend is a full 500 metres, and this coupled with the width of the track provides many thrilling contests in their closing stages in front of the stands. There is also a chute which allows for straight 1,000-metre races. Inside the grass track is a 75-foot wide sand track for racing, and inside that again a narrower sand track for slower training work. A second grandstand, for 32,000 additional people, is due to be opened in September 1985. The present stands, 8 storeys high, provide comfortable accommodation for 38,000 people. The view from the stands, looking directly across the tidal cove to the 2,700-foot peaks of Ma On Shan — Saddle Mountain — is dramatic, without parallel among racecourses. Everything about it is spectacular.

When the idea of a racecourse at Sha Tin was first mooted, misgivings were aired. It was felt that the Royal Hong Kong Jockey Club was going too far. As the Stewards saw it, however,

Happy Valley was a fairly small course, incapable of enlargement; and Hongkong, with its terrific interest in racing, needed something larger. More important than this, the New Territories, over which ponies formerly galloped in hunts through open countryside, was in due course going to have an urban population larger than that of Hongkong and Kowloon put together. Racing had to be brought nearer to this incipient urban community.

Prime mover in the resolve to go professional, and, as Chairman, the inspiration behind the creation of the magnificent Sha Tin racecourse, was Peter Williams, Chairman of the Board of Stewards from 1974 to 1981. The construction of the Sha Tin racecourse was a mammoth undertaking, conducted along the lines of a military operation. In March 1975, before the reclamation of the inlet had even begun, it was decided that the first race at Sha Tin would start at 2 p.m. on 7 October 1978; and it did.

Peter Williams was succeeded as head of the Jockey Club by Michael Sandberg, Chairman of the Hongkong and Shanghai Banking Corporation. This was the third time a head of 'The Bank' had been elected to this position. It is pleasant to be able to record that his horses have done well, with several wins.

The strange thing is that the China races, which in Shanghai were conducted on an immense financial scale, have passed into oblivion, while the present-day Hongkong races have become world-famous — for precisely their immense financial scale. The beauty of the night races, the splendour of the Sha Tin course, the fraternity existing between thousands of people of different races and nationalities . . . none of this is noticed abroad; only the betting. And as one is apt to discover when abroad, mention of the Hongkong races, and the scale of them, provokes amazement not unmixed with criticism, the latter usually unspoken, yet there just the same. There is the sense that undue attention is paid to the money side of racing.

Indisputably the average level of prize money for racing in Hongkong is among the highest offered by any country in the world. Against this must be seen the vast practical forward strides that have been made in the areas of racing control, veterinary care, and clinical research, not to mention the more mundane if huge area of offering an ever-improving service to betting customers — the Jockey Club runs 124 off-course betting centres throughout the territory.

However, a horse's name might be allowed a pertinent comment of its own at this stage. The first race at the new racecourse at Sha Tin was won by a 5-year-old mare, owned by Eric Cumine, and aptly named — or so cynics might declare — *Money No Object*.

At the present time the average turnover at a race in Hongkong is HK$23,100,000 — just over £2,000,000 a race. There are usually nine races per meeting. There are two meetings a week. And the season lasts for seven months.

To any in need of arithmetical assistance, the total turnover at the latest season was more than HK$10,313,000,000 — roughly £1,300,000,000.

Next year it will almost certainly be more.

At Sha Tin Racecourse, Spring 1983. From left to right, the author; the Hon. Michael Sandberg, CBE, JP, Chairman of the Board of Stewards of the Royal Hong Kong Jockey Club; and General Sir John Archer, KCB, OBE, the Club's Chief Executive. (By courtesy: Fung Kwai Yim, Esq.)

The Royal Hong Kong Jockey Club

THE CHAIRMEN OF THE BOARD OF STEWARDS

1884–1892 Phineas Ryrie, JP†

1892–1926 Sir Paul Chater, CMG, Chev. Leg. d'Hon., LL D, JP*†

1926–1929 Henry Percy White

1929–1935 Charles Gordon Stewart Mackie, JP†

1935–1939 Marcus Theodore Johnson, JP†

1940–1941 Thomas Ernest Pearce, JP† (killed in action)

1945–1946 Percy Tester

1946–1952 Sir Arthur Morse, CBE*

1953–1967 Donovan Benson, OBE

1967–1972 Sir John Saunders, CBE, DSO, MC*

1972–1974 Sir Douglas Clague, CBE, MC, QPM, CPM, JP*†

1974–1981 Peter Gordon Williams, OBE, JP†

1981– Michael Graham Ruddock Sandberg, CBE, JP*

* Member of the Governor's Executive Council
† Member of the Legislative Council

Acknowledgements

A great many people helped in the compilation of material for this book. I wish first of all to thank those who helped with interviews, letters, and so on, who figure in the text and will be clearly discernible to the reader, but who for reasons of space do not appear in what follows.

Among those who, with one or two exceptions, do not figure in the text, I owe my thanks to Mr James Buchanan-Jardine for giving me access to private family letters; Mrs I.A. (Midge) Macgregor for the loan of John Macgregor's invaluable Shanghai racing scrapbook; Professor C.R. Boxer, FBA, for introductions and suggestions on sources; Mr George Wright-Nooth for his help on early references; Mr Alan Reid and Mrs Margaret Reid for general guidance on research; Mr Michael Boycott for his reminiscences of the Tientsin races and for technical advice on racing in general; Andreas Baron von Delwig for material of particular value, written and verbal, and illustrations; Mr Roy Davis, 92 years old and blind, for a wonderful series of dictated letters from Canada; Mr Eric Cumine, OBE, FRIBA, for providing much valuable written and verbal material on the Shanghai races, and for his consistent interest; Miss Barbara Cumine, MBE, the architect's sister, for extending the scope of my inquiries in London; Mr Eric B. Moller for his reminiscences and advice; Mrs Clare Wadsworth for the provision of rare books and photographs; Mr Brian Ogden, of the Hongkong and Shanghai Banking Corporation, for putting me in contact with a wide range of people who took part in the China Races; Mr Yim Shui-yuen for providing the Chinese illustrations and for general advice; and Mr Christopher D'Almada e Castro for his reminiscences of pre-war racing in Hongkong.

Other friends who have helped, and to whom I owe my thanks, are Mr David Newbigging, CBE; Mr Horace Kadoorie, CBE, Chevalier Legion d'honneur; Colonel Henrique Alberto de Barros Botelho, OBE; Mr Leslie C. Smith, OBE; Mr Oswald Dallas; Mr Geoffrey Bonsall; the Revd Carl T. Smith; Mr Jack Hutton Potts; Senhor Rufino Ramos, of the Government of Macao; and that wise and delightful genius of the horse-racing world, Mr J.A. Allen.

In Hongkong I wish to thank Mr Ian Diamond, the Government Archivist; Mrs Robin McLean, assistant archivist at the Public Records Office; Mr Douglas Cheung, Librarian of the Government Secretariat; and at the University of Hongkong, Mr H.A. Rydings, the Librarian, and Mr Peter Yeung, in charge of the Hongkong Collection, all of them giving a degree of co-operation which would be hard to match.

Bibliography

The material for this book has come largely from newspapers published in China, and from personal interviews with people who remembered the China Races.

Among the books consulted were the following:

Bridge, Ann, *The Ginger Griffin*, Chatto & Windus, London, 1934.

Ching, Henry, *Pow Mah*, Royal Hong Kong Jockey Club, 1965.

Collis, Maurice, *Wayfoong*, Faber, London, 1965.

Davidson-Houston, J.V., *Yellow Creek, The Story of Shanghai*, Putnam, London, 1962.

Davis, C. Noel, *A History of the Shanghai Paper Hunt Club, 1863-1930*, Kelly and Walsh, Shanghai, 1930.

Drage, Charles, *Servants of the Dragon Throne*, Peter Dawnay, London, 1966.

Eitel, E.J., *Europe in China*, Kelly and Walsh, Hongkong, 1895.

Fleming, Peter, *The Siege at Peking*, Rupert Hart-Davis, London, 1959.

Hua Pao, Vols. I & II, Tien Shih Chai, Shanghai, 1884.

Hutcheon, Robin, *Chinnery, the man and the legend*, South China Morning Post Ltd., Hongkong, 1975.

Lo Kat, *Ma Cheung Sam-sap Nin (Thirty Years at the Racecourse)*, Ng Hing Kee, Hongkong, 1972.

Maclellan, J.W., *The Story of Shanghai*, North-China Herald, Shanghai, 1889.

Proulx, Benjamin, *Underground from Hong Kong*, Dutton, New York, 1943.

Rasmussen, A.H., *China Trader*, Constable, London, 1954.

Sapajou, Georges, *Early Birds, Shot at the Peking Race Course*, Peking, 1921.

Silver, Caroline, *Guide to the Horses of the World*, Elsevier Phaidon, Oxford, 1976.

Somers, Geoffrey V., *The Story of Racing in Hong Kong*, Michael Stevenson Ltd., Hongkong, 1975.

Teixeira, Padre Manuel, *Toponîmia de Macau, Vol. I. Ruas com nomes genericos*, Imprensa Nacional, Macao, 1979.

Woodcock, George, *The British in the Far East*, Atheneum, New York, 1969.

Index

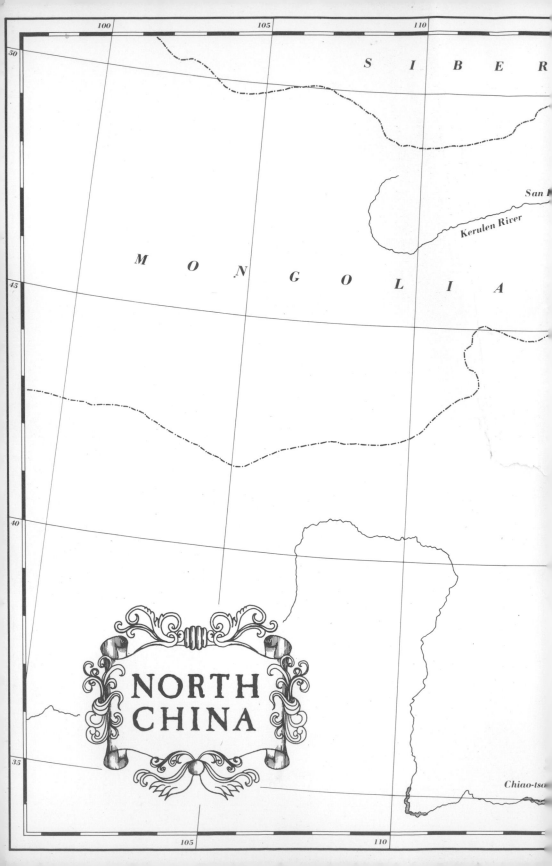

100 105 110

50

_S I B E R_

San

Kerulen River

_M O N G O L I A_

45

40

NORTH CHINA

35

Chiao-tso

105 110